Postal
Clerk and
Carrier

23rd Edition

John Gosney

Dawn Rosenberg McKay

Michele Lipson

THOMSON

ARCO

Australia • Canada • Mexico • Singapore • Spain • United Kingdom • United States

CONTENTS

PART III: CIVIL SERVICE TESTS FOR POSTAL CLERK AND CARRIER JOBS 47

PART IV: PRACTICE TESTS AND FULL-LENGTH PRACTICE EXAMS 135

Acknowledgments

Special thanks to Janette Young for providing the opportunity to work on this project. Thanks as well to Kangaroo Research Mavens for ensuring the accuracy and level of detail for much of the book's content.

—John Gosney

Thank you to John Gosney, our co-author, for asking the right questions and using the results of our research effort to put together a product we can all be proud of. Thanks to Janette Young and everyone at Peterson's for bringing us on board. A tremendous thank you to our husbands and families who have supported us and our efforts.

—Michele Lipson and Dawn Rosenberg McKay, Kangaroo Research Mavens (www.rooresearch.com)

INTRODUCTION

Congratulations on selecting ARCO's *Postal Clerk and Carrier.* You have in your hands a powerful tool to ensure your best chances at getting a great score on the U.S. Postal Exam. By working through the book, taking time to practice the sample exercises, and studying the various tips and techniques for tackling various question types, you can put yourself at a solid advantage for achieving your best score. This book also contains up-to-date information, including:

- Job requirements

- Benefits

- Working conditions

- Salaries

This is **your** book, written with **your success** in mind—enjoy reading it, and good luck on your exam!

WHAT THIS BOOK WILL DO FOR YOU

ARCO has followed testing trends and methods ever since the firm was founded in 1937. We *specialize* in books that prepare people for tests. Based on this experience, we have prepared the best possible book to help *you* score high. To write this book, we carefully analyzed every detail surrounding the forthcoming examinations. Since there is such variation in exams, we cannot predict exactly what your exam will be like. However, after studying many announcements and many exams, we have written this book to prepare you for the most probable question types. The instructional chapters will prepare you for questions that you are likely to face. The model exams, while they are not actual exams, will give you excellent practice and preparation for your civil service exam. Other features of this book include details about:

- The job itself

- Official and unofficial announcements concerning the examination

- All the previous examinations, although many are not available to the public

■ Related examinations

■ Technical literature that explains and forecasts the examination

CAN YOU PREPARE YOURSELF FOR YOUR TEST?

You want to pass this test. That's why you bought this book. Used correctly, your "self-tutor" will show you what to expect and give you a speedy brush-up on the subjects tested in your exam. Some of these are subjects not taught in schools at all. Even if your study time is very limited, you should:

■ Become familiar with the type of examination you will have

■ Improve your general test-taking skills

■ Improve your skill in analyzing and answering questions involving reasoning, judgment, comparison, and evaluation

■ Improve your speed and skill in reading and understanding what you read—an important part of your ability to learn and an important part of most tests

This book will:

■ **Present every type of question you will get on the actual test.** This will make you at ease with the test format.

■ **Find your weaknesses.** Once you know what subjects you're weak in, you can get right to work and concentrate on those areas. This kind of selective study yields maximum test results.

■ **Give you confidence** *now.* It will build your self-confidence while you are preparing for the test. As you proceed, it will prevent the kind of test anxiety that causes low test scores.

■ **Stress the multiple-choice type of question because that's the kind you'll have on your test.** You must not be satisfied with merely knowing the correct answer for each question. You must find out why the other choices are incorrect. This will help you remember a lot you thought you had forgotten.

After testing yourself, you may find that you are weak in a particular area. Concentrate on improving your skills by using the specific practice sections in this book that apply to you.

HOW DO I USE THIS BOOK?

Unlike many test-preparation books, you don't have to read through the book from front to back. If you prefer, you can jump right into the sample tests. Or, maybe you'd like to find out strategies for approaching the various exam questions. You may want to start out by looking up detailed, current information on jobs with the USPS, or perhaps check out Web sites containing valuable information about the U.S. Postal Service. This is your book—use it as you like!

If you already know what type of career you wish to pursue, this book will help you prepare for any of the major exams. If you don't know what type of job you'd like to apply for, you will also find information here about various types of careers, and perhaps it will narrow down your choices.

Following is a breakdown of what is offered in each section of this book.

PART I

There are five parts to this book. Part I covers the major employment sectors: federal, state, municipal (city), and private industry careers. There's more than enough for everyone here. Each sector has its own requirements and tests. However, as you will see, there are certain types of questions that will appear on most of these exams, regardless of the type of test you will take.

Also in this section is important information on test-taking techniques. This gives you the guidelines to help you prepare for the actual test. Feeling anxious before you take a test is a normal reaction. We provide you with tips on feeling relaxed and comfortable with your exam so you can get a great test score.

PART II

Part II is an overview of the various types of careers available. If you haven't already been in the field, you will be surprised by the number of different job opportunities there are as well as the varied jobs within an area. For example, did you know that there are almost 2,000 different job titles just within the U.S. Postal Service? This is just *one* federal agency.

If you are beginning your career or job shopping at this time, you should read this section carefully. It will help introduce you to the different jobs and the many opportunities that await you. We hope you will be inspired and excited and will be motivated to apply for, study for, and land one of those jobs. If this section helps you narrow your area of interest, you can then concentrate on the exams that will help you prepare for the job you want. If you are still wide open, give equal attention to each exam.

PART III

In this section, we detail test types and requirements. We've also given you a review section so that you can practice on a variety of different question types. We suggest you go through this chapter to get an idea of where your strengths lie and what weaknesses you'll have to deal with on the actual test. We've also provided you with a variety of different types of tests that you will encounter in almost any job you apply for in the civil service, since there are certain basics that need to be covered. For example, in most tests, you will be asked to understand vocabulary and the use of grammar. Some tests will test your memory abilities and your ability for recall. Can you alphabetize easily and quickly? That's an area also covered on many of these tests.

PART IV

In Part IV, there are real examinations (official sample examinations) and model examinations closely patterned after the actual exams. Timing, level of difficulty, question styles, and scoring methods all conform closely to the examinations for which they are meant to prepare. And a special feature of this book is that all the correct answers are explained.

When you do take the sample exams, try to set aside the full measure of time to take the exam in one sitting. Time yourself accurately (a stopwatch or a kitchen timer will work well), and stop working when the time is up. If you have not completed all of the questions when the time expires, stop anyway.

Check your answers against the provided answer key and score your paper. Then, continue with the remaining questions to get in all the practice you can. Carefully study all the answer explanations, even those for questions that you answered correctly. By reading all of the explanations, you can gain greater insight into methods of answering questions and the reasoning behind the correct choices.

One very important suggestion: We strongly believe that regardless of the test that you think you're planning to take—or the career path you want to follow—try to take *all* of the exams in this book. It may seem like a lot of extra work, but you never know where you may end up. You may think you're interested in a job with the local city government, and end up instead in a private company. Or perhaps the exam you were hoping to take is not being given for another year, but some other test is being given next month. It is always better to be prepared.

PART V

Finally, Part V contains civil service career information resources. Here you will find out how to go about looking for available jobs, as well as important addresses, phone numbers, and Internet Web sites that will help you pursue your career in civil service. The most important thing is to *use* this book. By going through all of the sections and reading them, reviewing question types, and taking the practice exams, you will be using what you learned here to the best of your ability to succeed in your intended career path.

APPENDIX

A glossary of Postal Service Terms is included to give you a quick definition of words and terms used in the Postal Service hiring process.

PART I

So You Want to Work for the Government

CHAPTER 1

FEDERAL CIVILIAN EMPLOYMENT

The federal government employs almost 3 million civilian workers in the United States and an additional 130,000 civilian workers—half of them U.S. citizens—in U.S. territories and international countries. The headquarters of most government departments and agencies are in the Washington, D.C., area, but only one out of eight federal employees works there.

Federal employees work in occupations that represent nearly every kind of job in private employment as well as some unique to the federal government, such as regulatory inspectors, foreign service officers, and Internal Revenue agents. Most federal employees work for the executive branch of the government.

The executive branch includes the Office of the President, the cabinet departments, and about 100 independent agencies, commissions, and boards. This branch is responsible for activities such as administering federal laws, handling international relations, conserving natural resources, treating and rehabilitating disabled veterans, delivering the mail, conducting scientific research, maintaining the flow of supplies to the armed forces, and administering other programs to promote the health and welfare of the people of the United States.

The Department of Defense, which includes the Departments of the Army, Navy, and Air Force, is the largest department. It employs about 1 million civilian workers. The Departments of Agriculture, Health and Human Services, and the Treasury are also big employers. The two largest independent agencies are the U.S. Postal Service and the Veterans Administration. There is also federal civilian employment available in the legislative branch, which includes Congress, the Government Printing Office, the General Accounting Office, and the Library of Congress. The judicial branch, the smallest employer, hires people for work within the court system.

WHITE-COLLAR OCCUPATIONS

Because of its wide range of responsibilities, the federal government employs white-collar workers in a great many occupational fields. About one of four of these are administrative and clerical workers.

General clerical workers are employed in all federal departments and agencies. These include office machine operators, secretaries, stenographers, clerk-typists, mail and file clerks, telephone operators, and workers in computer and related occupations. In addition, there are the half million postal clerks and mail carriers. Many government workers are employed in engineering and related fields. The engineers represent virtually every branch and specialty of engineering. There are large numbers of technicians in areas such as engineering, electronics, surveying, and drafting. Nearly two thirds of all engineers are in the Department of Defense. Of the more than 120,000 workers employed in accounting and budgeting work, 35,000 are professional accountants or Internal Revenue officers. Among technician and administrative occupations are accounting technicians, tax accounting technicians, and budget administrators.

There are also large numbers of clerks in specialized accounting work. Accounting workers are employed throughout the government, particularly in the Departments of Defense and the Treasury and in the General Accounting Office. Many federal employees work in hospitals or in medical, dental, and public health activities. Three out of five are either professional nurses or nursing assistants. Other professional occupations in this field include physicians, dieticians, technologists, and physical therapists. Technician and aide jobs include medical technicians, medical laboratory aides, and dental assistants. Employees in this field work primarily for the Veterans Administration; others work for the Departments of Defense and Health and Human Services.

Other government workers are engaged in administrative work related to private business and industry. They arrange and monitor contracts with the private sector and purchase goods and services needed by the federal government. Administrative occupations include contract and procurement specialists, production control specialists, and Internal Revenue officers. The Departments of Defense and Treasury employ two out of three of these workers. Another large group works in jobs concerned with the purchase, cataloging, storage, and distribution of supplies for the federal government. This field includes many managerial and administrative positions such as supply management officers, purchasing officers, and inventory management specialists, as well as large numbers of specialized clerical positions. Most of these jobs are in the Department of Defense.

Throughout the federal government, many people are employed in the field of law. They fill professional positions, such as attorneys or law clerks, and administrative positions, such as passport and visa examiners or tax law specialists. There also are many clerical positions that involve examining claims. The social sciences also employ many government employees. Economists are employed throughout the government, psychologists and social workers work primarily for the Veterans Administration, and foreign affairs and international relations specialists are employed by the Department of State. One third of the workers in this field are social insurance administrators employed largely in the Department of Health and Human Services.

About 50,000 biological and agricultural science workers are employed by the federal government, mostly in the Departments of Agriculture and Interior. Many of these work in forestry and soil conservation activities. Others administer farm assistance programs. The largest number is employed as biologists, forest and range fire controllers, soil conservationists, and forestry technicians.

The federal government employs another 50,000 people in investigative and inspection work. Large numbers of these are engaged in criminal investigations and health regulatory inspections, mostly in the Departments of Treasury, Justice, and Agriculture. Physical sciences is another area of government employment. The Departments of Defense, Interior, and Commerce employ three out of four workers in the physical sciences. Professional workers include chemists, physicists, meteorologists, cartographers, and geologists. Aides and technicians include physical science technicians, meteorological technicians, and cartography technicians. And in the mathematics field are professional mathematicians and statisticians and mathematics technicians and statistical clerks, employed primarily by the Departments of Defense, Agriculture, Commerce, and Health and Human Services.

ENTRANCE REQUIREMENTS

Entrance requirements for white-collar jobs vary widely. A college degree in a specified field or equivalent work experience is usually required for professional occupations such as physicists and engineers. Entrants into administrative and managerial occupations usually are not required to have knowledge of a specialized field but must, instead, indicate a potential for future development by having a degree from a four-year college or responsible job experience. They usually begin as trainees and learn their duties on the job.

Typical jobs in this group are budget analysts, claims examiners, purchasing specialists, administrative assistants, and personnel specialists. Technician, clerical, and aide-assistant jobs have entry-level positions for people with a high school education or the equivalent. For many of these positions, no previous experience or training is required. The entry-level position is usually that of trainee. Persons who have junior college or technical school training or those who have specialized skills may enter these occupations at higher levels. Typical jobs are engineering technicians, supply clerks, clerk-typists, and nursing assistants.

BLUE-COLLAR OCCUPATIONS

Blue-collar occupations—craft, operative, laborer, and some service jobs—provide full-time employment for more than half a million federal workers. The Department of Defense employs about three fourths of these workers in establishments such as naval shipyards, arsenals, and the Air or Army depots, as well as on construction, harbor, flood control, irrigation, or reclamation projects. Others work for the Veterans Administration, U.S. Postal Service, General Services Administration, Department of the Interior, and Tennessee Valley Authority.

The largest single blue-collar group consists of manual laborers. Large numbers are also employed in machine tool and metal work, motor vehicle operation, warehousing, and food preparation and serving. The federal government employs a wide variety of individuals in maintenance and repair work, such as electrical and electronic equipment installation and repair, and in vehicle and industrial equipment maintenance and repair. All these fields require a range of skill levels and include a variety of occupations comparable to the private sector.

Although the federal government employs blue-collar workers in many different fields, about half are concentrated in a small number of occupations. The largest group, the skilled mechanics, works as air-conditioning, aircraft, automobile, truck, electronics, sheet-metal, and general maintenance mechanics. Craft workers are also largely employed as painters, pipefitters, carpenters, electricians, and machinists. A similar number serves as warehouse workers, truck drivers, and general laborers. Workers are employed as janitors and food-service workers as well.

ENTRANCE REQUIREMENTS

Persons with previous training in a skilled trade may apply for a position with the federal government at the journey level. Those with no previous training may apply for appointment to one of several apprenticeship programs. Apprenticeship programs generally last four years; trainees receive both classroom and on-the-job training. After completing this training, a person is eligible for a position at the journey level. There are also a number of positions that require little or no prior training or experience, including janitors, maintenance workers, messengers, and many others.

THE MERIT SYSTEM

More than nine out of ten jobs in the federal government are under a merit system. The Civil Service Act, administered by the U.S. Office of Personnel Management, covers six out of ten federal titles. This act was passed by Congress to ensure that federal employees are hired on the basis of individual merit and fitness. It provides for competitive examinations and the selection of new employees from among the most qualified applicants.

Some federal jobs are exempt from civil service requirements either by law or by action of the Office of Personnel Management. However, most of these positions are covered by separate merit systems of other agencies, such as the Foreign Service of the Department of State, the Federal Bureau of Investigation, the Nuclear Regulatory Commission, and the Tennessee Valley Authority.

EARNINGS, ADVANCEMENT, AND WORKING CONDITIONS

Most federal civilian employees are paid according to one of three major pay systems: the **General Pay Schedule**, the **Wage System**, or the **Postal Service Schedule**.

GENERAL PAY SCHEDULE

More than half of all federal workers are paid under the General Schedule (GS), a pay scale for workers in professional, administrative, technical, and clerical jobs, and for workers such as guards and messengers. General Schedule jobs are classified by the U.S. Office of Personnel Management in one of fifteen grades, according to the difficulty of duties and responsibilities and the knowledge, experience, and skills required of the workers. GS pay rates are set by Congress and apply to government workers nationwide. They are reviewed annually to see whether they are comparable with salaries in private industry. They are generally subject to upward adjustment for very high cost of living regions. In low-cost areas, the GS pay scale may exceed that of most private-sector workers.

Most employees receive within-grade pay increases at one-, two-, or three-year intervals if their work is acceptable. Within-grade increases may also be given in recognition of high-quality service. Some managers and supervisors receive increases based on their job performance rather than on time in grade. High school graduates who have no related work experience usually start in GS-2 jobs, but some who have special skills begin at grade GS-3. Graduates of two-year colleges and technical schools often can begin at the GS-4 level. Most people with bachelor's degrees appointed to professional and administrative jobs such as statisticians, economists, writers and editors, budget analysts, accountants, and physicists, can enter at grades GS-5 or GS-7, depending on experience and academic record. Those who have a master's degree or Ph.D. or the equivalent education or experience may enter at the GS-9 or GS-11 level. Advancement to higher grades generally depends upon ability, work performance, and openings in jobs at higher grade levels.

GENERAL SCHEDULE

(Range of Salaries)

Effective as of January 2002

GS Rating	Low	High
1	$14,757	$18,456
2	$16,592	$20,876
3	$18,103	$23,530
4	$20,322	$26,415
5	$22,737	$29,559
6	$25,344	$32,949
7	$28,164	$36,615
8	$31,191	$40,551
9	$34,451	$44,783
10	$37,939	$49,324
11	$41,684	$54,185
12	$49,959	$64,944
13	$59,409	$77,229
14	$70,205	$91,265
15	$82,580	$107,357

FEDERAL WAGE SYSTEM

About one quarter of federal civilian workers are paid according to the Federal Wage System. Under this system, craft, service, and manual workers are paid hourly rates established on the basis of "prevailing" rates paid by private employers for similar work in the same locations. As a result, the federal government wage rate for an occupation varies by locality. This commitment to meeting the local wage scale allows the federal wage earner to bring home a weekly paycheck comparable to that which he or she would earn in the private sector and to enjoy the benefits and security of a government job at the same time. The federal wage earner has the best of all possible worlds in this regard.

Federal government employees work a standard 40-hour week. Employees who are required to work overtime may receive premium rates for the additional time or compensatory time off at a later date. Most employees work 8 hours a day, five days a week, Monday through Friday, but in some cases, the nature of the work requires a different workweek. Annual earnings for most full-time federal workers are not affected by seasonal factors.

Federal employees earn thirteen days of annual (vacation) leave each year during their first three years of service; twenty days each year until the end of fifteen years; after fifteen years, twenty-six days each year. Workers who are members of military reserve organizations also are granted up to fifteen days of paid military leave a year for training purposes. A federal worker who is laid off, though federal layoffs are uncommon, is entitled to unemployment compensation similar to that provided for employees in private industry. Other benefits available to most federal employees include: a contributory retirement system, optional participation in low-cost group life and health insurance programs that are partly supported by the government (as the employer), and training programs to develop maximum job proficiency and help workers achieve their highest potential. These training programs may be conducted in government facilities or in private educational facilities at government expense.

CHAPTER 2

STATE AND LOCAL EMPLOYMENT

State and local governments provide a very large and expanding source of job opportunities in a wide variety of occupational fields. About 15 million people work for state and local government agencies; nearly three fourths of them work in units of local government, such as counties, municipalities, towns, and school districts.

LARGEST JOB AREAS

The job distribution varies greatly from that in federal government service. Defense, international relations and commerce, immigration, and mail delivery are virtually nonexistent in state and local governments. On the other hand, there is great emphasis on education, health, social services, transportation, construction, and sanitation.

EDUCATIONAL SERVICES

About half of all jobs in state and local governments are in educational services. Educational employees work in public schools, colleges, and various extension services. About half of all education workers are instructional personnel. School systems, colleges, and universities also employ administrative personnel, librarians, guidance counselors, nurses, dieticians, clerks, and maintenance workers.

HEALTH SERVICES

The next largest field of state and local government employment is health services. Those employed in health and hospital work include physicians, nurses, medical laboratory technicians, dieticians, kitchen and laundry workers, and hospital attendants. Social services make up another aspect of health and welfare. Unfortunately, the need for welfare and human services has been increasing greatly. As the need grows, the opportunities for social workers and their affiliated administrative and support staff also grows.

GOVERNMENT CONTROL/FINANCIAL ACTIVITIES

Another million workers work in the areas of general governmental control and financial activities. These include chief executives and their staffs, legislative representatives, and persons employed in the administration of justice, tax enforcement and other financial work, and general administration. These functions require the services of individuals such as lawyers, judges and other court officers, city managers, property assessors, budget analysts, stenographers, and clerks.

STREETS AND HIGHWAYS

The movement of people is of concern to both state and local governments. Street and highway construction and maintenance are of major importance. Highway workers include civil engineers, surveyors, operators of construction machinery and equipment, truck drivers, concrete finishers, carpenters, construction laborers, and, where appropriate, snow removers. Toll collectors are relatively few in number, but they too are state or county employees or employees of independent authorities of the states or counties. Mass transportation within municipalities and between the cities and their outlying suburbs is also the province of local government. Maintaining vehicles, roadbeds and signaling systems, and staffing the vehicles themselves, requires a large and varied workforce.

POLICE AND FIRE PROTECTION SERVICES

Police and fire protection is another large field of employment. Along with uniformed officers, these services include extensive administrative, clerical, maintenance, and custodial personnel.

MISCELLANEOUS STATE AND LOCAL OCCUPATIONS

Other state and local government employees work in a wide variety of activities, including local utilities (water in most areas, electricity in some), natural resources, parks and recreation, sanitation, corrections, local libraries, sewage disposal, and housing and urban renewal. These activities require workers in diverse occupations such as economists, electrical engineers, electricians, pipefitters, clerks, foresters, and bus drivers.

CLERICAL, ADMINISTRATIVE, MAINTENANCE, AND CUSTODIAL WORKERS

A large percentage of employment in most government agencies is made up of clerical, administrative, maintenance, and custodial workers. Among the workers involved in these activities are word processors, secretaries, data processors, computer specialists, office managers, fiscal and budget administrators, bookkeepers, accountants, carpenters, painters, plumbers, guards, and janitors. The list is endless. Residents of the state or locality fill most positions in state and local governments. Many localities have residency requirements. Exceptions are generally made for persons with skills that are in special demand.

EARNINGS

Job conditions and earnings of state and local government employees vary widely, depending upon occupation and locality. Salary differences from state to state and even within some states tend to reflect differences in the general wage level and cost of living in the various localities.

As with the federal government, a majority of state and local government positions are filled through some type of formal civil service test; that is, personnel are hired and promoted on the basis of merit. State and local government workers have the same protections as federal government workers: they cannot be refused employment because of their race; they cannot be denied promotion because someone else made a greater political contribution; and they cannot be fired because the boss's son needs a job. Jobs tend to be classified according to job description and pegged to a salary schedule that is based upon the job classifications. Periodic performance reviews also are standard expectations. Nearly every group of employees has some sort of union or organization, but the functions and powers of these units vary greatly.

Since states and local entities are independent, the benefits packages they offer their employees can be quite different. Most state and local government employees are covered by retirement systems or by the federal social security program. Most have some sort of health coverage. They usually work a standard week of 40 hours or less with overtime pay or compensatory time benefits for additional hours of work.

CHAPTER 3

PREPARING YOURSELF FOR THE CIVIL SERVICE EXAMINATION

Most federal, state, and municipal units have recruitment procedures for filling civil service positions. They have developed a number of methods to make job opportunities known. Places where such information may be obtained include:

1. The offices of the State Employment Services. There are almost two thousand throughout the country. These offices are administered by the state in which they are located, with the financial assistance of the federal government. You will find the address of the one nearest you in your telephone book.

2. Your state Civil Service Commission. Address your inquiry to the capital city of your state.

3. Your city Civil Service Commission. It is sometimes called by another name, such as the Department of Personnel, but you will be able to identify it in your telephone directory under the listing of city departments.

4. Your municipal building and your local library. Complete listings are carried by such newspapers as *The Chief-Leader* (published in New York City), as well as by other city and statewide publications devoted to civil service employees. Many local newspapers run a section on regional civil service news.

5. State and local agencies looking for competent employees will contact schools, professional societies, veterans organizations, unions, and trade associations.

6. School boards and boards of education, which employ the greatest proportion of all state and local personnel, should be asked directly for information about job openings. You will find more in-depth information at the end of this book.

THE FORMAT OF THE JOB ANNOUNCEMENT

When a position is open and a civil service examination is to be given for it, a job announcement is drawn up. This generally contains everything an applicant has to know about the job. The announcement begins with the job title and salary. A typical announcement then describes the work, the location of the position, the education and experience requirements, the kind of examination to be given, and the system of rating. It may also have something to say about veteran preference and the age limit. It tells which application form is to be filled out, where to get the form, and where and when to file it.

Study the job announcement carefully. It will answer many of your questions and help you decide whether you like the position and are qualified for it. We have included sample job announcements in a later chapter. There is no point in applying for a position and taking the examination if you do not want to work where the job is. The job may be in your community or hundreds of miles away at the other end of the state. If you are not willing to work where the job is, study other announcements that will give you an opportunity to work in a place of your choice. A civil service job close to your home has an additional advantage, since local residents usually receive preference in appointments.

The words **Optional Fields**—sometimes just the word **Options**—may appear on the front page of the announcement. You then have a choice to apply for that particular position in which you are especially interested. This is because the duties of various positions are quite different even though they bear the same broad title. A public relations clerk, for example, does different work from a payroll clerk, although they are considered broadly in the same general area. Not every announcement has options. But whether or not it has them, the precise duties are described in detail, usually under the heading, **Description of Work.** Make sure that these duties come within the range of your experience and ability.

Most job requirements give a **deadline for filing** an application. Others bear the words **No Closing Date** at the top of the first page; this means that applications will be accepted until the needs of the agency are met. In some cases a public notice is issued when a certain number of applications has been received. No application mailed past the deadline date will be considered.

Every announcement has a detailed section on **education and experience requirements** for the particular job and for the optional fields. Make sure that in both education and experience you meet the minimum qualifications. If you do not meet the given standards for one job, there may be others open where you stand a better chance of making the grade.

If the job announcement does not mention **veteran preference,** it would be wise to inquire if there is such a provision in your state or municipality. There may be none or it may be limited to disabled veterans. In some jurisdictions, surviving spouses of disabled veterans are given preference. All such information can be obtained through the agency that issues the job announcement. Applicants may be denied examinations and eligible candidates may be denied appointments for any of the following reasons:

- Intentional false statements

- Deception or fraud in examination or appointment

- Use of intoxicating beverages to the extent that ability to perform the duties of the position is impaired

- Criminal, infamous, dishonest, immoral, or notoriously disgraceful conduct

The announcement describes the **kind of test** given for the particular position. Please pay special attention to this section. It tells what areas are to be covered in the written test and lists the specific subjects on which questions will be asked. Sometimes sample questions are given.

Usually the announcement states whether the examination is to be **assembled** or **unassembled.** In an assembled examination, applicants assemble in the same place at the same time to take a written or performance test. The unassembled examination is one where an applicant does not take a test; instead, he or she is rated on his or her education and experience and whatever records of past achievement the applicant is asked to provide.

In the competitive examination, all applicants for a position compete with each other; the better the mark, the better the chance of being appointed. Also, competitive examinations are given to determine desirability for promotion among employees. Civil service written tests are rated on a scale of 100, with 70 usually as the passing mark.

FILLING OUT THE APPLICATION FORM

Having studied the job announcement and having decided that you want the position and are qualified for it, your next step is to get an application form. The job announcement tells you where to send for it. On the whole, civil service application forms differ little from state to state and locality to locality. The questions that have been worked out after years of experimentation are simple and direct, designed to elicit a maximal amount of information about you.

Many prospective civil service employees have failed to get a job because of slipshod, erroneous, incomplete, misleading, or untruthful answers. Give the application serious attention, for it is the first important step toward getting the job you want. Here, along with some helpful comments, are the questions usually asked on the average application form, although not necessarily in this order.

- **Name of examination or kind of position applied for.** This information appears in large type on the first page of the job announcement.

- **Optional job** (if mentioned in the announcement). If you wish to apply for an option, simply copy the title from the announcement. If you are not interested in an option, write *None*.

- **Primary place of employment applied for.** The location of the position was probably contained in the announcement. You must consider whether you want to work there. The announcement may list more than one location where the job is open. If you would accept employment in any of the places, list them all; otherwise list the specific place or places where you would be willing to work.

- **Name and address.** Give in full, including your middle name if you have one, and your maiden name as well if you are a married woman.

- **Home and office phones.** If none, write *None*.

- **Legal or voting residence.** The state in which you vote is the one you list here.

- **Height without shoes, weight, sex.** Answer accurately.

- **Date of birth.** Give the exact day, month, and year.

- **Lowest grade or pay you will accept.** Although the salary is clearly stated in the job announcement, there may be a quicker opening in the same occupation but carrying less responsibility and thus a lower basic entrance salary. You will not be considered for a job paying less than the amount you give in answer to this question.

- **Will you accept temporary employment if offered you for (a) one month or less, (b) one to four months, (c) four to twelve months?** Temporary positions come up frequently and it is important to know whether you are available.

- **Will you accept less than full-time employment?** Part-time work comes up now and then. Consider whether you want to accept such a position while waiting for a full-time appointment.

- **Were you in active military service in the Armed Forces of the United States?** Veterans' preference, if given, is usually limited to active service during the following periods: 12/7/41–12/31/46; 6/27/50–1/31/55; 6/1/63–5/7/75; 6/1/83–12/1/87; 10/23/83–11/21/83; 12/20/89–1/3/90; 8/2/90 to end of Persian Gulf hostilities.

■ **Do you claim disabled veterans credit?** If you do, you have to show proof of a war-incurred disability compensable by at least 10 percent. This is done through certification by the Veterans Administration.

■ **Special qualifications and skills.** Even though not directly related to the position for which you are applying, information about licenses and certificates obtained for teacher, pilot, registered nurse, and so on, is requested. List your experience in the use of machines and equipment and whatever other skills you have acquired.

Also list published writings, public speaking experience, membership in professional societies, and honors and fellowships received.

■ **Education.** List your entire educational history, including all diplomas, degrees, and special courses taken in any accredited or armed forces school. Also give your credits toward a college or a graduate degree.

■ **References.** The names of people who can give information about you, with their occupations and business and home addresses, are often requested.

■ **Your health.** Questions are asked concerning your medical record. You are expected to have the physical and psychological capacity to perform the job for which you are applying. Standards vary, of course, depending on the requirements of the position. A physical handicap usually will not bar an applicant from a job he can perform adequately unless the safety of the public is involved.

■ **Work history.** Considerable space is allotted on the form for the applicant to tell about all his past employment. Examiners check all such answers closely. Do not embellish or falsify your record. If you were ever fired, say so. It is better for you to state this openly than for the examiners to find out the truth from your former employer.

Following are samples of a New York City Application for Examination and a state application from Louisiana.

NEW YORK CITY APPLICATION FOR EXAMINATION

DEPARTMENT OF CITYWIDE ADMINISTRATIVE SERVICES
DIVISION OF CITYWIDE PERSONNEL SERVICES
1 Centre Street, 14th floor
New York, NY 10007

APPLICATION FOR EXAMINATION

(Directions for completing this application are on the *back* of this form. Additional information is on the Special Circumstances Sheet)

Download this form on-line: nyc.gov/html/dcas

FOLLOW DIRECTIONS ON BACK
Fill in all requested information clearly, accurately, and completely.

The City will only process applications with complete, correct, legible information which are accompanied by correct payment or waiver documentation.

All unprocessed applications will be returned to the applicant.

1. EXAM #:

2. EXAM TITLE:

Check One:
☐ Open Competitive
☐ Promotion

4. LAST NAME:

5. FIRST NAME:

6. MIDDLE INITIAL:

3. SOCIAL SECURITY NUMBER:

7. MAILING ADDRESS:

8. APT. #:

9. CITY OR TOWN:

10. STATE:

11. ZIP CODE:

12. PHONE:

13. OTHER NAMES USED IN CITY SERVICE:

14. RACE/ETHNICITY (Check One):
☐ White
☐ American Indian/Alaskan Native
☐ Black
☐ Asian/Pacific Islander
☐ Hispanic

15. SEX (Check One):
☐ Male
☐ Female

16. ARE YOU EMPLOYED BY THE HEALTH AND HOSPITALS CORPORATION? (Check One)
☐ YES   ☐ NO

17. CHECK ALL BOXES THAT APPLY TO YOU: (Directions for this section are found on the "Special Circumstances" Sheet)
☐ I AM A SABBATH OBSERVER AND WILL REQUEST AN ALTERNATE TEST DATE (Verification required. See Item A on Special Circumstances Sheet)
☐ I HAVE A DISABILITY AND WILL REQUEST SPECIAL ACCOMMODATIONS (Verification required. See item B on Special Circumstances Sheet).
☐ I CLAIM VETERANS' CREDIT (For qualifications see item C on Special Circumstances Sheet)
☐ I CLAIM DISABLED VETERANS' CREDIT (For qualifications see item C on Special Circumstances Sheet)

Questions 14 & 15:
Discrimination on the basis of sex, sexual orientation, race, creed, color, age, disability status, veteran status or religious observance is prohibited by law. The City of New York is an equal opportunity employer. The identifying information requested on this form is to be used to determine the representation of protected groups among applicants. This information is voluntary and will not be made available to individuals making hiring decisions.

18. Your Signature: _____   Date: _____

STATE OF LOUISIANA APPLICATION—PAGE 1

SF10
(Page 1)
REV. 1/97

STATE PRE-EMPLOYMENT APPLICATION

STATE OF LOUISIANA
DEPARTMENT OF CIVIL SERVICE
P.O. Box 94111, Capitol Station
Baton Rouge, Louisiana 70804-9111

FOR OFFICE USE

Special _____
Promo _____
Action(s) _____

Session _____

Data Entry Completed _____

AN EQUAL OPPORTUNITY EMPLOYER

1. TEST LOCATION-Check only one.

Baton Rouge (3) (Weekday) ☐	New Orleans (6) (Weekday) ☐	Lafayette (4) (Sat. only) ☐	Shreveport (7) (Sat. only) ☐
☐	New Orleans (12) (Saturday) ☐	Lake Charles (5) (Sat. only) ☐	West Monroe (8) (Sat. only) ☐

2. Enter Name and Complete Address below.

3. Parish of Residence

4. Are you 18 or older? ☐ Yes ☐ No

5. Other names ever used on SF-10

6. Social Security Number (For identification purpose)

NAME - First   Middle   Last

Mailing Address

City   State   Zip Code

Work Telephone No.

Home Telephone No.

7. REGISTER TITLE(S) APPLIED FOR	FOR OFFICE USE					**ADDITIONAL TITLES**	FOR OFFICE USE				
	SER	CD	REJ	GRD	TR		SER	CD	REJ	GRD	TR

LAST PRINT FIRST NAME MIDDLE

JS No.

V.P.

S.R.

ALL TITLES LISTED ABOVE MUST HAVE THE SAME SERIES NO.

8. JOB LOCATION AVAILABILITY - IMPORTANT: Read Item 9 on the Instruction Page before completing this item. Mark at least one (1), but no more than twenty (20) parishes.

☐ 01 Acadia	☐ 09 Caddo	☐ 17 E. Baton Rouge	☐ 25 Jackson	☐ 33 Madison	☐ 41 Red River	☐ 49 St. Landry	☐ 57 Vermillion
☐ 02 Allen	☐ 10 Calcasieu	☐ 18 E. Carroll	☐ 26 Jefferson	☐ 34 Morehouse	☐ 42 Richland	☐ 50 St. Martin	☐ 58 Vernon
☐ 03 Ascension	☐ 11 Caldwell	☐ 19 E. Feliciana	☐ 27 Jeff Davis	☐ 35 Natchitoches	☐ 43 Sabine	☐ 51 St. Mary	☐ 59 Washington
☐ 04	☐ 12 Cameron	☐ 20 Evangeline	☐ 28 Lafayette	☐ 36 Orleans	☐ 44 St. Bernard	☐ 52 St. Tammany	☐ 60 Webster
☐ 05 Avoyelles	☐ 13 Catahoula	☐ 21 Franklin	☐ 29 Lafourche	☐ 37 Ouachita	☐ 45 St. Charles	☐ 53 Tangipahoa	☐ 61 W. Baton Rouge
☐ 06 Beauregard	☐ 14 Claiborne	☐ 22 Grant	☐ 30 LaSalle	☐ 38 Plaquemines	☐ 46 St. Helena	☐ 54 Tensas	☐ 62 W. Carroll
☐ 07 Bienville	☐ 15 Concordia	☐ 23 Iberia	☐ 31 Lincoln	☐ 39 Pte. Coupee	☐ 47 St. James	☐ 55 Terrebonne	☐ 63 W. Feliciana
☐ 08 Bossier	☐ 16 DeSoto	☐ 24 Iberville	☐ 32 Livingston	☐ 40 Rapides	☐ 48 St. John	☐ 56 Union	☐ 64 Winn

9. ☐ Permanent ☐ Temporary—Type of employment you will accept

NOTE: Most Temporary Appointments are 3 - 12 months

10. ☐ YES ☐ NO Do you possess a valid driver's license?

11. ☐ YES ☐ NO Do you possess a valid commercial driver's license?

12. ☐ YES ☐ NO Are you currently holding or running for an elective public office?

13. ☐ YES ☐ NO Have you ever been on probation or sentenced to jail/prison as a result of a felony conviction or guilty plea?

14. ☐ YES ☐ NO Have you ever been fired from a job or resigned to avoid dismissal?

NOTE: If answers to Items 13 and/or 14 are "YES", you MUST complete Item 24 on Page 2 of this application

15. ☐ YES ☐ NO Are you claiming Veteran's Preference points on this application? (If "YES", see Item 20 on Page 2.)

The following information is collected to complete Equal Opportunity Reports required by law. You ARE NOT LEGALLY OBLIGATED to provide this information.

16. RACIAL/ETHNIC GROUP   **16A.** DATE OF BIRTH   **17.** SEX

_____   _____   ☐ Male ☐ Female

I HAVE READ THE FOLLOWING STATEMENTS CAREFULLY BEFORE SIGNING THIS APPLICATION:

18. Date   Social Security No. (for verification)

19. Signature of Applicant

AUTHORITY TO RELEASE INFORMATION: I consent to the release of information concerning my capacity and/or all aspects of prior job performance by employers, educational institutions, law enforcement agencies, and other individuals and agencies to duly accredited investigators, personnel technicians, and other authorized employees of the state government for the purpose of determining my eligibility and suitability for employment.

I certify that all statements made on this application and any attached papers are true and complete to the best of my knowledge. I understand that information on this application may be subject to investigation and verification and that any misrepresentation or material omission may cause my application to be rejected, my name to be removed from the eligible register and/or subject me to dismissal from state service.

STATE OF LOUISIANA APPLICATION—PAGE 2

20. ACTIVE MILITARY SERVICE/VETERAN'S PREFERENCE

See Item 10 on the Instruction Page to determine your eligibility for Veteran's Preference. If you are a first-time applicant or if you are claiming Veteran's Preference for the first time, required PROOF MUST BE ATTACHED to this application to have preference points added to your score.

List the dates (month and year) and branch for all ACTIVE DUTY military service. Was this service performed on an active, full-time basis with full pay and allowances? (Check YES or NO for each period of service.)

FROM	TO	BRANCH OF SERVICE	YES	NO

List all GRADES held and dates of each grade. Begin with the highest grade. IMPORTANT: Use E-, O-, or WO-grade.

FROM	TO	GRADE HELD	FROM	TO	GRADE HELD

21. TRAINING AND EDUCATION

Have you received a high school diploma or equivalency certificate?

☐ YES   Date received _____

☐ NO   Highest grade completed _____

A. LIST *BUSINESS OR* TECHNICAL COLLEGES ATTENDED

NAME/LOCATION OF SCHOOL	Dates Attended (Month & Year) FROM — TO	Did You Graduate? YES — NO	TITLE OF PROGRAM	CLOCK HOURS PER WEEK

List any accounting practice sets completed:

B. LIST COLLEGES *OR* UNIVERSITIES ATTENDED (Include graduate or professional schools)

NAME OF COLLEGE OR UNIVERSITY/ CITY AND STATE	Dates Attended (Month & Year) FROM — TO	Total Credit Hours Earned Semester — Quarter	Type of Degree Earned	Major Field of Study	Date Degree Received (Month & Yr.)

C. MAJOR SUBJECTS

	CHIEF UNDERGRADUATE SUBJECTS (Show Major on Line 1.)	Total Credit Hours Earned Semester — Quarter	CHIEF GRADUATE SUBJECTS (Show Major on Line 1.)	Total Credit Hours Earned Semester or Qtr.
1				
2				
3				

22. LICENSES AND CERTIFICATION

List any job-related licenses or certificates that you have (CPA, lawyer, registered nurse, etc.)

	TYPE OF LICENSE OR CERTIFICATE (Specify Which One)	DATE ORIGINALLY LICENSED/ CERTIFIED	EXPIRATION DATE	NAME AND ADDRESS OF LICENSING OR CERTIFYING AGENCY
1				
2				

23. TYPING SPEED

_____ WPM

DICTATION SPEED

_____ WPM

24. Explain a "YES" answer to Items 13 and/or 14 here. A "YES" ANSWER WILL NOT NECESSARILY BAR YOU FROM STATE EMPLOYMENT. WE WILL CONSIDER THE DATE, FACTS, AND CIRCUMSTANCES OF EACH INDIVIDUAL CASE. For Item 13, give the law enforcement authority (city police, sherrif, FBI, etc.), the offense, date of offense, place, and disposition of case.

_____

_____

Name _____

STATE OF LOUISIANA APPLICATION—PAGE 3

Name _____

25. WORK EXPERIENCE — <u>IMPORTANT</u>: Read Item 11 of Instruction Page carefully before completing these items. List all jobs and activities including military service, part-time employment, self-employment, and volunteer work. **BEGIN** with your **FIRST** job in Block A; **END** with your **MOST RECENT or PRESENT** job.

A | EMPLOYER/COMPANY NAME | | KIND OF BUSINESS |

| STREET ADDRESS | YOUR OFFICIAL JOB TITLE |

| CITY AND STATE | BEGINNING SALARY | ENDING SALARY |

| DATES OF EMPLOYMENT (MO/DA/YR) | AVERAGE HOURS WORKED PER WEEK | REASON FOR LEAVING | NO. OF EMPLOYEES YOU DIRECTLY SUPERVISED |
| FROM | TO |

| NAME/TITLE OF YOUR SUPERVISOR) | LIST JOB TITLES OF EMPLOYEES YOU DIRECTLY SUPERVISED |

| NAME/TITLE OF PERSON WHO CAN VERIFY THIS EMPLOYMENT (IF OTHER THAN SUPERVISOR) |

DUTIES: List the major duties involved with job and give an approximate percentage of time spent on each duty.

% OF TIME	MAJOR DUTIES
100%	

B | EMPLOYER/COMPANY NAME | | KIND OF BUSINESS |

| STREET ADDRESS | YOUR OFFICIAL JOB TITLE |

| CITY AND STATE | BEGINNING SALARY | ENDING SALARY |

| DATES OF EMPLOYMENT (MO/DA/YR) | AVERAGE HOURS WORKED PER WEEK | REASON FOR LEAVING | NO. OF EMPLOYEES YOU DIRECTLY SUPERVISED |
| FROM | TO |

| NAME/TITLE OF YOUR SUPERVISOR) | LIST JOB TITLES OF EMPLOYEES YOU DIRECTLY SUPERVISED |

| NAME/TITLE OF PERSON WHO CAN VERIFY THIS EMPLOYMENT (IF OTHER THAN SUPERVISOR) |

DUTIES: List the major duties involved with job and give an approximate percentage of time spent on each duty.

% OF TIME	MAJOR DUTIES

STATE OF LOUISIANA APPLICATION—PAGE 4

100%

USE REVERSE SIDE OF THIS PAGE IF ADDITIONAL SPACE REQUIRED FOR WORK EXPERIENCE

Name _____

25. WORK EXPERIENCE (Continued)

C | EMPLOYER/COMPANY NAME | KIND OF BUSINESS |

STREET ADDRESS | YOUR OFFICIAL JOB TITLE

CITY AND STATE | BEGINNING SALARY | ENDING SALARY

| DATES OF EMPLOYMENT (MO/DA/YR) | AVERAGE HOURS WORKED PER WEEK | REASON FOR LEAVING | NO. OF EMPLOYEES YOU DIRECTLY SUPERVISED |

FROM | TO

NAME/TITLE OF YOUR SUPERVISOR | LIST JOB TITLES OF EMPLOYEES YOU DIRECTLY SUPERVISED

NAME/TITLE OF PERSON WHO CAN VERIFY THIS EMPLOYMENT
(IF OTHER THAN SUPERVISOR)

DUTIES: List the major duties involved with job and give an approximate percentage of time spent on each duty.

% OF TIME	MAJOR DUTIES

100%

D | EMPLOYER/COMPANY NAME | KIND OF BUSINESS |

STREET ADDRESS | YOUR OFFICIAL JOB TITLE

CITY AND STATE | BEGINNING SALARY | ENDING SALARY

| DATES OF EMPLOYMENT (MO/DA/YR) | AVERAGE HOURS WORKED PER WEEK | REASON FOR LEAVING | NO. OF EMPLOYEES YOU DIRECTLY SUPERVISED |

FROM | TO

NAME/TITLE OF YOUR SUPERVISOR) | LIST JOB TITLES OF EMPLOYEES YOU DIRECTLY SUPERVISED

NAME/TITLE OF PERSON WHO CAN VERIFY THIS EMPLOYMENT
(IF OTHER THAN SUPERVISOR)

DUTIES: List the major duties involved with job and give an approximate percentage of time spent on each duty.

% OF TIME	MAJOR DUTIES

CHAPTER 4

TEST-TAKING TECHNIQUES

Many factors enter into a test score. The most important factor is the ability to answer the questions, which indicates the ability to learn and perform the duties of the job. Assuming that you have this ability, knowing what to expect on the exam and familiarity with techniques of effective test taking will give you the confidence you need to do your best on the exam.

HOW TO BE TEST-WISE

There is no quick substitute for long-term study and development of your skills to prepare you for doing well on tests. However, there are some steps you can take to help you do your very best. Knowing these steps is often called being **test-wise**. *Test-wise* is a general term that simply means being familiar with some good procedures to follow when getting ready for and taking a test. The procedures fall into four major areas:

1. Being prepared

2. Avoiding careless errors

3. Managing your time

4. Guessing

Following these steps may help you feel more confident as you take the actual test.

BE PREPARED

Don't make the test harder than it has to be by not preparing yourself. You are taking a very important step in preparation by reading this book and taking the sample tests that are included. This will help you to become familiar with the tests and the kinds of questions you will have to answer. As you use this book, read the sample questions and directions for taking the test carefully. Then, when you take the sample tests, time yourself as you will be timed on the real test.

As you are working on the sample questions, don't look at the correct answers before you try to answer them on your own. This can fool you into thinking you understand a question when you really don't. Try it on your own first, then compare your answer with the one given. Remember, in a sample test, you are your own grader; you don't gain anything by pretending to understand something you really don't.

On the examination day assigned to you, allow the test itself to be the main attraction of the day. Do not squeeze it in between other activities. Be sure to bring your admission card, identification, and pencils, as instructed. Prepare these the night before so that you are not flustered by a last-minute search. Arrive rested, relaxed, and on time. In fact, plan to arrive a little bit early. Leave plenty of time for traffic tie-ups or other complications that might upset you and interfere with your test performance.

In the test room, the examiner will hand out forms for you to fill out. He or she will give you the instructions that you must follow in taking the examination. The examiner will tell you how to fill in the grids on the forms. Time limits and timing signals will be explained. If you do not understand any of the examiner's instructions, ASK QUESTIONS. It would be ridiculous to score less than your best because of poor communication. At the examination, you must follow instructions exactly. Fill in the grids on the forms carefully and accurately. Gridding incorrectly may lead to loss of veterans' credits to which you may be entitled or misaddressing of your test results. Do not begin until you are told to begin. Stop as soon as the examiner tells you to stop. Do not turn pages until you are told to do so. Do not go back to parts you have already completed. Any infraction of the rules is considered cheating. If you cheat, your test paper will not be scored, and you will not be eligible for appointment. The answer sheet for most multiple-choice exams is machine scored. You cannot give any explanations to the machine, so you must fill out the answer sheet clearly and correctly.

HOW TO MARK YOUR ANSWER SHEET

1. **Blacken your answer space firmly and completely.** ● is the only correct way to mark the answer sheet. ◖, ⊗, ⊘, and ⊘ are all unacceptable. The machine might not read them at all.

2. **Mark only one answer for each question.** If you mark more than one answer, you will be considered wrong, even if one of the answers is correct.

3. **If you change your mind, you must erase your mark.** Attempting to cross out an incorrect answer like this ✸ will not work. You must erase any incorrect answer completely. An incomplete erasure might be read as a second answer.

4. **All of your answering should be in the form of blackened spaces.** The machine cannot read English. Do not write any notes in the margins.

5. **MOST IMPORTANT: Answer each question in the right place.** Question 1 must be answered in space 1; question 52 in space 52. If you should skip an answer space and mark a series of answers in the wrong places, you must erase all those answers and do the questions over, marking your answers in the proper places. You cannot afford to use the limited time in this way. Therefore, as you answer *each* question, look at its number and check that you are marking your answer in the space with the same number.

6. **For the typing tests, type steadily and carefully.** Just don't rush, since that's when the errors occur. Keep in mind that each error subtracts one word per minute (wpm) from your final score.

AVOID CARELESS ERRORS

Don't reduce your score by making careless mistakes. Always read the instructions for each test section carefully, even when you think you already know what the directions are. It's why we stress throughout this book that it's important to fully understand the directions for these different question types *before* you go into the actual exam. It will not only reduce errors, but it will save you time—time you will need for the questions.

What if you don't understand the directions? You will have risked getting the answers wrong for a whole test section. As an example, vocabulary questions can sometimes test synonyms (words that have similar meanings) and sometimes test antonyms (words with opposite meanings). You can easily see how a mistake in understanding in this case could make a whole set of answers incorrect.

If you have time, reread any complicated instructions after you do the first few questions to check that you really do understand them. Of course, whenever you are allowed to, ask the examiner to clarify anything you don't understand. Other careless mistakes affect only the response to particular questions. This often happens with arithmetic questions, but can happen with other questions as well. This type of error, called a *response error*, usually stems from a momentary lapse of concentration.

Example

The question reads: "The capital of Massachusetts is . . . ."

The answer is (D), Boston, and you mark (B) because "B" is the first letter of the word "Boston."

Example

The question reads: "8 – 5 = ..."

The answer is (A), 3, but you mark (C) thinking "third letter."

A common error in Reading Comprehension questions is bringing your own information into the subject. For example, you may encounter a passage that discusses a subject you know something about. While this can make the passage easier to read, it can also tempt you to rely on your own knowledge about the subject. You must rely on information within the passage for your answers—in fact, sometimes the "wrong answer" for the questions are based on true information about the subject *not* given in the passage. Since the test makers are testing your reading ability, rather than your general knowledge of the subject, an answer based on information not contained in the passage is considered incorrect.

MANAGE YOUR TIME

Before you begin, take a moment to plan your progress through the test. Although you are usually not expected to finish all of the questions given on a test, you should at least get an idea of how much time you should spend on each question in order to answer them all. For example, if there are sixty questions to answer and you have 30 minutes, you will have about one-half minute to spend on each question.

Keep track of the time on your watch or the room clock, but do not fixate on the time remaining. Your task is to answer questions. Do not spend too much time on any one question. If you find yourself stuck, do not take the puzzler as a personal challenge. Either guess and mark the question in the question booklet or skip the question entirely, marking the question as a skip and taking care to skip the answer space on the answer sheet. If there is time at the end of the exam or exam part, you can return and give marked questions another try.

MULTIPLE-CHOICE QUESTIONS

Almost all of the tests given on civil service exams are multiple-choice format. This means that you normally have four or five answer choices. But it's not something that should be overwhelming. There is a basic technique to answering these types of questions. Once you've understood this technique, it will make your test-taking far less stressful. First, there should only be one correct answer. Since these tests have been given time and again, and the test developers have a sense of which questions work and which questions don't work, it will be rare that your choices will be ambiguous. They may be complex, and somewhat confusing, but there will still be only one right answer.

The first step is to look at the question without looking at the answer choices. Now think about the correct answer. That may sound somewhat simplistic, but it's usually the case that your first choice is the correct one. Thus, follow your instinct. Once you have come up with the answer, look at the answer choices. If your answer is one of the choices, you're probably correct.

If you go back and change it, it's more likely that you'll end up with the wrong answer. It's not 100 percent infallible, but there's a strong possibility that you've selected the right answer.

With math questions you should first solve the problem. If your answer is among the choices, you're probably correct. Don't ignore things like the proper function signs (adding, subtracting, multiplying, and dividing), negative and positive numbers, and so on. But suppose you don't know the correct answer. You then use the *process of elimination*. It's a time-honored technique for test takers. There is always one correct answer.

There is usually one answer choice that is totally incorrect—a *distracter*. If you look at that choice and it seems highly unlikely, then eliminate it. You've just cut down the number of choices to make. Now weigh the remaining choices. They may seem incorrect or they may be correct. If they seem incorrect, eliminate them. You've now increased your odds at getting the correct answer. In the end, you may be left with only two choices. At that point, it's just a matter of guessing. But with only two choices left, you now have a 50 percent chance of getting it right. With four choices, you only have a 25 percent chance, and with five choices, only a 20 percent chance at guessing correctly. That's why the process of elimination is important.

SHOULD YOU GUESS?

You may be wondering whether or not it is wise to guess when you are not sure of an answer (even if you've reduced the odds to 50 percent) or whether it is better to skip the question when you are not certain. The wisdom of guessing depends on the scoring method for that particular examination part. If the scoring is *rights only*, that is, one point for each correct answer and no subtraction for wrong answers, then by all means you should guess. Read the question and all of the answer choices carefully. Eliminate those answer choices that you are certain are wrong. Then guess from among the remaining choices. You cannot gain a point if you leave the answer space blank; you may gain a point with an educated guess or even with a lucky guess. In fact, it is foolish to leave any spaces blank on a test that counts only right answers. If it appears that you are about to run out of time before completing such an exam, mark all the remaining blanks with the same letter. According to the law of averages, you should get some portion of those questions right.

If the scoring method is *rights minus wrongs*, such as the address checking test found on Postal Clerk Exam 470, DO NOT GUESS. A wrong answer counts heavily against you. On this type of test, do not rush to fill answer spaces randomly at the end. Work as quickly as possible while concentrating on accuracy. Keep working carefully until time is called. Then stop and leave the remaining answer spaces blank.

In guessing the answers to multiple-choice questions, take a second to eliminate those answers that are obviously wrong, then quickly consider and guess from the remaining choices. The fewer choices from which you guess, the better the odds of guessing correctly.

Once you decide to make a guess, be it an educated guess or a wild stab, do it right away and move on; don't keep thinking about it and wasting time. You should always mark the test questions at which you guess so that you can return later. For those questions that are scored by subtracting a fraction of a point for each wrong answer, or *rights minus a fraction of wrongs*, the decision as to whether or not to guess is really up to you. A correct answer gives you one point; a skipped space gives you nothing at all, but costs you nothing except the chance of getting the answer right; a wrong answer costs you 1/4 point.

If you are really uncomfortable with guessing, you may skip a question, *but* you must then remember to skip its answer space as well. The risk of losing your place if you skip questions is so great that we advise you to guess even if you are not sure of the answer. Our suggestion is that you answer every question in order, even if you have to guess. It is better to lose a few points for wrong guesses than to lose valuable seconds figuring where you started marking answers in the wrong place, erasing, and re-marking answers. On the other hand, do not mark random answers at the end. Work steadily until time is up.

One of the questions you should ask in the testing room is what scoring method will be used on your particular exam. You can then guide your guessing procedure accordingly.

TEST-TAKING TIPS

1. Get to the test center early. Make sure you give yourself plenty of extra time to get there, park your car, if necessary, and even grab a cup of coffee before the test.

2. Listen to the test monitors and follow their instructions carefully. Read every word of the instructions.

3. Read every word of every question.

4. Mark your answers by completely darkening the answer space of your choice. Do not use the test paper to work out your answers.

5. Mark only ONE answer for each question, even if you think that more than one answer is correct. You must choose only one. If you mark more than one answer, the scoring machine will consider you wrong.

6. If you change your mind, erase completely. Leave no doubt as to which answer you mean.

7. If your exam permits you to use scratch paper or the margins of the test booklet for figuring, don't forget to mark the answer on the answer sheet. Only the answer sheet is scored.

8. Check often to be sure that the question number matches the answer space and that you have not skipped a space by mistake.

9. Guess according to the guessing suggestions we have made.

10. Stay alert. Be careful not to mark a wrong answer just because you were not concentrating.

11. Do not panic. If you cannot finish any part before time is up, do not worry. If you are accurate, you can do well even without finishing. It is even possible to earn a scaled score of 100 without entirely finishing an exam part if you are very accurate. At any rate, do not let your performance on any one part affect your performance on any other part.

12. Check and recheck, time permitting. If you finish any part before time is up, use the remaining time to check that each question is answered in the right space and that there is only one answer for each question. Return to the difficult questions and rethink them.

SCORING

If your exam is a short-answer exam such as those often used by companies in the private sector, your answers will be graded by a personnel officer trained in grading test questions. If you blackened spaces on the separate answer sheet accompanying a multiple-choice exam, your answer sheet will be machine scanned or will be hand scored using a punched card stencil. Then a raw score will be calculated using the scoring formula that applies to that test or test portion—rights only, rights minus wrongs, or rights minus a fraction of wrongs. Raw scores on test parts are then added together for a total raw score.

A raw score is *not* a final score. The raw score is not the score that finds its way onto an eligibility list. The civil service testing authority, Postal Service, or other testing body converts raw scores to a scaled score according to an unpublicized formula of its own. The scaling formula allows for slight differences in difficulty of questions from one form of the exam to another and allows for equating the scores of all candidates. Regardless of the number of questions and possible different weights of different parts of the exam, most civil service clerical test scores are reported on a scale of 1 to 10. The entire process of conversion from raw to scaled score is confidential information.

The score you receive is not your number right, is not your raw score, and, despite being on a scale of 1 to 100, is not a percentage. It is a scaled score. If you are entitled to veterans' service points, these are added to your passing scaled score to boost your rank on the eligibility list. Veterans' points are added only to passing scores. A failing score cannot be brought to passing level by adding veterans' points. The score earned plus veterans' service points, if any, is the score that finds its place on the rank order eligibility list. Highest scores go to the top of the list.

PART II

Postal Clerk and Carrier Careers

CHAPTER 5

Working for the U.S. Postal Service

WELCOME TO THE U.S. POSTAL SERVICE

Remember when you were a kid and you took a field trip to your local post office? More than likely, a friendly employee gave you a tour of the mail sorting area, demonstrated how the various computers are used (depending, of course, on your age at the time of the tour!), and perhaps gave you a peek into one of the mail trucks. And, if you're like many people, you left with the impression that the only thing postal employees do is "sort the mail." Maybe this impression stayed with you into adulthood.

Most people are familiar with the duties of the city carrier and post-office window clerk (the same friendly employees who may have given you the tour when you were young). However, very few people are aware of the many different tasks required in "sorting the mail," not to mention the enormous variety of occupations in the U.S. Postal Service.

Twenty-four hours a day mail (consisting of packages, magazines, and other assorted papers) moves through the typical large post office. It takes a lot of hard work to keep that mail moving, and all that hard work requires the involvement of many different people performing many different tasks:

Almost 85 percent of all postal workers are in jobs directly related to processing and delivering mail. This group includes postal clerks, city carriers, mail handlers, rural carriers, and truck drivers. Postmasters and supervisors make up nearly 10 percent of total employment, and maintenance workers about 4 percent. The remainder includes such workers as postal inspectors, guards, personnel workers, and secretaries.

- City carriers have collected some of this mail from neighborhood mailboxes; some has been trucked in from surrounding towns or from the airport. When a truck arrives at the post office, mail handlers unload the mail.

- Postal clerks then sort it according to destination. After being sorted, outgoing mail is loaded into trucks for delivery to the airport or nearby towns. Local mail is left for carriers to deliver the next morning.

- To keep buildings and equipment clean and in good working order, the Postal Service employs a variety of service and maintenance workers, including janitors, laborers, truck mechanics, electricians, carpenters, and painters. Some workers specialize in repairing machines that process mail.

- Postal inspectors audit the operations of post offices to see that they are run efficiently, that funds are spent properly, and that postal laws and regulations are observed. They also prevent and detect crimes such as theft, forgery, and fraud involving use of the mail.

- Postmasters and supervisors are responsible for the day-to-day operation of the post office, for hiring and promoting employees, and for setting up work schedules.

As you can see, there are lots of exciting positions within the U.S. Postal Service. However, the focus of this book will be on the positions of Postal Clerk and Carrier. Not only will you receive up-to-date information on these positions, but you also learn specific techniques for how to get your best score on the exams. You'll also get plenty of opportunity to practice on each exam question type.

BENEFITS, SALARIES, HOLIDAYS, AND LEAVE TIME

The United States Postal Service is an independent agency of the Federal Government. As such, employees of the Postal Service are federal employees who enjoy the generous benefits offered by the government. These benefits include an automatic raise at least once a year, regular cost-of-living adjustments, liberal paid vacation and sick leave, life insurance, hospitalization, and the opportunity to join a credit union.

At the same time, the operation of the Postal Service is businesslike and independent of politics. A postal worker's job is secure even though presidential administrations change. An examination system is used to fill vacancies. This system provides opportunities for those who are able and motivated to enter the Postal Service and to move within it.

BENEFITS

Post Office employees are covered by the same benefits as employees of the Federal Government, including Federal Employees Health Benefits (FEHB), Federal Employees Retirement System (FERS), and Life Insurance.

The table below illustrates the general benefits offered by the USPS.

Type of Benefits	Who Is Covered	Available Options
Health: *Federal Employees Health Benefits (FEHB)*	Postal Employees and Retirees and their survivors. Coverage may include: • Self only; or • Family coverage for yourself, your spouse, and unmarried dependant children under age 22	• Managed Fee for Service Plans; • Point of Service (POP) options; or • Health Maintenance Organizations (HMOs)
Retirement: *Federal Employees Retirement System (FERS)*	Almost all new employees hired after 1983 are automatically covered. Employees who leave may still qualify for benefits. Builds on the Social Security Benefits employees may earn in the future, or may already have earned, from non-Federal work.	FERS is a three-tiered retirement plan, consisting of these components: • Social Security Benefits (available for those age 62 and retired) • Basic Benefits Plan (financed by a small contribution from the employee and the government) • A Special Retirement Supplement for employees who meet the criteria is paid as a monthly benefit until the employee reaches age 62 • Thrift Savings Plan (tax-deferred retirement savings and investment plan; similar to 401K plans)

Type of Benefits	Who Is Covered	Available Options
Life: *The Federal Employees' Group Life Insurance Program (FEGLI)*	Postal employees and retirees, as well as many of their family members, are eligible for this group life insurance program.	• Basic Insurance (automatic unless employee opts out; insured pays 2/3 of cost and the government pays) • Optional Insurance (not automatic; insured pays 100% of cost)
Social Security and Medicare	All postal employees including those who have just been hired are covered.	
Flexible Spending Accounts	All postal employees who have over one year of service are eligible.	• Tax-free contributions that can be used to cover health-care expenses

SALARIES

Salaries within the USPS are "graded." The amount of time you've been employed, any promotions you might have achieved, as well as whether or not you work full-time or part-time are all factors that determine your salary.

The following tables illustrate salary levels for various positions with the USPS. You are assigned a "Grade"(e.g., Grade 5) depending on the type of position you fill (note that each position has different grade levels). Moving between steps (e.g., B to C) requires that you be in the previous position for a specified number of weeks (more details on these "step" requirements are defined after the tables).

LETTER CARRIER PAY SCHEDULE – 11/17/01 (YEARLY)

STEPS	A	B	C	D	E
Grade 1	$32,735	$36,013	$37,285	$39,721	$40,056
Grade 2	$34,411	$37,897	$37,976	$40,471	$40,834
STEPS	F	G	H	I	J
Grade 1	$40,393	$40,724	$41,060	$41,395	$41,726
Grade 2	$41,197	$41,555	$41,916	$42,280	$42,633
STEPS	K	L	M	N	O
Grade 1	$42,063	$42,397	$42,732	$43,069	$43,402
Grade 2	$42,997	$43,360	$43,719	$44,086	$44,446

MAIL HANDLER PAY SCHEDULE – 11/17/2001 (YEARLY)

STEPS	A	B	C	D	E
Level 4	$26,273	$31,167	$33,479	$36,885	$37,159
Level 5	$27,650	$32,879	$35,256	$37,557	$37,853

STEPS	F	G	H	I	J
Level 4	$37,438	$37,712	$37,988	$38,264	$38,544
Level 5	$38,153	$38,446	$38,745	$39,045	$39,339

STEPS	K	L	M	N	O
Level 4	$38,819	$39,095	$39,371	$39,647	$39,922
Level 5	$39,638	$39,931	$40,231	$40,528	$40,825

RURAL CARRIER EVALUATED SCHEDULE – 9/2002

Full-Time Annual Basic Rates (Partial Schedule)

Hours	A	B	C	1	2	3	4
12	$9,357	$10,295	$10,620	$11,320	$11,427	$11,531	$11,637
18	$14,034	$15,445	$15,933	$16,979	$17,138	$17,297	$17,456
24	$18,712	$20,588	$21,241	$22,640	$22,848	$23,058	$23,268
30	$23,389	$25,745	$26,558	$28,303	$28,564	$28,833	$29,091
40	$31,185	$34,316	$35,404	$37,730	$38,082	$38,435	$38,782
48	$40,542	$44,612	$46,024	$49,050	$49,509	$49,967	$50,419

Hours	5	6	7	8	9	10	11
12	$11,742	$11,851	$11,954	$12,058	$12,166	$12,271	$12,378
18	$17,614	$17,772	$17,930	$18,088	$18,250	$18,407	$18,568
24	$23,478	$23,690	$23,899	$24,108	$24,320	$24,531	$24,744
30	$29,353	$29,618	$29,880	$30,143	$30,407	$30,670	$30,937
40	$39,136	$39,487	$39,835	$40,189	$40,539	$40,891	$41,245
48	$50,877	$51,339	$51,789	$52,247	$52,707	$53,163	$53,622

FULL TIME REGULAR APWU SALARY SCHEDULE (PS) – 9/7/02
(APPLIES TO ALL POSTAL CLERKS)

Steps	D	E	F	G	H
2	$36,678	$36,922	$37,166	$37,411	$37,660
3	$37,270	$37,533	$37,802	$38,063	$38,329
4	$37,912	$38,197	$38,487	$38,772	$39,055
5	$38,608	$38,916	$39,225	$39,530	$39,841
6	$39,358	$39,693	$40,030	$40,361	$40,698
7	$40,172	$40,532	$40,891	$41,252	$41,615

SALARY STEP INCREASE WAITING PERIODS FOR BARGAINING UNIT POSITIONS

To be eligible for a periodic step increase, an employee:

■ Must have received and currently be serving under a career appointment

■ Must have performed in a satisfactory or outstanding manner during the waiting period

■ Cannot have received an equivalent increase during the waiting period

■ Must have completed the required waiting period (see tables below)

POSTAL SERVICE (PS) SCHEDULE

Steps (From→To)	Grades 1–3	Grades 4–7	Grades 8–10	Steps (From→To)	Grades 1–3	Grades 4–7	Grades 8–10
A → B	96	96	—	H → I	44	44	44
B → C	88	96	—	I → J	44	44	44
C → D	88	44	52	J → K	34	34	34
D → E	44	44	44	K → L	34	34	34
E → F	44	44	44	L → M	26	26	26
F → G	44	44	44	M → N	26	26	26
G → H	44	44	44	N → O	24	24	24

MAIL HANDLER (MH) SCHEDULE

Steps (From → To)	Grades 4–6	Steps (From → To)	Grades 4–6
A → B	96	H → I	44
B → C	96	I → J	44
C → D	44	J → K	34
D → E	44	K → L	34
E → F	44	L → M	26
F → G	44	M → N	26
G → H	44	N → O	24

RURAL CARRIER SCHEDULES*

Steps (From → To)	A to B	B to C	C to 1	1 to 2	2 to 3	3 to 4	4 to 5	5 to 6	6 to 7	7 to 8	8 to 9	9 to 10	10 to 11	11 to 12
Hours/Miles	96	96	44	44	44	44	44	44	44	34	34	26	26	24

*NOTE: Waiting periods for these step increases apply to all hours on the Rural Carrier Evaluated Schedule, all miles on the Rural Mileage Schedule, and Grade 5 of the Rural Auxiliary Schedule.**

CITY CARRIER (CC) SCHEDULE

Steps (From → To)	Grades 4–6	Steps (From → To)	Grades 4–6
A → B	96	H → I	44
B → C	96	I → J	44
C → D	44	J → K	34
D → E	44	K → L	34
E → F	44	L → M	26
F → G	44	M → N	26
G → H	44	N → O	24

HOLIDAYS

All USPS offices observe the following holidays:

- New Year's Day
- Martin Luther King, Jr.'s Birthday
- George Washington's Birthday
- Memorial Day
- Independence Day
- Labor Day
- Columbus Day
- Veterans' Day
- Thanksgiving Day
- Christmas Day

LEAVE TIME

In addition to the benefits listed above, employees of the postal service are also granted leave time for a variety of purposes. The following table illustrates the amount of leave time you can expect, depending on the reason for leave and your years of service.

Type of Leave	Use of This Type of Leave	Amount of Time You May Use
Annual Leave	For rest, recreation, and for personal and emergency purposes *Must be approved in advance by appropriate supervisor*	Employees earn 13, 20, or 26 days of annual leave each leave year, according to their years of service.
Sick Leave	• Medical, dental, or optical examination or treatment • You are incapacitated by physical or mental illness, injury, or pregnancy or confinement • Contagious disease: If the employee himself or herself has a contagious disease or must care for a family member with a contagious disease • Medical leave for disabled veterans	Full-time employee: 13 days per year (employees accrue 4 hours for each full biweekly pay period, without limitation)

Type of Leave	Use of This Type of Leave	Amount of Time You May Use
Family and Medical Leave	According to the Family and Medical Leave Act of 1993 (FMLA), employees are entitled to 12 weeks of unpaid leave for the following reasons: • The birth and care of your child • Placement of a child with you for adoption or foster care • Care of your spouse, child, or parent with a serious health condition • Your own serious health condition *You may substitute Annual Leave for unpaid leave*	Twelve administrative work weeks during any 12-month period
Court Leave	For employees who are summoned, in connection with a judicial proceeding, to serve as a juror or to serve a witness, in a nonofficial capacity, in a case involving the Federal Government or Postal Service	
Military Leave	For reservists or for members of the National Guard	Up to 15 days
Leave Sharing	Allows career postal employees to donate their leave to other career postal employees for a medical emergency when the recipient has exhausted his or her own leave	

TRAINING AND QUALIFICATIONS

An applicant for a Postal Service job must pass an examination and meet minimum age requirements. Generally, the minimum age is 18 years, but a high school graduate may begin work at 16 years if the job is not hazardous and does not require the use of a motor vehicle. Many Postal Service jobs do not require formal education or special training. Applicants for these jobs are hired on the basis of their examination scores. Note that some postal jobs do have special education or experience requirements, and some are open only to veterans. Any special requirements are stated on the announcement of examination.

Here is a list of the general requirements for qualification for a USPS position:

■ Job applicants must pass an exam and must be 18 years old at the time of appointment or 16 years old with a high school diploma.

■ Employees must be U. S. citizens or permanent resident aliens.

■ Basic competency in English is required.

Advancement opportunities are available for most postal workers because there is a management commitment to provide career development. Also, employees can get preferred assignments, such as the day shift or a more desirable delivery route, as their seniority increases. When an opening occurs, employees may submit written requests, called "bids," for assignment to the vacancy. The bidder who meets the qualifications and has the most seniority gets the job.

■ Males born after December 31, 1959 must be registered with the Selective Service System.

■ Applicants must provide the names of their current employer and all previous employers for the ten year period leading up to the date of application or to their 16th birthday, whichever is most recent.

■ Military service is treated as prior employment. Veterans must indicate service and submit Copy 4 of the DD Form 214, Certificate of Release or Discharge from Active Duty.

■ A local criminal check is required prior to employment; at employment, a more extensive criminal history check is completed.

■ Employees must be drug free; this is determined through a urinalysis drug screen.

■ Applicants must demonstrate an ability to physically or mentally perform in a specific position; this ability is determined by a medical examination.

■ Employees who drive at work, i.e. city carriers, motor vehicle operators, etc., must have a safe driving record.

■ If there are special educational or experience requirements, it will be stated in the job announcement.

ADDITIONAL QUALIFICATION ISSUES

When a job opens, the appointing officer chooses one of the top three applicants. Others are left on the list to be considered for future openings. New employees are trained either on the job by supervisors and other experienced employees, or in local training centers. Training ranges from a few days to several months, depending on the job. For example, mail handlers and mechanics' helpers can learn their jobs in a relatively short time. Postal inspectors, on the other hand, need months of training.

Chapter 6

Postal Service Job Descriptions

Remember that your goal of landing your first-choice job must be tempered with the realities of the real world. However, career advancement is encouraged within the USPS, so you can always "work your way up" to that great job you've been dreaming of, even if you don't get it when you first start.

Deciding on a job within the USPS is like deciding on any other job. Each position is unique and appeals to different individuals for different reasons. Do you enjoy a specific type of work? If you don't really like being outdoors, then a courier route is probably not the right position for you. Perhaps you enjoy a position that is more routine from day to day, as compared to one that changes every minute. A mail sorting position might be the best fit for you. The point is that you should try to match the job descriptions listed in this chapter with your own interests, keeping in mind that all positions within the USPS are competitive. You might want to look for two or three positions that interest you in case your "first choice position" isn't available right away.

POST OFFICE CLERK

JOB DUTIES

Remember that trip to the post office when you were a kid (we're not letting you forget, are we)? You might remember thinking the only duties of a postal clerk are to sell stamps and to take packages.

Actually, the majority of postal clerks are distribution clerks who sort incoming and outgoing mail in workrooms. Only in a small post office does a postal clerk perform "double duty" of sitting behind the counter and sorting mail.

Generally speaking, postal clerks are responsible for the following tasks:

- Sorting and distributing mail to post offices and to carrier routes

- Completing a variety of services at public windows of post offices, post office branches, or stations (usually only in small post offices)

- Performing related duties as assigned

WORKING CONDITIONS

The postal clerk performs more or less manual work, depending on the size of the post office where he or she works, as well as the equipment in place (chutes, sorting machines) to help with this task. In general, the work involves continuous standing, stretching, and reaching. In addition, the postal clerk might be required to handle heavy sacks of letter mail or parcel post weighing up to 70 pounds.

However, if your duties also include those of a window clerk, you more than likely experience a wider variety of duties. You have frequent contact with the public (which might be viewed as a benefit or drawback, depending on your personality), your work is normally not physically strenuous, and you won't have to work much at night. Again, each post office is unique in what duties are assigned to the postal clerk.

As was mentioned at the beginning of this chapter, different jobs appeal to different people, all for different reasons. However, you should be aware that some distribution clerks (which again can be the primary role of the postal clerk) could become bored with the routine of sorting mail. Also, postal clerks might be required to work at night (especially at large post offices, where sorting and distributing the mail is a "24/7" activity).

QUALIFICATION REQUIREMENTS

Qualification requirements for the position of postal clerk closely mirror the working conditions described previously. Note that no experience is necessary for the position of postal clerk.

A successful applicant must show, on a physical examination, that he or she is able to perform the duties of the position, which include:

- Prolonged standing, walking, and reaching

- Handling of heavy sacks of mail

- Testing 20/40 (Snellen) for distance vision in one eye (corrective lenses permitted)

- Reading without strain printed material the size of typewritten characters (corrective lenses permitted)

- Ability to hear the conversational voice, with or without a hearing aid (for window positions)

- Maintaining emotional and mental stability

TESTING REQUIREMENT

The testing requirement for postal clerks is *Postal Service Test 470*. You must attain a rating of at least 70 out of 100. The subjects on which you are tested include:

- Memory for addresses

- Address checking

ADDITIONAL PROVISIONS

You should also be aware of the following additional provisions for postal clerks:

- Duties of newly appointed part-time clerks and carriers are interchangeable.

- Clerks must maintain pleasant and effective public relations with customers and others, which requires a general familiarity with postal laws, regulations, and procedures commonly used and with the geography of the area.

- Clerks must maintain neat and proper personal attire and grooming, including wearing a uniform when required.

> Postal Clerks are represented by:
> **The American Postal Workers Union, AFL-CIO**
> 1300 L Street NW
> Washington, DC 20005
> 202-842-4200
> On the Web: www.apwu.org

CITY CARRIER

Perhaps the most familiar of positions within the USPS is the role of "mailperson." This brings to mind a wealth of feelings. How many times have you anxiously waited for the "postman" to deliver a letter or package? Maybe it was the results of your college entrance exams? Or perhaps one of the many items (and items of exceptionally high quality, of course) that you impulsively purchased from an advertisement you saw on television. Indeed, the "postman" is a fixture in our culture, the person who delivers good and bad news, letters, bills, magazine subscriptions, and more. It is an exceptionally crucial job. Despite the rise in popularity of e-mail, can we really imagine a world where there was no daily postal delivery? Postal couriers are definitely worthy of the attention they receive.

You might be surprised to learn, however, that much of the postal carrier's work is done at the post office. Often carriers start their day at the post office as early as 6 a.m., where they spend a few hours arranging their mail for delivery, re-addressing letters to be forwarded, and taking care of other details.

JOB DUTIES

A carrier typically covers his or her route on foot, toting a heavy load of mail in a satchel or pushing it in a cart. In outlying areas, a carrier might drive a car or small truck. Carriers or Special Delivery Messengers perform the following tasks:

- Promptly and efficiently deliver and collect mail on foot or by vehicle under varying conditions in a prescribed area or on various routes

- Deliver parcel post from trucks and make collections of mail from various boxes or other locations

- Maintain pleasant and effective public relations with customers

WORKING CONDITIONS

The mail is always delivered, come rain or shine. There must be an extreme weather situation for the mail to be postponed for an entire day. It might be late, of course, but that's a big difference from not going out at all. With that thought in mind, carriers may be required to:

- Drive motor vehicles in all kinds of traffic and road conditions (obviously, you need a driver's license)

- Carry mail in shoulder satchels weighing as much as 35 pounds

- Load and unload sacks of mail weighing up to 70 pounds

- Serve in all kinds of weather

Despite these tough requirements, the job has some key advantages. Carriers who begin work early in the morning are through by early afternoon. They are also free to work at their own pace as long as they cover their routes within a certain period of time.

QUALIFICATION REQUIREMENTS

As with many positions with the USPS, a carrier must be in such physical condition as to enable him or her to do potentially strenuous and physically taxing work. No experience is necessary for the position of city or special carrier.

You must, upon physical examination, be able to perform the following duties:

- Endure prolonged standing, walking, and reaching

- Handle heavy sacks of mail

- Test 20/40 (Snellen) for distance vision in one eye (corrective lenses permitted)

- Read, without strain, printed material the size of typewritten characters (corrective lenses permitted)

- Maintain emotional and mental stability

- Have no irremediable defect or incurable disease that prevents efficient performance of duty that renders you a hazard to yourself, fellow employees, or others

- If driving of a vehicle weighing less than 10,000 pounds (GVW) is required, applicant must have vision of 20/40 in one eye and be able to read, without strain, printed material the size of typewritten characters (corrective lenses permitted). The ability to hear is not required to operate a vehicle weighing less than 10,000 pounds (GVW).

TESTING REQUIREMENT

The testing requirement for postal carriers is *Postal Service Test 470*. You must attain a rating of at least 70 out of 100. The subjects you will be tested on include:

- Memory for addresses

- Address checking

ADDITIONAL PROVISIONS

In addition to the information listed previously, if you wish to be a carrier for the USPS you are also required to adhere to the following:

- Maintain pleasant and effective public relations with customers and others, which requires a general familiarity with postal laws, regulations, and procedures commonly used, and with the geography of the area

- Must maintain neat and proper personal attire and grooming, including wearing a uniform when required

- For positions requiring driving, applicants must have a valid state driver's license and demonstrate and maintain a safe driving record. Applicants must pass the Postal Service road test to show the ability to safely drive a vehicle of the type used on the job.

- Note that duties of newly appointed part-time clerks and carriers are interchangeable.

> City Carriers are represented by:
> **National Association of Letter Carriers, AFL-CIO**
> 100 Indian Avenue, NW
> Washington, DC 20001-2144
> 202-393-4695
> On the Web: www.nalc.org

FLAT SORTING MACHINE OPERATOR

JOB DUTIES

A flat sorting machine operator's work is very similar to that of the Distribution Clerk position. However, as a flat sorting machine operator, you work with large, bulky packages.

You might guess that, with this requirement, you have to possess greater physical strength and stamina. Like the Distribution Clerk machine operator's position, increasing automation adds a good degree of security to this position, which is a definite plus that might offset the "physically taxing" requirements of the position.

QUALIFICATION REQUIREMENTS

In order to qualify for this position, you must possess sufficient levels of the following Knowledge, Skills, and Abilities (KSAs):

- Work without immediate supervision

- Work in cooperation with fellow employees to efficiently perform the duties of the position

- Observe and act on visual information such as names, addresses, numbers, and shapes

- Learn and recall pairings of addresses with numbers, letters, or positions

- Sequence or place mail in the proper numerical, alphabetical, or geographic order

- Perform routine troubleshooting, such as removing jams

- Be physically able to efficiently perform the duties of the position

- Test 20/40 (Snellen) for vision in one eye, have a near acuity of 7 or higher in either eye (Titmus or Bausch and Lomb), and read, without strain, printed material the size of typewritten characters (corrective lenses permitted)

- Ability to distinguish basic colors and shades is desirable

TESTING REQUIREMENT

The testing requirement for flat sorting machine operator is *Postal Service Test 470* as a requirement for the trainee position. Other requirements include:

- Successful completion of the appropriate training program for the flat sorting machine operation

- Demonstration of the ability to key at 45 items per minute with 98 percent accuracy

> Flat Sorting Machine Operators are represented by:
> **The American Postal Workers Union, AFL-CIO**
> 1300 L Street NW
> Washington, DC 20005
> 202-842-4200
> On the Web: www.apwu.org

MAIL HANDLER

Because of the extreme physical nature of this job, if you have certain physical conditions you won't be permitted to take the strength and stamina test without prior approval of your doctor (which is a requirement for this position). These conditions include hernia or rupture, back trouble, heart trouble, pregnancy, or any other condition that makes it dangerous for you to lift and carry 70-pound weights.

If you fail to qualify on the strength and stamina test, you won't be tested again in the same group of hires. If you fail this test a second time, your eligibility for the position is canceled.

JOB DUTIES

Mail handlers unload and move bulk mail, and perform other duties incidental to the movement and processing of mail.

QUALIFICATION REQUIREMENTS

As a mail handler, you must:

- Demonstrate sufficient levels of Knowledge, Skills, and Abilities (KSAs), which include at least minimum competency for senior-qualified positions

- Demonstrate these KSAs by describing examples of experience, education, or training, any of which may be non-postal

- Be physically able to perform efficiently the duties of the position

- Have vision of 20/40 (Snellen) in one eye and the ability to read, without strain, printed material the size of typewritten characters (corrective lenses permitted)

- Be able to hear the conversational voice in at least one ear (hearing aid permitted)

TESTING REQUIREMENT

Testing requirements for the position of mail handler include:

- Successful completion of the *Postal Service Test 470,* which measures the applicant's ability to understand simple word meanings, check names and numbers, and follow oral directions

- Passing a test of physical abilities prior to appointment.

Mail Handlers are represented by:
National Postal Mail Handlers Union, AFL-CIO
1101 Connecticut Avenue, NW, Suite 500
Washington, DC 20036
202-833-9095
On the Web: www.npmhu.org

MARK-UP CLERK, AUTOMATED

JOB DUTIES

A mark-up clerk, automated operates an electro-mechanical operator-paced machine to process mail as undeliverable as addressed. In doing this, you operate the keyboard of a computer terminal to enter and extract dates to several databases. Although you don't have to be a computer programmer to qualify for this position, you should feel comfortable working with computers, as you need to enter into several potentially different programs in order to enter, view, and change data.

QUALIFICATION REQUIREMENTS

Qualifications include demonstration of a sufficient level of the following KSAs:

> *The ability to type will prove invaluable for your role as a mark-up clerk, automated.*

- Use reference materials and manuals relevant to the position

- Perform effectively under the pressures of the position

- Operate any office equipment appropriate to the position

- Work well with others

- Six months of clerical or office machine operating experience (Successful completion of a four-year high school course or successful completion of business school may be substituted for the six months of clerical or office machine operating requirements

- Physically able to perform efficiently the duties of the position

- Test 20/40 (Snellen) for vision in one eye with the ability to read, without strain, printed material the size of typewritten characters (corrective lenses permitted)

- Ability to distinguish basic colors and shades is desirable

TESTING REQUIREMENT

You must have good date entry skills and must pass a typing test. You also need to successfully complete *Postal Service Test 470, Configuration 2*.

> Mark-Up Clerks are represented by:
> **The American Postal Workers Union, AFL-CIO**
> 1300 L Street NW
> Washington, DC 20005
> 202-842-4200
> On the Web: www.apwu.org

RURAL CARRIER

JOB DUTIES

> *Because many of your patrons live in remote locations (hence "rural" in your job title), you are also required, on occasion, to perform all the duties of a window clerk, including accepting, collecting, and delivering all classes of mail and selling stamp supplies and money orders.*

The work of the rural carrier combines the work of the window clerk and the letter carrier. However, the job also has special characteristics of its own.

As a rural carrier, you begin the day with sorting and loading the mail for delivery. Then comes your drive (which might be over tough roads during rough weather). Given the "rural" nature of your job, you deliver most of your mail from the car. At the end of your day, you return to the post office with outgoing mail and money collected in various transactions.

As you might guess, you enjoy a great deal of independence with this position since there is no one "looking over your shoulder." However, the work can be taxing, and you have to endure the inherent dilemmas that come with spending lots of time in the car.

WORKING CONDITIONS

In general, you should expect the following working conditions as a rural carrier:

- Loading and delivering parcels weighing up to 70 pounds

- Placing letters and parcels in mail boxes with careful handling of the vehicle and frequent shifting from one side of the vehicle to the other

- Maintaining pleasant and effective working relations with customers and an acceptable appearance

QUALIFICATION REQUIREMENTS

Requirements for this position include that you have the ability to:

The ability to hear is not required for this position.

- Read, understand, and apply written instructions

- Perform basic arithmetic computations

- Prepare reports and maintain records

- Communicate effectively with customers

- Work effectively without close supervision

You must also:

- Be physically able to perform efficiently the arduous duties of the position

- Have vision of 20/40 (Snellen) in one eye and the ability to read, without strain, printed material the size of typewritten characters (corrective lenses permitted)

TESTING REQUIREMENT

You must successfully complete *Postal Service Test 460*.

ADDITIONAL PROVISIONS

In addition to the requirements listed previously, you must have a valid state driver's license and a safe driving record and must pass the Postal Service road test, which shows the ability to safely drive the type of vehicle used on the job.

Rural carriers also furnish all necessary vehicle equipment for prompt handling of the mail, unless supplied by the employer. Note that rural carriers are paid for equipment maintenance.

> Rural Carriers are represented by:
> **National Rural Letter Carriers Association**
> Fourth Floor
> 1630 Duke Street
> Alexandria, VA 22314-3465
> 703-684-5545
> On the Web: www.nrlca.org

MAIL PROCESSING CLERK

JOB DUTIES

This is a newer position with the Postal Service, as it merges two existing positions: Distribution Clerk (Machine) and Mail Processor. The Mail Processing Clerk may use either automated mail processing equipment or manual methods of sorting and distribution.

WORKING CONDITIONS

In general, you should expect the following working conditions with this position:

- Continuous standing, stretching, and/or reaching

- Possible handling of heavy sacks of letter mail and/or parcel post weighing up to 70 pounds

QUALIFICATION REQUIREMENTS

Since this position is a combination of two existing positions, the requirements are a conglomeration of the previous position requirements. Specifically, the applicant must possess sufficient levels of the following KSAs:

- Knowledge of multi-position letter sorting machine

- Work without immediate supervision

- Work in cooperation with fellow employees to efficiently perform the duties of the position

- Observe and act on visual information such as names, addresses, numbers, and shapes

- Learn and recall pairings of addresses with numbers, letters, or positions

- Sequence or place mail in the proper numerical, alphabetical, or geographic order

- Must be physically able to efficiently perform the duties of the position

- Must have vision of 20/40 (Snellen) in one eye, near acuity of 7 or higher in either eye (Titmus or Bausch and Lomb), and the ability to read, without strain, printed material the size of typewritten character (corrective lenses permitted)

- Ability to distinguish basic colors and shades is desirable

TESTING REQUIREMENT

Applicants for this position must take and successfully pass *Postal Service Test 470*. You must obtain a rating of at least 70 out of 100.

> Mail Processing Clerks are represented by:
> **The American Postal Workers Union, AFL-CIO**
> 1300 L Street NW
> Washington, DC 20005
> 202-842-4200
> On the Web: www.apwu.org

PART III

Civil Service Tests for Postal Clerk and Carrier Jobs

CHAPTER 7

BEFORE YOU TAKE THE PRELIMINARY EXAM

The purpose of the Preliminary Exam is to establish a base upon which you can build your studies for your postal exam. The preliminary exam will give you an idea of the demands of the exam, of how well you can meet these demands now, and of how much preparation you need to do to succeed on the exam. By starting out with a full-length exam, you see from the beginning how many questions you must answer and how quickly you must work to score high on this exam.

DIRECTIONS FOR TAKING THE PRELIMINARY EXAM

- Arrange for a friend or family member to read the oral instructions for Part D. If you are unable to find a reader, skip ahead and read the chapter entitled "Strategies for Following Oral Instructions." Prepare a tape according to the instructions in that chapter.

- Choose a workspace that is quiet and well lit.

- Clear your desk or tabletop of all clutter.

- Bring a stopwatch or kitchen timer and two or three number-two pencils with good erasers to your study area. Although the pencils should have plenty of exposed lead, you will find that it is easier and doesn't take as long to fill in the answer circles if the pencils are not razor sharp. The little circles on the answer sheet must be completely filled in, and the fewer strokes needed to fill them, the faster you will be able to work. Scribble a bit to dull the points now. At the actual exam, you will dull the points as you fill out the grids before the exam begins.

- Tear out the answer sheets for the preliminary exam and place them on the desk or table beside your book, to the right if you are right-handed, to the left if you are left-handed.

- Turn to the first page of Part A. Read over the sample Address Checking questions and fill in your answer in the sample answer sheet. Then set the timer and begin work on Part A.

- Stop as soon as time is up and draw a line on your answer sheet at your stopping place. You want an accurate measure of how many questions you were able to answer correctly within the time limit. However, you may go back and get extra practice later on by answering the remaining questions without including them in your score.

- Proceed through the entire exam in this manner. First, answer the sample questions for the part just as you will at the exam site; then set the timer and answer as many questions as possible within the time limit. Mark your stopping place on the answer sheet and move on.

DIRECTIONS FOR SCORING YOUR EXAM

■ When you have completed the entire preliminary exam, check your answers against the correct answer keys beginning on page 81. Circle all wrong answers in red so that you can easily locate them when you analyze your errors.

■ Calculate your raw score for each part of the exam as instructed on the score sheet on page 55.

■ Check to see where your scores fall on the self-evaluation chart on page 56.

■ Now you can analyze your errors and begin to learn from them. You may be able to identify a pattern of errors in address checking and in following oral instructions. And you can begin developing expertise at number series as you study the explanations.

After you have completed the preliminary exam and have analyzed your results, you should have a good idea of where you stand and of how much you need to do to prepare for the exam. Plan to spend many hours with the four instructional chapters in Part III. Each will give you valuable help with answering the four distinct question types. Absorb all the information. Follow through with the drills and exercises. Do not jump ahead to the model exams until you are really prepared. Then, go on and develop skill and speed with the model exams.

PRELIMINARY MODEL EXAM ANSWER SHEET

PART A—ADDRESS CHECKING

1. Ⓐ Ⓓ	20. Ⓐ Ⓓ	39. Ⓐ Ⓓ	58. Ⓐ Ⓓ	77. Ⓐ Ⓓ
2. Ⓐ Ⓓ	21. Ⓐ Ⓓ	40. Ⓐ Ⓓ	59. Ⓐ Ⓓ	78. Ⓐ Ⓓ
3. Ⓐ Ⓓ	22. Ⓐ Ⓓ	41. Ⓐ Ⓓ	60. Ⓐ Ⓓ	79. Ⓐ Ⓓ
4. Ⓐ Ⓓ	23. Ⓐ Ⓓ	42. Ⓐ Ⓓ	61. Ⓐ Ⓓ	80. Ⓐ Ⓓ
5. Ⓐ Ⓓ	24. Ⓐ Ⓓ	43. Ⓐ Ⓓ	62. Ⓐ Ⓓ	81. Ⓐ Ⓓ
6. Ⓐ Ⓓ	25. Ⓐ Ⓓ	44. Ⓐ Ⓓ	63. Ⓐ Ⓓ	82. Ⓐ Ⓓ
7. Ⓐ Ⓓ	26. Ⓐ Ⓓ	45. Ⓐ Ⓓ	64. Ⓐ Ⓓ	83. Ⓐ Ⓓ
8. Ⓐ Ⓓ	27. Ⓐ Ⓓ	46. Ⓐ Ⓓ	65. Ⓐ Ⓓ	84. Ⓐ Ⓓ
9. Ⓐ Ⓓ	28. Ⓐ Ⓓ	47. Ⓐ Ⓓ	66. Ⓐ Ⓓ	85. Ⓐ Ⓓ
10. Ⓐ Ⓓ	29. Ⓐ Ⓓ	48. Ⓐ Ⓓ	67. Ⓐ Ⓓ	86. Ⓐ Ⓓ
11. Ⓐ Ⓓ	30. Ⓐ Ⓓ	49. Ⓐ Ⓓ	68. Ⓐ Ⓓ	87. Ⓐ Ⓓ
12. Ⓐ Ⓓ	31. Ⓐ Ⓓ	50. Ⓐ Ⓓ	69. Ⓐ Ⓓ	88. Ⓐ Ⓓ
13. Ⓐ Ⓓ	32. Ⓐ Ⓓ	51. Ⓐ Ⓓ	70. Ⓐ Ⓓ	89. Ⓐ Ⓓ
14. Ⓐ Ⓓ	33. Ⓐ Ⓓ	52. Ⓐ Ⓓ	71. Ⓐ Ⓓ	90. Ⓐ Ⓓ
15. Ⓐ Ⓓ	34. Ⓐ Ⓓ	53. Ⓐ Ⓓ	72. Ⓐ Ⓓ	91. Ⓐ Ⓓ
16. Ⓐ Ⓓ	35. Ⓐ Ⓓ	54. Ⓐ Ⓓ	73. Ⓐ Ⓓ	92. Ⓐ Ⓓ
17. Ⓐ Ⓓ	36. Ⓐ Ⓓ	55. Ⓐ Ⓓ	74. Ⓐ Ⓓ	93. Ⓐ Ⓓ
18. Ⓐ Ⓓ	37. Ⓐ Ⓓ	56. Ⓐ Ⓓ	75. Ⓐ Ⓓ	94. Ⓐ Ⓓ
19. Ⓐ Ⓓ	38. Ⓐ Ⓓ	57. Ⓐ Ⓓ	76. Ⓐ Ⓓ	95. Ⓐ Ⓓ

PART B—MEMORY FOR ADDRESSES—SCORED TEST

1 Ⓐ Ⓑ Ⓒ Ⓓ Ⓔ   23 Ⓐ Ⓑ Ⓒ Ⓓ Ⓔ   45 Ⓐ Ⓑ Ⓒ Ⓓ Ⓔ   67 Ⓐ Ⓑ Ⓒ Ⓓ Ⓔ

2 Ⓐ Ⓑ Ⓒ Ⓓ Ⓔ   24 Ⓐ Ⓑ Ⓒ Ⓓ Ⓔ   46 Ⓐ Ⓑ Ⓒ Ⓓ Ⓔ   68 Ⓐ Ⓑ Ⓒ Ⓓ Ⓔ

3 Ⓐ Ⓑ Ⓒ Ⓓ Ⓔ   25 Ⓐ Ⓑ Ⓒ Ⓓ Ⓔ   47 Ⓐ Ⓑ Ⓒ Ⓓ Ⓔ   69 Ⓐ Ⓑ Ⓒ Ⓓ Ⓔ

4 Ⓐ Ⓑ Ⓒ Ⓓ Ⓔ   26 Ⓐ Ⓑ Ⓒ Ⓓ Ⓔ   48 Ⓐ Ⓑ Ⓒ Ⓓ Ⓔ   70 Ⓐ Ⓑ Ⓒ Ⓓ Ⓔ

5 Ⓐ Ⓑ Ⓒ Ⓓ Ⓔ   27 Ⓐ Ⓑ Ⓒ Ⓓ Ⓔ   49 Ⓐ Ⓑ Ⓒ Ⓓ Ⓔ   71 Ⓐ Ⓑ Ⓒ Ⓓ Ⓔ

6 Ⓐ Ⓑ Ⓒ Ⓓ Ⓔ   28 Ⓐ Ⓑ Ⓒ Ⓓ Ⓔ   50 Ⓐ Ⓑ Ⓒ Ⓓ Ⓔ   72 Ⓐ Ⓑ Ⓒ Ⓓ Ⓔ

7 Ⓐ Ⓑ Ⓒ Ⓓ Ⓔ   29 Ⓐ Ⓑ Ⓒ Ⓓ Ⓔ   51 Ⓐ Ⓑ Ⓒ Ⓓ Ⓔ   73 Ⓐ Ⓑ Ⓒ Ⓓ Ⓔ

8 Ⓐ Ⓑ Ⓒ Ⓓ Ⓔ   30 Ⓐ Ⓑ Ⓒ Ⓓ Ⓔ   52 Ⓐ Ⓑ Ⓒ Ⓓ Ⓔ   74 Ⓐ Ⓑ Ⓒ Ⓓ Ⓔ

9 Ⓐ Ⓑ Ⓒ Ⓓ Ⓔ   31 Ⓐ Ⓑ Ⓒ Ⓓ Ⓔ   53 Ⓐ Ⓑ Ⓒ Ⓓ Ⓔ   75 Ⓐ Ⓑ Ⓒ Ⓓ Ⓔ

10 Ⓐ Ⓑ Ⓒ Ⓓ Ⓔ   32 Ⓐ Ⓑ Ⓒ Ⓓ Ⓔ   54 Ⓐ Ⓑ Ⓒ Ⓓ Ⓔ   76 Ⓐ Ⓑ Ⓒ Ⓓ Ⓔ

11 Ⓐ Ⓑ Ⓒ Ⓓ Ⓔ   33 Ⓐ Ⓑ Ⓒ Ⓓ Ⓔ   55 Ⓐ Ⓑ Ⓒ Ⓓ Ⓔ   77 Ⓐ Ⓑ Ⓒ Ⓓ Ⓔ

12 Ⓐ Ⓑ Ⓒ Ⓓ Ⓔ   34 Ⓐ Ⓑ Ⓒ Ⓓ Ⓔ   56 Ⓐ Ⓑ Ⓒ Ⓓ Ⓔ   78 Ⓐ Ⓑ Ⓒ Ⓓ Ⓔ

13 Ⓐ Ⓑ Ⓒ Ⓓ Ⓔ   35 Ⓐ Ⓑ Ⓒ Ⓓ Ⓔ   57 Ⓐ Ⓑ Ⓒ Ⓓ Ⓔ   79 Ⓐ Ⓑ Ⓒ Ⓓ Ⓔ

14 Ⓐ Ⓑ Ⓒ Ⓓ Ⓔ   36 Ⓐ Ⓑ Ⓒ Ⓓ Ⓔ   58 Ⓐ Ⓑ Ⓒ Ⓓ Ⓔ   80 Ⓐ Ⓑ Ⓒ Ⓓ Ⓔ

15 Ⓐ Ⓑ Ⓒ Ⓓ Ⓔ   37 Ⓐ Ⓑ Ⓒ Ⓓ Ⓔ   59 Ⓐ Ⓑ Ⓒ Ⓓ Ⓔ   81 Ⓐ Ⓑ Ⓒ Ⓓ Ⓔ

16 Ⓐ Ⓑ Ⓒ Ⓓ Ⓔ   38 Ⓐ Ⓑ Ⓒ Ⓓ Ⓔ   60 Ⓐ Ⓑ Ⓒ Ⓓ Ⓔ   82 Ⓐ Ⓑ Ⓒ Ⓓ Ⓔ

17 Ⓐ Ⓑ Ⓒ Ⓓ Ⓔ   39 Ⓐ Ⓑ Ⓒ Ⓓ Ⓔ   61 Ⓐ Ⓑ Ⓒ Ⓓ Ⓔ   83 Ⓐ Ⓑ Ⓒ Ⓓ Ⓔ

18 Ⓐ Ⓑ Ⓒ Ⓓ Ⓔ   40 Ⓐ Ⓑ Ⓒ Ⓓ Ⓔ   62 Ⓐ Ⓑ Ⓒ Ⓓ Ⓔ   84 Ⓐ Ⓑ Ⓒ Ⓓ Ⓔ

19 Ⓐ Ⓑ Ⓒ Ⓓ Ⓔ   41 Ⓐ Ⓑ Ⓒ Ⓓ Ⓔ   63 Ⓐ Ⓑ Ⓒ Ⓓ Ⓔ   85 Ⓐ Ⓑ Ⓒ Ⓓ Ⓔ

20 Ⓐ Ⓑ Ⓒ Ⓓ Ⓔ   42 Ⓐ Ⓑ Ⓒ Ⓓ Ⓔ   64 Ⓐ Ⓑ Ⓒ Ⓓ Ⓔ   86 Ⓐ Ⓑ Ⓒ Ⓓ Ⓔ

21 Ⓐ Ⓑ Ⓒ Ⓓ Ⓔ   43 Ⓐ Ⓑ Ⓒ Ⓓ Ⓔ   65 Ⓐ Ⓑ Ⓒ Ⓓ Ⓔ   87 Ⓐ Ⓑ Ⓒ Ⓓ Ⓔ

22 Ⓐ Ⓑ Ⓒ Ⓓ Ⓔ   44 Ⓐ Ⓑ Ⓒ Ⓓ Ⓔ   66 Ⓐ Ⓑ Ⓒ Ⓓ Ⓔ   88 Ⓐ Ⓑ Ⓒ Ⓓ Ⓔ

PART C—NUMBER SERIES

1. Ⓐ Ⓑ Ⓒ Ⓓ Ⓔ   7. Ⓐ Ⓑ Ⓒ Ⓓ Ⓔ   13. Ⓐ Ⓑ Ⓒ Ⓓ Ⓔ   19. Ⓐ Ⓑ Ⓒ Ⓓ Ⓔ

2. Ⓐ Ⓑ Ⓒ Ⓓ Ⓔ   8. Ⓐ Ⓑ Ⓒ Ⓓ Ⓔ   14. Ⓐ Ⓑ Ⓒ Ⓓ Ⓔ   20. Ⓐ Ⓑ Ⓒ Ⓓ Ⓔ

3. Ⓐ Ⓑ Ⓒ Ⓓ Ⓔ   9. Ⓐ Ⓑ Ⓒ Ⓓ Ⓔ   15. Ⓐ Ⓑ Ⓒ Ⓓ Ⓔ   21. Ⓐ Ⓑ Ⓒ Ⓓ Ⓔ

4. Ⓐ Ⓑ Ⓒ Ⓓ Ⓔ   10. Ⓐ Ⓑ Ⓒ Ⓓ Ⓔ   16. Ⓐ Ⓑ Ⓒ Ⓓ Ⓔ   22. Ⓐ Ⓑ Ⓒ Ⓓ Ⓔ

5. Ⓐ Ⓑ Ⓒ Ⓓ Ⓔ   11. Ⓐ Ⓑ Ⓒ Ⓓ Ⓔ   17. Ⓐ Ⓑ Ⓒ Ⓓ Ⓔ   23. Ⓐ Ⓑ Ⓒ Ⓓ Ⓔ

6. Ⓐ Ⓑ Ⓒ Ⓓ Ⓔ   12. Ⓐ Ⓑ Ⓒ Ⓓ Ⓔ   18. Ⓐ Ⓑ Ⓒ Ⓓ Ⓔ   24. Ⓐ Ⓑ Ⓒ Ⓓ Ⓔ

PART D—FOLLOWING ORAL INSTRUCTIONS

1 Ⓐ Ⓑ Ⓒ Ⓓ Ⓔ   23 Ⓐ Ⓑ Ⓒ Ⓓ Ⓔ   45 Ⓐ Ⓑ Ⓒ Ⓓ Ⓔ   67 Ⓐ Ⓑ Ⓒ Ⓓ Ⓔ
2 Ⓐ Ⓑ Ⓒ Ⓓ Ⓔ   24 Ⓐ Ⓑ Ⓒ Ⓓ Ⓔ   46 Ⓐ Ⓑ Ⓒ Ⓓ Ⓔ   68 Ⓐ Ⓑ Ⓒ Ⓓ Ⓔ
3 Ⓐ Ⓑ Ⓒ Ⓓ Ⓔ   25 Ⓐ Ⓑ Ⓒ Ⓓ Ⓔ   47 Ⓐ Ⓑ Ⓒ Ⓓ Ⓔ   69 Ⓐ Ⓑ Ⓒ Ⓓ Ⓔ
4 Ⓐ Ⓑ Ⓒ Ⓓ Ⓔ   26 Ⓐ Ⓑ Ⓒ Ⓓ Ⓔ   48 Ⓐ Ⓑ Ⓒ Ⓓ Ⓔ   70 Ⓐ Ⓑ Ⓒ Ⓓ Ⓔ
5 Ⓐ Ⓑ Ⓒ Ⓓ Ⓔ   27 Ⓐ Ⓑ Ⓒ Ⓓ Ⓔ   49 Ⓐ Ⓑ Ⓒ Ⓓ Ⓔ   71 Ⓐ Ⓑ Ⓒ Ⓓ Ⓔ
6 Ⓐ Ⓑ Ⓒ Ⓓ Ⓔ   28 Ⓐ Ⓑ Ⓒ Ⓓ Ⓔ   50 Ⓐ Ⓑ Ⓒ Ⓓ Ⓔ   72 Ⓐ Ⓑ Ⓒ Ⓓ Ⓔ
7 Ⓐ Ⓑ Ⓒ Ⓓ Ⓔ   29 Ⓐ Ⓑ Ⓒ Ⓓ Ⓔ   51 Ⓐ Ⓑ Ⓒ Ⓓ Ⓔ   73 Ⓐ Ⓑ Ⓒ Ⓓ Ⓔ
8 Ⓐ Ⓑ Ⓒ Ⓓ Ⓔ   30 Ⓐ Ⓑ Ⓒ Ⓓ Ⓔ   52 Ⓐ Ⓑ Ⓒ Ⓓ Ⓔ   74 Ⓐ Ⓑ Ⓒ Ⓓ Ⓔ
9 Ⓐ Ⓑ Ⓒ Ⓓ Ⓔ   31 Ⓐ Ⓑ Ⓒ Ⓓ Ⓔ   53 Ⓐ Ⓑ Ⓒ Ⓓ Ⓔ   75 Ⓐ Ⓑ Ⓒ Ⓓ Ⓔ
10 Ⓐ Ⓑ Ⓒ Ⓓ Ⓔ   32 Ⓐ Ⓑ Ⓒ Ⓓ Ⓔ   54 Ⓐ Ⓑ Ⓒ Ⓓ Ⓔ   76 Ⓐ Ⓑ Ⓒ Ⓓ Ⓔ
11 Ⓐ Ⓑ Ⓒ Ⓓ Ⓔ   33 Ⓐ Ⓑ Ⓒ Ⓓ Ⓔ   55 Ⓐ Ⓑ Ⓒ Ⓓ Ⓔ   77 Ⓐ Ⓑ Ⓒ Ⓓ Ⓔ
12 Ⓐ Ⓑ Ⓒ Ⓓ Ⓔ   34 Ⓐ Ⓑ Ⓒ Ⓓ Ⓔ   56 Ⓐ Ⓑ Ⓒ Ⓓ Ⓔ   78 Ⓐ Ⓑ Ⓒ Ⓓ Ⓔ
13 Ⓐ Ⓑ Ⓒ Ⓓ Ⓔ   35 Ⓐ Ⓑ Ⓒ Ⓓ Ⓔ   57 Ⓐ Ⓑ Ⓒ Ⓓ Ⓔ   79 Ⓐ Ⓑ Ⓒ Ⓓ Ⓔ
14 Ⓐ Ⓑ Ⓒ Ⓓ Ⓔ   36 Ⓐ Ⓑ Ⓒ Ⓓ Ⓔ   58 Ⓐ Ⓑ Ⓒ Ⓓ Ⓔ   80 Ⓐ Ⓑ Ⓒ Ⓓ Ⓔ
15 Ⓐ Ⓑ Ⓒ Ⓓ Ⓔ   37 Ⓐ Ⓑ Ⓒ Ⓓ Ⓔ   59 Ⓐ Ⓑ Ⓒ Ⓓ Ⓔ   81 Ⓐ Ⓑ Ⓒ Ⓓ Ⓔ
16 Ⓐ Ⓑ Ⓒ Ⓓ Ⓔ   38 Ⓐ Ⓑ Ⓒ Ⓓ Ⓔ   60 Ⓐ Ⓑ Ⓒ Ⓓ Ⓔ   82 Ⓐ Ⓑ Ⓒ Ⓓ Ⓔ
17 Ⓐ Ⓑ Ⓒ Ⓓ Ⓔ   39 Ⓐ Ⓑ Ⓒ Ⓓ Ⓔ   61 Ⓐ Ⓑ Ⓒ Ⓓ Ⓔ   83 Ⓐ Ⓑ Ⓒ Ⓓ Ⓔ
18 Ⓐ Ⓑ Ⓒ Ⓓ Ⓔ   40 Ⓐ Ⓑ Ⓒ Ⓓ Ⓔ   62 Ⓐ Ⓑ Ⓒ Ⓓ Ⓔ   84 Ⓐ Ⓑ Ⓒ Ⓓ Ⓔ
19 Ⓐ Ⓑ Ⓒ Ⓓ Ⓔ   41 Ⓐ Ⓑ Ⓒ Ⓓ Ⓔ   63 Ⓐ Ⓑ Ⓒ Ⓓ Ⓔ   85 Ⓐ Ⓑ Ⓒ Ⓓ Ⓔ
20 Ⓐ Ⓑ Ⓒ Ⓓ Ⓔ   42 Ⓐ Ⓑ Ⓒ Ⓓ Ⓔ   64 Ⓐ Ⓑ Ⓒ Ⓓ Ⓔ   86 Ⓐ Ⓑ Ⓒ Ⓓ Ⓔ
21 Ⓐ Ⓑ Ⓒ Ⓓ Ⓔ   43 Ⓐ Ⓑ Ⓒ Ⓓ Ⓔ   65 Ⓐ Ⓑ Ⓒ Ⓓ Ⓔ   87 Ⓐ Ⓑ Ⓒ Ⓓ Ⓔ
22 Ⓐ Ⓑ Ⓒ Ⓓ Ⓔ   44 Ⓐ Ⓑ Ⓒ Ⓓ Ⓔ   66 Ⓐ Ⓑ Ⓒ Ⓓ Ⓔ   88 Ⓐ Ⓑ Ⓒ Ⓓ Ⓔ

SCORE SHEET

ADDRESS CHECKING: Your score on the Address Checking section is based on the number of questions you answered correctly minus the number of questions you answered incorrectly. To determine your score, subtract the number of wrong answers from the number of correct answers.

Number Right   –   Number Wrong   =   Raw Score

_____   –   _____   =   _____

MEMORY FOR ADDRESSES: Your score on the Memory for Addresses section is based upon the number of questions you answered correctly minus one-fourth of the questions you answered incorrectly (number wrong divided by 4). Calculate this now:

Number Wrong   ÷   4   =   _____

Number Right   –   Number Wrong   ÷   4   =   Raw Score

_____   –   _____   =   _____

NUMBER SERIES: Your score on the Number Series section is based only on the number of questions you answered correctly. Wrong answers do not count against you.

Number Right   =   Raw Score

_____   =   _____

FOLLOWING ORAL INSTRUCTIONS: Your score on the Following Oral Instructions section is based only upon the number of questions you marked correctly on the answer sheet. The worksheet is not scored, and wrong answers on the answer sheet do not count against you.

Number Right   =   Raw Score

_____   =   _____

TOTAL SCORE: To find your total raw score, add together the raw scores for each section of the exam.

Address Checking Score   _____
+
Memory for Addresses Score   _____
+
Number Series Score   _____
+
Following Oral Instructions Score   _____

=   _____

Total Raw Score   _____

SELF-EVALUATION CHART

Calculate your raw score for each test as shown on the previous page. Then, check to see where your score falls on the scale from Poor to Excellent. Lightly shade in the boxes in which your scores fall.

Part	Excellent	Good	Average	Fair	Poor
Address Checking	80–95	65–79	50–64	35–49	1–34
Memory for Addresses	75–88	60–74	45–59	30–44	1–29
Number Series	21–24	18–20	14–17	11–13	1–10
Following Oral Instructions	27–31	23–26	19–22	14–18	1–13

Chapter 8

Preliminary Model Exam

PART A—ADDRESS CHECKING

SAMPLE QUESTIONS

You will be allowed 3 minutes to read the directions and answer the 5 sample questions that follow. On the actual test, however, you will have only 6 minutes to answer 95 questions, so see how quickly you can compare addresses and still get the correct answer.

> **Directions:** *Each question consists of two addresses. If the two addresses are alike in EVERY way, darken space (A) on your answer sheet. If the two addresses are different in ANY way, darken space (D) on your answer sheet.*

1	...3380 Federal Street	3380 S Federal Street
2	...1618 Highland Way	1816 Highland Way
3	...Greenvale NY 11548	Greenvale NY 11548
4	...Ft. Collins CO 80523	Ft. Collings CO 80523
5	...7214 NW 83rd St	7214 NW 83rd St

SAMPLE ANSWER SHEET		CORRECT ANSWERS	
1. (A)(D)	4. (A)(D)	1. (A)●	4. (A)●
2. (A)(D)	5. (A)(D)	2. (A)●	5. ●(D)
3. (A)(D)		3. ●(D)	

ADDRESS CHECKING

Time: 6 Minutes • 95 Questions

> **Directions:** *For each question, compare the address in the left column with the address in the right column. If the two addresses are ALIKE IN EVERY WAY, darken space (A) on your answer sheet. If the two addresses are DIFFERENT IN ANY WAY, darken space (D) on your answer sheet. Correct answers for this test are on page 81.*

1	...197 Wonderview Dr NW	197 Wonderview Dr NW
2	...243 S Capistano Ave	234 S Capistrano Ave
3	...4300 Las Pillas Rd	4300 Las Pillas Rd
4	...5551 N Ramara Ave	5551 N Ramara St
5	...Walden Col 80480	Waldon Col 80480
6	...2200 E Dunnington St	2200 E Dowington St
7	...2700 Helena Way	2700 Helena Way
8	...3968 S Zeno Ave	3968 S Zemo Ave
9	...14011 Costilla Ave NE	14011 Costilla Ave SE
10	...1899 N Dearborn Dr	1899 N Dearborn Dr
11	...8911 Scranton Way	8911 Scranton Way
12	...365 Liverpool St	356 Liverpool St
13	...1397 Lewiston Pl	1297 Lewiston Pl
14	...4588 Crystal Way	4588 Crystal Rd
15	...Muscle Shoals AL 35660	Muscle Shoals AL 35660
16	...988 Larkin Johson Ave SE	988 Larkin Johnson Ave SE
17	...5501 Greenville Blvd NE	5501 Greenview Blvd NE
18	...7133 N Baranmor Pky	7133 N Baranmor Pky
19	...10500 Montana Rd	10500 Montana Rd
20	...4769 E Kalispell Dr	4769 E Kalispell Cir
21	...Daytona Beach Fla 32016	Daytona Beach FL 32016
22	...2227 W 94th Ave	2272 W 94th Ave
23	...6399 E Ponce De Leon St	6399 E Ponce De Leon Ct
24	...20800 N Rainbow Pl	20800 N Rainbow Pl
25	...Sasser GA 31785	Sasser GA 31785
26	...Washington DC 20018	Washington DC 20013

27	...6500 Milwaukee NE	6500 Milwaukee SE
28	...1300 Strasburg Dr	1300 Strasburg Dr
29	...Burnettsville IN 47926	Bornettsville IN 47926
30	...1594 S Frontage St	1594 S Frontage Ave
31	...37099 Oliphant Ln	37909 Oliphant Ln
32	...2248 Avonsdale Cir NW	2248 Avonsdale Cir NE
33	...1733 Norlander Dr SE	1733 Norlander Dr SW
34	...15469 W Oxalida Dr	15469 W Oxalido Dr
35	...4192 E Commonwealth Ave	4192 E Commonwealth Ave
36	...Kingsfield Maine 04947	Kingsfield Maine 04947
37	...246 East Ramsdell Rd	246 East Ramsdale Rd
38	...8456 Vina Del Maro Blvd	8456 Vina Del Maro Blvd
39	...6688 N 26th Street	6888 N 26th Street
40	...1477 Woodrow Wilson Blvd	1477 Woodrow Wilson Blvd
41	...3724 S 18th Ave	3724 S 18th Ave
42	...11454 S Lake Maggiore Blvd	11454 S Lake Maggiore Blvd
43	...4832 N Bougainnvilla Ave	4832 N Bougainnvillia Ave
44	...3713 Coffee Pot Riviera	3773 Coffee Pot Riviera
45	...2800 S Freemont Ter	2800 S Freemond Ter
46	...3654 S Urbane Dr	3654 S Urbane Cir
47	...1408 Oklahoma Ave NE	1408 Oklahoma Ave NE
48	...6201 Meadowland Ln	6201 Meadowlawn Ln
49	...5799 S Augusta Ln	15799 S Augusta Ln
50	...5115 Winchester Rd	5115 Wcstehester Rd
51	...4611 N Kendall Pl	4611 N Kcnall Pl
52	...17045 Dormieone Cir	17045 Dormieone Cir
53	...3349 Palma Del Mar Blvd	3345 Palma Del Mar Blvd
54	...13211 E 182nd Ave	12311 E 182nd Ave
55	...Evansville WY 82636	Evansville WI 82636
56	...6198 N Albritton Rd	6198 N Albretton Rd
57	...11230 Twinflower Cir	11230 Twintower Cir
58	...6191 Lockett Station Rd	6191 Lockett Station Rd

59	...1587 Vanderbilt Dr N	1587 Vanderbilt Dr S
60	...Ontarioville IL 60103	Ontarioville IL 60103
61	...4204 Bridgeton Ave	4204 Bridgeton Ave
62	...31215 N Emerald Dr	31215 N Emerald Cir
63	...4601 N Peniman Ave	4601 N Peniman Ave
64	...3782 SE Verrazanna Bay	3782 SE Verrazana Bay
65	...2766 N Thunderbird Ct	2766 N Thunderbird Ct
66	...2166 N Elmorado Ct	2166 N Eldorado Ct
67	...10538 Innsbruck Ln	1058 Innsbruck Ln
68	...888 Lonesome Rd	8888 Lonesome Rd
69	...4023 N Brainbridge Ave	4023 N Brainbridge Ave
70	...3000 E Roberta Rd	30000 E Roberta Rd
71	...Quenemo KS 66528	Quenemo KS 66528
72	...13845 Donahoo St	13345 Donahoo St
73	...10466 Gertrude NE	10466 Gertrude NE
74	...2733 N 105th Ave	2733 S 105th Ave
75	...3100 N Wyandotte Cir	3100 N Wyandotte Ave
76	...11796 Summittcrest Dr	11769 Summittcrest Dr
77	...Viburnum Miss 65566	Viburnom Miss 65566
78	...9334 Kindleberger Rd	9334 Kindleberger Road
79	...4801 Armourdale Pky	8401 Armourdale Pky
80	...9392 Northrup Ave	9392 Northrop Ave
81	...11736 Rottinghaus Rd	11736 Rottinghaus Rd
82	...3878 Flammang Dr	3878 Flammang Dr
83	...2101 Johnstontown Way	2101 Johnsontown Way
84	...1177 Ghentwoodrow St	1177 Ghentwoodrow Ct
85	...888 Onadaga Ct	888 Onadaga Ct
86	...3205 N Rastetter Ave	3205 N Rastetter Ave
87	...1144 Yellowsands Dr NE	1144 Yellowsands Dr NW
88	...3197 Clerkenwell Ct	3197 Clerkenwell Ct
89	...3021 Pemaquid Way	3210 Pemaquid Way
90	...1398 Angelina Rd	1398 Angelino Rd

91	...4331 NW Zoeller Ave	4881 NW Zoeller Ave
92	...1805 Jeassamine Ln	1805 Jassamine Ln
93	...14411 Bellemeade Ave	14411 Bellemeade Ave
94	...Noquochoke MA 02790	Noguochoke MA 02790
95	...11601 Hagamann Cir	11601 Hagamann Ct

PART B—MEMORY FOR ADDRESSES

SAMPLE QUESTIONS

The sample questions for this section are based upon the addresses in the five boxes below. Your task is to mark on your answer sheet the letter of the box in which each address belongs. You will have 5 minutes now to study the locations of the addresses. Cover the boxes and try to mark the location of the sample questions. You may look back at the boxes if you cannot yet mark the address locations from memory.

The exam itself provides three practice sessions before the question set that really counts. Practice I and Practice III supply you with the boxes and permit you to refer to them if necessary. Practice II and the Memory for Addresses test do not permit you to look at the boxes. The test itself is based on memory.

A	B	C	D	E
8300–8699 Ball	9100–9799 Ball	9800–9999 Ball	8200–8299 Ball	8700–9099 Ball
Meadow	Swing	Winter	Checker	Ford
9800–9999 Wren	8700–9099 Wren	8300–8699 Wren	9100–9799 Wren	8200–8299 Wren
Denim	Vapor	Artisan	Zenith	Hammock
8200–8299 Slug	9800–9999 Slug	8700–9099 Slug	8300–8699 Slug	9100–9799 Slug

1. 8700–9099 Wren
2. 9100–9799 Slug
3. Denim
4. 9800–9999 Ball
5. Checker
6. Hammock
7. 9800–9999 Slug
8. 8300–8699 Ball
9. 8200–8299 Wren
10. Vapor
11. 8700–9099 Slug
12. Artisan
13. 8200–8299 Ball
14. 9100–9799 Wren

```
SAMPLE ANSWER SHEET
1. Ⓐ Ⓑ Ⓒ Ⓓ Ⓔ        8. Ⓐ Ⓑ Ⓒ Ⓓ Ⓔ
2. Ⓐ Ⓑ Ⓒ Ⓓ Ⓔ        9. Ⓐ Ⓑ Ⓒ Ⓓ Ⓔ
3. Ⓐ Ⓑ Ⓒ Ⓓ Ⓔ       10. Ⓐ Ⓑ Ⓒ Ⓓ Ⓔ
4. Ⓐ Ⓑ Ⓒ Ⓓ Ⓔ       11. Ⓐ Ⓑ Ⓒ Ⓓ Ⓔ
5. Ⓐ Ⓑ Ⓒ Ⓓ Ⓔ       12. Ⓐ Ⓑ Ⓒ Ⓓ Ⓔ
6. Ⓐ Ⓑ Ⓒ Ⓓ Ⓔ       13. Ⓐ Ⓑ Ⓒ Ⓓ Ⓔ
7. Ⓐ Ⓑ Ⓒ Ⓓ Ⓔ       14. Ⓐ Ⓑ Ⓒ Ⓓ Ⓔ
```

```
CORRECT ANSWERS
1. Ⓐ ● Ⓒ Ⓓ Ⓔ        8. ● Ⓑ Ⓒ Ⓓ Ⓔ
2. Ⓐ Ⓑ Ⓒ Ⓓ ●        9. Ⓐ Ⓑ Ⓒ Ⓓ ●
3. ● Ⓑ Ⓒ Ⓓ Ⓔ       10. Ⓐ ● Ⓒ Ⓓ Ⓔ
4. Ⓐ Ⓑ ● Ⓓ Ⓔ       11. Ⓐ Ⓑ ● Ⓓ Ⓔ
5. Ⓐ Ⓑ Ⓒ ● Ⓔ       12. Ⓐ Ⓑ ● Ⓓ Ⓔ
6. Ⓐ Ⓑ Ⓒ Ⓓ ●       13. Ⓐ Ⓑ Ⓒ ● Ⓔ
7. Ⓐ ● Ⓒ Ⓓ Ⓔ       14. Ⓐ Ⓑ Ⓒ ● Ⓔ
```

MEMORY FOR ADDRESSES

> **Directions:** *The five boxes below are labeled A, B, C, D, and E. In each box are three sets of number spans with names and two names that are not associated with numbers. In the next 3 MINUTES, you must try to memorize the box location of each name and number span. The position of a name or number span within its box is not important. You need only remember the letter of the box in which the item is to be found. You will use these names and numbers to answer three sets of practice questions that are NOT scored and one actual test that IS scored. Correct answers are on page 82.*

A	B	C	D	E
8300–8699 Ball	9100–9799 Ball	9800–9999 Ball	8200–8299 Ball	8700–9099 Ball
Meadow	Swing	Winter	Checker	Ford
9800–9999 Wren	8700–9099 Wren	8300–8699 Wren	9100–9799 Wren	8200–8299 Wren
Denim	Vapor	Artisan	Zenith	Hammock
8200–8299 Slug	9800–9999 Slug	8700–9099 Slug	8300–8699 Slug	9100–9799 Slug

PRACTICE I

> **Directions:** *Use the next 3 MINUTES to mark on the answer sheet at the end of Practice 1 the letter of the box in which each item that follows is to be found. Try to mark each item without looking back at the boxes. If, however, you get stuck, you may refer to the boxes during this practice exercise. If you find that you must look at the boxes, try to memorize as you do so. This test is for practice only. It will not be scored.*

1. 9100–9799 Wren
2. 8700–9099 Slug
3. Winter
4. 8700–9099 Ball
5. 9800–9999 Wren
6. 9800–9999 Slug
7. 8700–9099 Wren
8. Meadow
9. Vapor
10. 9100–9799 Ball
11. 9100–9799 Slug
12. 8700–9099 Wren
13. 9800–9999 Ball
14. 8200–8299 Wren
15. Checker
16. Hammock
17. 8300–8699 Ball

18. 9100–9799 Wren
19. 8300–8699 Slug
20. 8700–9099 Wren
21. 8200–8299 Slug
22. Ford
23. Denim
24. 9800–9999 Wren
25. 9100–9799 Ball
26. Artisan
27. 8700–9099 Ball
28. 8200–8299 Ball
29. 8200–8299 Wren
30. Zenith
31. Vapor
32. Meadow
33. 8700–9099 Slug
34. 9800–9999 Slug

35. 9800–9999 Wren
36. Winter
37. Swing
38. 9100–9799 Slug
39. 9800–9999 Ball
40. 8300–8699 Wren
41. 8300–8699 Ball
42. Swing
43. Zenith
44. 9100–9799 Slug
45. 8700–9099 Ball
46. Checker
47. 8300–8699 Wren
48. Vapor
49. 8200–8299 Slug
50. 9800–9999 Wren
51. 9100–9799 Wren

52. Artisan
53. Swing
54. Hammock
55. 8300–8699 Slug
56. 8300–8699 Ball
57. 9800–9999 Ball
58. 8700–9099 Slug
59. Meadow
60. Denim
61. 9100–9799 Ball
62. 8200–8299 Ball
63. Ford
64. 9100–9799 Slug

65. 9800–9999 Slug
66. Winter
67. Zenith
68. 8700–9099 Wren
69. 8200–8299 Wren
70. Checker
71. 8700-9099 Ball
72. 8300–8699 Slug
73. 9100–9799 Wren
74. 9800–9999 Ball
75. Meadow
76. 8700–9099 Wren
77. 8300–8699 Ball

78. 9100–9799 Slug
79. Hammock
80. Vapor
81. 9800–9999 Slug
82. 8200–8299 Wren
83. Artisan
84. Swing
85. 9800–9999 Ball
86. 9100–9799 Wren
87. 8200–8299 Slug
88. 8700–9099 Ball

PRACTICE I ANSWER SHEET

1 Ⓐ Ⓑ Ⓒ Ⓓ Ⓔ	23 Ⓐ Ⓑ Ⓒ Ⓓ Ⓔ	45 Ⓐ Ⓑ Ⓒ Ⓓ Ⓔ	67 Ⓐ Ⓑ Ⓒ Ⓓ Ⓔ
2 Ⓐ Ⓑ Ⓒ Ⓓ Ⓔ	24 Ⓐ Ⓑ Ⓒ Ⓓ Ⓔ	46 Ⓐ Ⓑ Ⓒ Ⓓ Ⓔ	68 Ⓐ Ⓑ Ⓒ Ⓓ Ⓔ
3 Ⓐ Ⓑ Ⓒ Ⓓ Ⓔ	25 Ⓐ Ⓑ Ⓒ Ⓓ Ⓔ	47 Ⓐ Ⓑ Ⓒ Ⓓ Ⓔ	69 Ⓐ Ⓑ Ⓒ Ⓓ Ⓔ
4 Ⓐ Ⓑ Ⓒ Ⓓ Ⓔ	26 Ⓐ Ⓑ Ⓒ Ⓓ Ⓔ	48 Ⓐ Ⓑ Ⓒ Ⓓ Ⓔ	70 Ⓐ Ⓑ Ⓒ Ⓓ Ⓔ
5 Ⓐ Ⓑ Ⓒ Ⓓ Ⓔ	27 Ⓐ Ⓑ Ⓒ Ⓓ Ⓔ	49 Ⓐ Ⓑ Ⓒ Ⓓ Ⓔ	71 Ⓐ Ⓑ Ⓒ Ⓓ Ⓔ
6 Ⓐ Ⓑ Ⓒ Ⓓ Ⓔ	28 Ⓐ Ⓑ Ⓒ Ⓓ Ⓔ	50 Ⓐ Ⓑ Ⓒ Ⓓ Ⓔ	72 Ⓐ Ⓑ Ⓒ Ⓓ Ⓔ
7 Ⓐ Ⓑ Ⓒ Ⓓ Ⓔ	29 Ⓐ Ⓑ Ⓒ Ⓓ Ⓔ	51 Ⓐ Ⓑ Ⓒ Ⓓ Ⓔ	73 Ⓐ Ⓑ Ⓒ Ⓓ Ⓔ
8 Ⓐ Ⓑ Ⓒ Ⓓ Ⓔ	30 Ⓐ Ⓑ Ⓒ Ⓓ Ⓔ	52 Ⓐ Ⓑ Ⓒ Ⓓ Ⓔ	74 Ⓐ Ⓑ Ⓒ Ⓓ Ⓔ
9 Ⓐ Ⓑ Ⓒ Ⓓ Ⓔ	31 Ⓐ Ⓑ Ⓒ Ⓓ Ⓔ	53 Ⓐ Ⓑ Ⓒ Ⓓ Ⓔ	75 Ⓐ Ⓑ Ⓒ Ⓓ Ⓔ
10 Ⓐ Ⓑ Ⓒ Ⓓ Ⓔ	32 Ⓐ Ⓑ Ⓒ Ⓓ Ⓔ	54 Ⓐ Ⓑ Ⓒ Ⓓ Ⓔ	76 Ⓐ Ⓑ Ⓒ Ⓓ Ⓔ
11 Ⓐ Ⓑ Ⓒ Ⓓ Ⓔ	33 Ⓐ Ⓑ Ⓒ Ⓓ Ⓔ	55 Ⓐ Ⓑ Ⓒ Ⓓ Ⓔ	77 Ⓐ Ⓑ Ⓒ Ⓓ Ⓔ
12 Ⓐ Ⓑ Ⓒ Ⓓ Ⓔ	34 Ⓐ Ⓑ Ⓒ Ⓓ Ⓔ	56 Ⓐ Ⓑ Ⓒ Ⓓ Ⓔ	78 Ⓐ Ⓑ Ⓒ Ⓓ Ⓔ
13 Ⓐ Ⓑ Ⓒ Ⓓ Ⓔ	35 Ⓐ Ⓑ Ⓒ Ⓓ Ⓔ	57 Ⓐ Ⓑ Ⓒ Ⓓ Ⓔ	79 Ⓐ Ⓑ Ⓒ Ⓓ Ⓔ
14 Ⓐ Ⓑ Ⓒ Ⓓ Ⓔ	36 Ⓐ Ⓑ Ⓒ Ⓓ Ⓔ	58 Ⓐ Ⓑ Ⓒ Ⓓ Ⓔ	80 Ⓐ Ⓑ Ⓒ Ⓓ Ⓔ
15 Ⓐ Ⓑ Ⓒ Ⓓ Ⓔ	37 Ⓐ Ⓑ Ⓒ Ⓓ Ⓔ	59 Ⓐ Ⓑ Ⓒ Ⓓ Ⓔ	81 Ⓐ Ⓑ Ⓒ Ⓓ Ⓔ
16 Ⓐ Ⓑ Ⓒ Ⓓ Ⓔ	38 Ⓐ Ⓑ Ⓒ Ⓓ Ⓔ	60 Ⓐ Ⓑ Ⓒ Ⓓ Ⓔ	82 Ⓐ Ⓑ Ⓒ Ⓓ Ⓔ
17 Ⓐ Ⓑ Ⓒ Ⓓ Ⓔ	39 Ⓐ Ⓑ Ⓒ Ⓓ Ⓔ	61 Ⓐ Ⓑ Ⓒ Ⓓ Ⓔ	83 Ⓐ Ⓑ Ⓒ Ⓓ Ⓔ
18 Ⓐ Ⓑ Ⓒ Ⓓ Ⓔ	40 Ⓐ Ⓑ Ⓒ Ⓓ Ⓔ	62 Ⓐ Ⓑ Ⓒ Ⓓ Ⓔ	84 Ⓐ Ⓑ Ⓒ Ⓓ Ⓔ
19 Ⓐ Ⓑ Ⓒ Ⓓ Ⓔ	41 Ⓐ Ⓑ Ⓒ Ⓓ Ⓔ	63 Ⓐ Ⓑ Ⓒ Ⓓ Ⓔ	85 Ⓐ Ⓑ Ⓒ Ⓓ Ⓔ
20 Ⓐ Ⓑ Ⓒ Ⓓ Ⓔ	42 Ⓐ Ⓑ Ⓒ Ⓓ Ⓔ	64 Ⓐ Ⓑ Ⓒ Ⓓ Ⓔ	86 Ⓐ Ⓑ Ⓒ Ⓓ Ⓔ
21 Ⓐ Ⓑ Ⓒ Ⓓ Ⓔ	43 Ⓐ Ⓑ Ⓒ Ⓓ Ⓔ	65 Ⓐ Ⓑ Ⓒ Ⓓ Ⓔ	87 Ⓐ Ⓑ Ⓒ Ⓓ Ⓔ
22 Ⓐ Ⓑ Ⓒ Ⓓ Ⓔ	44 Ⓐ Ⓑ Ⓒ Ⓓ Ⓔ	66 Ⓐ Ⓑ Ⓒ Ⓓ Ⓔ	88 Ⓐ Ⓑ Ⓒ Ⓓ Ⓔ

PRACTICE II

Directions: The next 88 questions constitute another practice exercise. Mark your answers on the Practice II answer sheet. Again, the time limit is 3 MINUTES. This time, however, you must NOT look at the boxes while answering the questions. You must rely on your memory in marking the box location of each item. This practice test will not be scored.

1.	8200–8299 Ball	31.	8700–9099 Ball	61.	9800–9999 Wren
2.	8300–8699 Wren	32.	9100–9799 Wren	62.	8700–9099 Slug
3.	9800–9999 Slug	33.	9800–9999 Slug	63.	Meadow
4.	Hammock	34.	8200–8299 Slug	64.	8200–8299 Ball
5.	Meadow	35.	Denim	65.	9100–9799 Ball
6.	8700–9099 Ball	36.	Winter	66.	Ford
7.	8700–9099 Slug	37.	Hammock	67.	8200–8299 Wren
8.	9800–9999 Wren	38.	9100–9799 Slug	68.	8300–8699 Wren
9.	Zenith	39.	9100–9799 Ball	69.	8300–8699 Slug
10.	Swing	40.	9800–9999 Ball	70.	Checker
11.	8200–8299 Wren	41.	Artisan	71.	Artisan
12.	8200–8299 Slug	42.	Meadow	72.	8700–9099 Wren
13.	8300–8699 Slug	43.	9800–9999 Wren	73.	8200–8299 Slug
14.	9100–9799 Ball	44.	8300–8699 Wren	74.	8700–9099 Slug
15.	Ford	45.	8300–8699 Slug	75.	Winter
16.	Checker	46.	8300–8699 Ball	76.	Vapor
17.	Artisan	47.	Swing	77.	8300–8699 Ball
18.	8300–8699 Ball	48.	Vapor	78.	8700–9099 Ball
19.	8700–9099 Wren	49.	9800–9999 Ball	79.	8700–9099 Slug
20.	9800–9999 Wren	50.	9100–9799 Wren	80.	Vapor
21.	Vapor	51.	9100–9799 Slug	81.	Swing
22.	Meadow	52.	8700–9099 Wren	82.	9800–9999 Wren
23.	8200–8299 Ball	53.	8300–8699 Ball	83.	9800–9999 Ball
24.	Winter	54.	Swing	84.	8300–8699 Wren
25.	Ford	55.	Zenith	85.	8300–8699 Ball
26.	8300–8699 Ball	56.	Hammock	86.	8300–8699 Slug
27.	8700–9099 Wren	57.	Denim	87.	Hammock
28.	8700–9099 Slug	58.	8700–9099 Ball	88.	Denim
29.	Zenith	59.	8300–8699 Slug		
30.	Checker	60.	9800–9999 Slug		

PRACTICE II ANSWER SHEET

1 Ⓐ Ⓑ Ⓒ Ⓓ Ⓔ	23 Ⓐ Ⓑ Ⓒ Ⓓ Ⓔ	45 Ⓐ Ⓑ Ⓒ Ⓓ Ⓔ	67 Ⓐ Ⓑ Ⓒ Ⓓ Ⓔ
2 Ⓐ Ⓑ Ⓒ Ⓓ Ⓔ	24 Ⓐ Ⓑ Ⓒ Ⓓ Ⓔ	46 Ⓐ Ⓑ Ⓒ Ⓓ Ⓔ	68 Ⓐ Ⓑ Ⓒ Ⓓ Ⓔ
3 Ⓐ Ⓑ Ⓒ Ⓓ Ⓔ	25 Ⓐ Ⓑ Ⓒ Ⓓ Ⓔ	47 Ⓐ Ⓑ Ⓒ Ⓓ Ⓔ	69 Ⓐ Ⓑ Ⓒ Ⓓ Ⓔ
4 Ⓐ Ⓑ Ⓒ Ⓓ Ⓔ	26 Ⓐ Ⓑ Ⓒ Ⓓ Ⓔ	48 Ⓐ Ⓑ Ⓒ Ⓓ Ⓔ	70 Ⓐ Ⓑ Ⓒ Ⓓ Ⓔ
5 Ⓐ Ⓑ Ⓒ Ⓓ Ⓔ	27 Ⓐ Ⓑ Ⓒ Ⓓ Ⓔ	49 Ⓐ Ⓑ Ⓒ Ⓓ Ⓔ	71 Ⓐ Ⓑ Ⓒ Ⓓ Ⓔ
6 Ⓐ Ⓑ Ⓒ Ⓓ Ⓔ	28 Ⓐ Ⓑ Ⓒ Ⓓ Ⓔ	50 Ⓐ Ⓑ Ⓒ Ⓓ Ⓔ	72 Ⓐ Ⓑ Ⓒ Ⓓ Ⓔ
7 Ⓐ Ⓑ Ⓒ Ⓓ Ⓔ	29 Ⓐ Ⓑ Ⓒ Ⓓ Ⓔ	51 Ⓐ Ⓑ Ⓒ Ⓓ Ⓔ	73 Ⓐ Ⓑ Ⓒ Ⓓ Ⓔ
8 Ⓐ Ⓑ Ⓒ Ⓓ Ⓔ	30 Ⓐ Ⓑ Ⓒ Ⓓ Ⓔ	52 Ⓐ Ⓑ Ⓒ Ⓓ Ⓔ	74 Ⓐ Ⓑ Ⓒ Ⓓ Ⓔ
9 Ⓐ Ⓑ Ⓒ Ⓓ Ⓔ	31 Ⓐ Ⓑ Ⓒ Ⓓ Ⓔ	53 Ⓐ Ⓑ Ⓒ Ⓓ Ⓔ	75 Ⓐ Ⓑ Ⓒ Ⓓ Ⓔ
10 Ⓐ Ⓑ Ⓒ Ⓓ Ⓔ	32 Ⓐ Ⓑ Ⓒ Ⓓ Ⓔ	54 Ⓐ Ⓑ Ⓒ Ⓓ Ⓔ	76 Ⓐ Ⓑ Ⓒ Ⓓ Ⓔ
11 Ⓐ Ⓑ Ⓒ Ⓓ Ⓔ	33 Ⓐ Ⓑ Ⓒ Ⓓ Ⓔ	55 Ⓐ Ⓑ Ⓒ Ⓓ Ⓔ	77 Ⓐ Ⓑ Ⓒ Ⓓ Ⓔ
12 Ⓐ Ⓑ Ⓒ Ⓓ Ⓔ	34 Ⓐ Ⓑ Ⓒ Ⓓ Ⓔ	56 Ⓐ Ⓑ Ⓒ Ⓓ Ⓔ	78 Ⓐ Ⓑ Ⓒ Ⓓ Ⓔ
13 Ⓐ Ⓑ Ⓒ Ⓓ Ⓔ	35 Ⓐ Ⓑ Ⓒ Ⓓ Ⓔ	57 Ⓐ Ⓑ Ⓒ Ⓓ Ⓔ	79 Ⓐ Ⓑ Ⓒ Ⓓ Ⓔ
14 Ⓐ Ⓑ Ⓒ Ⓓ Ⓔ	36 Ⓐ Ⓑ Ⓒ Ⓓ Ⓔ	58 Ⓐ Ⓑ Ⓒ Ⓓ Ⓔ	80 Ⓐ Ⓑ Ⓒ Ⓓ Ⓔ
15 Ⓐ Ⓑ Ⓒ Ⓓ Ⓔ	37 Ⓐ Ⓑ Ⓒ Ⓓ Ⓔ	59 Ⓐ Ⓑ Ⓒ Ⓓ Ⓔ	81 Ⓐ Ⓑ Ⓒ Ⓓ Ⓔ
16 Ⓐ Ⓑ Ⓒ Ⓓ Ⓔ	38 Ⓐ Ⓑ Ⓒ Ⓓ Ⓔ	60 Ⓐ Ⓑ Ⓒ Ⓓ Ⓔ	82 Ⓐ Ⓑ Ⓒ Ⓓ Ⓔ
17 Ⓐ Ⓑ Ⓒ Ⓓ Ⓔ	39 Ⓐ Ⓑ Ⓒ Ⓓ Ⓔ	61 Ⓐ Ⓑ Ⓒ Ⓓ Ⓔ	83 Ⓐ Ⓑ Ⓒ Ⓓ Ⓔ
18 Ⓐ Ⓑ Ⓒ Ⓓ Ⓔ	40 Ⓐ Ⓑ Ⓒ Ⓓ Ⓔ	62 Ⓐ Ⓑ Ⓒ Ⓓ Ⓔ	84 Ⓐ Ⓑ Ⓒ Ⓓ Ⓔ
19 Ⓐ Ⓑ Ⓒ Ⓓ Ⓔ	41 Ⓐ Ⓑ Ⓒ Ⓓ Ⓔ	63 Ⓐ Ⓑ Ⓒ Ⓓ Ⓔ	85 Ⓐ Ⓑ Ⓒ Ⓓ Ⓔ
20 Ⓐ Ⓑ Ⓒ Ⓓ Ⓔ	42 Ⓐ Ⓑ Ⓒ Ⓓ Ⓔ	64 Ⓐ Ⓑ Ⓒ Ⓓ Ⓔ	86 Ⓐ Ⓑ Ⓒ Ⓓ Ⓔ
21 Ⓐ Ⓑ Ⓒ Ⓓ Ⓔ	43 Ⓐ Ⓑ Ⓒ Ⓓ Ⓔ	65 Ⓐ Ⓑ Ⓒ Ⓓ Ⓔ	87 Ⓐ Ⓑ Ⓒ Ⓓ Ⓔ
22 Ⓐ Ⓑ Ⓒ Ⓓ Ⓔ	44 Ⓐ Ⓑ Ⓒ Ⓓ Ⓔ	66 Ⓐ Ⓑ Ⓒ Ⓓ Ⓔ	88 Ⓐ Ⓑ Ⓒ Ⓓ Ⓔ

PRACTICE III

A	B	C	D	E
8300–8699 Ball	9100–9799 Ball	9800–9999 Ball	8200–8299 Ball	8700–9099 Ball
Meadow	Swing	Winter	Checker	Ford
9800–9999 Wren	8700–9099 Wren	8300–8699 Wren	9100–9799 Wren	8200–8299 Wren
Denim	Vapor	Artisan	Zenith	Hammock
8200–8299 Slug	9800–9999 Slug	8700–9099 Slug	8300–8699 Slug	9100–9799 Slug

1. 8200–8299 Ball
2. 9100–9799 Wren
3. 8300–8699 Slug
4. 8700–9099 Wren
5. Denim
6. Ford
7. 8300–8699 Ball
8. 9100–9799 Slug
9. 8200–8299 Slug
10. Meadow
11. Zenith
12. 8700–9099 Slug
13. 9800–9999 Ball
14. 9100–9799 Ball
15. 8700–9099 Wren
16. 9100–9799 Slug
17. 9100–9799 Ball
18. 9100–9799 Wren
19. Artisan
20. Vapor
21. 8300–8699 Wren
22. Meadow
23. 9800–9999 Slug
24. 8700–9099 Wren
25. 8700–9099 Ball
26. Winter
27. Denim
28. 8200–8299 Ball
29. 8300–8699 Slug
30. Hammock
31. Ford
32. 8300–8699 Ball
33. 8700–9099 Wren
34. 8700–9099 Slug
35. Meadow
36. Vapor
37. 8700–9099 Ball
38. 9100–9799 Wren
39. 9800–9999 Ball
40. 9800–9999 Slug
41. Hammock
42. Winter
43. Swing
44. 9100–9799 Ball
45. 9100–9799 Slug
46. 8300–8699 Wren
47. 8200–8299 Wren
48. Ford
49. Zenith
50. 8200–8299 Slug
51. 8300–8699 Slug
52. Denim
53. 8200–8299 Ball
54. 9800–9999 Wren
55. Artisan
56. Checker
57. 9100–9799 Slug
58. 9700–9799 Ball
59. 8200–8299 Wren
60. 8300–8699 Wren
61. 9800–9999 Ball
62. 8200–8299 Wren
63. 8200–8299 Slug
64. 8700–9099 Wren
65. Hammock
66. Zenith

67. 9100–9799 Ball	75. 8300–8699 Slug	83. Swing
68. 9800–9999 Slug	76. Checker	84. Artisan
69. 8300–8699 Ball	77. Winter	85. Ford
70. 8300–8699 Wren	78. Vapor	86. 9800–9999 Ball
71. Denim	79. 9100–9799 Slug	87. 8200–8299 Wren
72. Meadow	80. 9100–9799 Wren	88. 8300–8699 Ball
73. 9800–9999 Wren	81. 8700–9099 Ball	
74. 8200–8299 Ball	82. 8700–9099 Slug	

PRACTICE III ANSWER SHEET

1 Ⓐ Ⓑ Ⓒ Ⓓ Ⓔ   23 Ⓐ Ⓑ Ⓒ Ⓓ Ⓔ   45 Ⓐ Ⓑ Ⓒ Ⓓ Ⓔ   67 Ⓐ Ⓑ Ⓒ Ⓓ Ⓔ
2 Ⓐ Ⓑ Ⓒ Ⓓ Ⓔ   24 Ⓐ Ⓑ Ⓒ Ⓓ Ⓔ   46 Ⓐ Ⓑ Ⓒ Ⓓ Ⓔ   68 Ⓐ Ⓑ Ⓒ Ⓓ Ⓔ
3 Ⓐ Ⓑ Ⓒ Ⓓ Ⓔ   25 Ⓐ Ⓑ Ⓒ Ⓓ Ⓔ   47 Ⓐ Ⓑ Ⓒ Ⓓ Ⓔ   69 Ⓐ Ⓑ Ⓒ Ⓓ Ⓔ
4 Ⓐ Ⓑ Ⓒ Ⓓ Ⓔ   26 Ⓐ Ⓑ Ⓒ Ⓓ Ⓔ   48 Ⓐ Ⓑ Ⓒ Ⓓ Ⓔ   70 Ⓐ Ⓑ Ⓒ Ⓓ Ⓔ
5 Ⓐ Ⓑ Ⓒ Ⓓ Ⓔ   27 Ⓐ Ⓑ Ⓒ Ⓓ Ⓔ   49 Ⓐ Ⓑ Ⓒ Ⓓ Ⓔ   71 Ⓐ Ⓑ Ⓒ Ⓓ Ⓔ
6 Ⓐ Ⓑ Ⓒ Ⓓ Ⓔ   28 Ⓐ Ⓑ Ⓒ Ⓓ Ⓔ   50 Ⓐ Ⓑ Ⓒ Ⓓ Ⓔ   72 Ⓐ Ⓑ Ⓒ Ⓓ Ⓔ
7 Ⓐ Ⓑ Ⓒ Ⓓ Ⓔ   29 Ⓐ Ⓑ Ⓒ Ⓓ Ⓔ   51 Ⓐ Ⓑ Ⓒ Ⓓ Ⓔ   73 Ⓐ Ⓑ Ⓒ Ⓓ Ⓔ
8 Ⓐ Ⓑ Ⓒ Ⓓ Ⓔ   30 Ⓐ Ⓑ Ⓒ Ⓓ Ⓔ   52 Ⓐ Ⓑ Ⓒ Ⓓ Ⓔ   74 Ⓐ Ⓑ Ⓒ Ⓓ Ⓔ
9 Ⓐ Ⓑ Ⓒ Ⓓ Ⓔ   31 Ⓐ Ⓑ Ⓒ Ⓓ Ⓔ   53 Ⓐ Ⓑ Ⓒ Ⓓ Ⓔ   75 Ⓐ Ⓑ Ⓒ Ⓓ Ⓔ
10 Ⓐ Ⓑ Ⓒ Ⓓ Ⓔ   32 Ⓐ Ⓑ Ⓒ Ⓓ Ⓔ   54 Ⓐ Ⓑ Ⓒ Ⓓ Ⓔ   76 Ⓐ Ⓑ Ⓒ Ⓓ Ⓔ
11 Ⓐ Ⓑ Ⓒ Ⓓ Ⓔ   33 Ⓐ Ⓑ Ⓒ Ⓓ Ⓔ   55 Ⓐ Ⓑ Ⓒ Ⓓ Ⓔ   77 Ⓐ Ⓑ Ⓒ Ⓓ Ⓔ
12 Ⓐ Ⓑ Ⓒ Ⓓ Ⓔ   34 Ⓐ Ⓑ Ⓒ Ⓓ Ⓔ   56 Ⓐ Ⓑ Ⓒ Ⓓ Ⓔ   78 Ⓐ Ⓑ Ⓒ Ⓓ Ⓔ
13 Ⓐ Ⓑ Ⓒ Ⓓ Ⓔ   35 Ⓐ Ⓑ Ⓒ Ⓓ Ⓔ   57 Ⓐ Ⓑ Ⓒ Ⓓ Ⓔ   79 Ⓐ Ⓑ Ⓒ Ⓓ Ⓔ
14 Ⓐ Ⓑ Ⓒ Ⓓ Ⓔ   36 Ⓐ Ⓑ Ⓒ Ⓓ Ⓔ   58 Ⓐ Ⓑ Ⓒ Ⓓ Ⓔ   80 Ⓐ Ⓑ Ⓒ Ⓓ Ⓔ
15 Ⓐ Ⓑ Ⓒ Ⓓ Ⓔ   37 Ⓐ Ⓑ Ⓒ Ⓓ Ⓔ   59 Ⓐ Ⓑ Ⓒ Ⓓ Ⓔ   81 Ⓐ Ⓑ Ⓒ Ⓓ Ⓔ
16 Ⓐ Ⓑ Ⓒ Ⓓ Ⓔ   38 Ⓐ Ⓑ Ⓒ Ⓓ Ⓔ   60 Ⓐ Ⓑ Ⓒ Ⓓ Ⓔ   82 Ⓐ Ⓑ Ⓒ Ⓓ Ⓔ
17 Ⓐ Ⓑ Ⓒ Ⓓ Ⓔ   39 Ⓐ Ⓑ Ⓒ Ⓓ Ⓔ   61 Ⓐ Ⓑ Ⓒ Ⓓ Ⓔ   83 Ⓐ Ⓑ Ⓒ Ⓓ Ⓔ
18 Ⓐ Ⓑ Ⓒ Ⓓ Ⓔ   40 Ⓐ Ⓑ Ⓒ Ⓓ Ⓔ   62 Ⓐ Ⓑ Ⓒ Ⓓ Ⓔ   84 Ⓐ Ⓑ Ⓒ Ⓓ Ⓔ
19 Ⓐ Ⓑ Ⓒ Ⓓ Ⓔ   41 Ⓐ Ⓑ Ⓒ Ⓓ Ⓔ   63 Ⓐ Ⓑ Ⓒ Ⓓ Ⓔ   85 Ⓐ Ⓑ Ⓒ Ⓓ Ⓔ
20 Ⓐ Ⓑ Ⓒ Ⓓ Ⓔ   42 Ⓐ Ⓑ Ⓒ Ⓓ Ⓔ   64 Ⓐ Ⓑ Ⓒ Ⓓ Ⓔ   86 Ⓐ Ⓑ Ⓒ Ⓓ Ⓔ
21 Ⓐ Ⓑ Ⓒ Ⓓ Ⓔ   43 Ⓐ Ⓑ Ⓒ Ⓓ Ⓔ   65 Ⓐ Ⓑ Ⓒ Ⓓ Ⓔ   87 Ⓐ Ⓑ Ⓒ Ⓓ Ⓔ
22 Ⓐ Ⓑ Ⓒ Ⓓ Ⓔ   44 Ⓐ Ⓑ Ⓒ Ⓓ Ⓔ   66 Ⓐ Ⓑ Ⓒ Ⓓ Ⓔ   88 Ⓐ Ⓑ Ⓒ Ⓓ Ⓔ

MEMORY FOR ADDRESSES—SCORED TEST

Time: 5 minutes • 88 Questions

> **Directions:** *Mark your answers on the answer sheet provided on page 52. This test will be scored. You are NOT permitted to look at the boxes. Work from memory, as quickly and as accurately as you can. Correct answers are on page 83.*

1.	9800–9999 Wren	31.	8300–8699 Ball	61.	8200–8299 Ball
2.	9100–9799 Ball	32.	8700–9099 Ball	62.	9100–9799 Wren
3.	Meadow	33.	9100–9799 Wren	63.	Checker
4.	Hammock	34.	Denim	64.	9800–9999 Slug
5.	9100–9799 Slug	35.	Checker	65.	8200–8299 Wren
6.	8200–8299 Ball	36.	8200–8299 Slug	66.	8300–8699 Slug
7.	9800–9999 Slug	37.	8700–9099 Slug	67.	Vapor
8.	Zenith	38.	8200–8299 Wren	68.	Zenith
9.	Vapor	39.	Zenith	69.	9800–9999 Ball
10.	8200–8299 Wren	40.	Hammock	70.	9800–9999 Wren
11.	8300–8699 Wren	41.	8200–8299 Ball	71.	Artisan
12.	9800–9999 Ball	42.	Swing	72.	8200–8299 Ball
13.	8300–8699 Slug	43.	9800–9999 Slug	73.	8300–8699 Slug
14.	Ford	44.	9800–9999 Ball	74.	9100–9799 Ball
15.	Artisan	45.	Vapor	75.	Vapor
16.	Denim	46.	8700–9099 Ball	76.	Meadow
17.	9800–9999 Slug	47.	9100–9799 Wren	77.	8200–8299 Wren
18.	8200–8299 Slug	48.	8700–9099 Slug	78.	8700–9099 Slug
19.	8700–9099 Wren	49.	8700–9099 Wren	79.	9100–9799 Ball
20.	9100–9799 Wren	50.	8300–8699 Ball	80.	Swing
21.	Checker	51.	Winter	81.	Artisan
22.	Swing	52.	Hammock	82.	9800–9999 Wren
23.	8300–8699 Slug	53.	Meadow	83.	Hammock
24.	Winter	54.	8200–8299 Slug	84.	8300–8699 Wren
25.	9100–9799 Ball	55.	8300–8699 Wren	85.	8300–8699 Ball
26.	8700–9099 Wren	56.	9100–9799 Slug	86.	9100–9799 Slug
27.	9100–9799 Slug	57.	Denim	87.	Checker
28.	8300–8699 Wren	58.	Swing	88.	Ford
29.	Artisan	59.	Ford		
30.	Ford	60.	9100–9799 Ball		

PART C—NUMBER SERIES

SAMPLE QUESTIONS

The following sample questions show you the type of question that will be used in Part C. You will have 3 minutes to answer the sample questions below and to study the explanations.

> **Directions:** *Each number series question consists of a series of numbers that follows some definite order. The numbers progress from left to right according to some rule. One pair of numbers to the right of the series comprises the next two numbers in the series. Study each series to try to find a pattern to the series and to figure out the rule that governs the progression. Choose the answer pair that continues the series according to the pattern established and mark its letter on your answer sheet.*

    1.   21 21 19 17 17 15 13 .... (A) 11 11 (B) 13 11 (C) 11 9 (D) 9 7 (E) 13 13

The pattern of this series is: repeat the number, then subtract 2 and subtract 2 again; repeat the number, then subtract 2 and subtract 2 again, and so on. Following the pattern, the series should continue with choice (B) 13 11, and then go on 9 9 7 5 5 3 1 1.

    2.   23 22 20 19 16 15 11 .... (A) 6 5 (B) 10 9 (C) 6 1 (D) 10 6 (E) 10 5

If you write in the changes between the numbers of the series, you can see that the pattern being established is: –1, –2, –1, –3, –1, –4, –1, –5 . . . . Fitting the pattern to the remaining numbers, it is apparent that choice (E) is the answer because 11 – 1 = 10 and 10 – 5 = 5.

    3.   5 6 8 9 11 12 14 .... (A) 15 16 (B) 16 17 (C) 15 17 (D) 16 18 (E) 17 19

The pattern here is: +1, +2; +1, +2; +1, +2, and so on. The correct answer is (C) because 14 + 1 = 15 and 15 + 2 = 17.

    4.   7 10 8 13 16 8 19 .... (A) 22 8 (B) 8 22 (C) 20 21 (D) 22 25 (E) 8 25

Marking the changes between numbers is not sufficient for solving this series. You must first notice that the number 8 is repeated after each two numbers. If you disregard the 8's, you can see that the series is increasing by a factor of +3. With this information, you can choose choice (A) as the correct answer because 19 + 3 = 22, and the two numbers, 19 and 22, are then followed by 8.

    5.   1 35 2 34 3 33 4 .... (A) 4 5 (B) 32 31 (C) 32 5 (D) 5 32 (E) 31 6

This series is, in reality, two alternating series. One series, beginning with 1, increases at the rate of +1. The other series alternates with the first. It begins with 35 and decreases by –1. The correct answer is choice (C) because the next number in the decreasing series is 32 and the next number in the increasing series is 5.

SAMPLE ANSWER SHEET	CORRECT ANSWERS
1. Ⓐ Ⓑ Ⓒ Ⓓ Ⓔ	1. Ⓐ ● Ⓒ Ⓓ Ⓔ
2. Ⓐ Ⓑ Ⓒ Ⓓ Ⓔ	2. Ⓐ Ⓑ Ⓒ Ⓓ ●
3. Ⓐ Ⓑ Ⓒ Ⓓ Ⓔ	3. Ⓐ Ⓑ ● Ⓓ Ⓔ
4. Ⓐ Ⓑ Ⓒ Ⓓ Ⓔ	4. ● Ⓑ Ⓒ Ⓓ Ⓔ
5. Ⓐ Ⓑ Ⓒ Ⓓ Ⓔ	5. Ⓐ Ⓑ ● Ⓓ Ⓔ

NUMBER SERIES

Time: 20 Minutes • 24 Questions

> **Directions:** *Each number series question consists of a series of numbers that follows some definite order. The numbers progress from left to right according to some rule. One pair of numbers to the right of the series comprises the next two numbers in the series. Study each series to try to find a pattern to the series and to figure out the rule that governs the progression. Choose the answer pair that continues the series according to the pattern established and mark its letter on your answer sheet. Correct answers are on page 83.*

1. 8 9 10 8 9 10 8 .... (A) 8 9   (B) 9 10   (C) 9 8   (D) 10 8   (E) 8 10

2. 3 4 4 3 5 5 3 .... (A) 3 3   (B) 6 3   (C) 3 6   (D) 6 6   (E) 6 7

3. 7 7 3 7 7 4 7 .... (A) 7 7   (B) 7 8   (C) 5 7   (D) 8 7   (E) 7 5

4. 18 18 19 20 20 21 22 .... (A) 22 23   (B) 23 24   (C) 23 23   (D) 22 22   (E) 21 22

5. 2 6 10 3 7 11 4 .... (A) 12 16   (B) 5 9   (C) 8 5   (D) 12 5   (E) 8 12

6. 11 8 15 12 19 16 23 .... (A) 27 20   (B) 24 20   (C) 27 24   (D) 20 24   (E) 20 27

7. 16 8 15 9 14 10 13 .... (A) 12 11   (B) 13 12   (C) 11 13   (D) 11 12   (E) 11 14

8. 4 5 13 67 12 8 .... (A) 9 11   (B) 13 9   (C) 9 13   (D) 11 9   (E) 11 10

9. 19 24 20 25 21 26 22 .... (A) 18 27   (B) 22 24   (C) 23 29   (D) 27 23   (E) 28 32

10. 25 25 22 22 19 19 16 .... (A) 18 18   (B) 16 16   (C) 16 13   (D) 15 15   (E) 15 13

11. 1 1 2 3 5 8 13 .... (A) 21 29   (B) 21 34   (C) 18 27   (D) 21 27   (E) 24 32

12. 1 3 2 4 3 5 4 .... (A) 6 5   (B) 5 6   (C) 3 1   (D) 3 5   (E) 4 3

13. 1 2 2 3 3 3 4 .... (A) 4 5   (B) 5 5   (C) 3 5   (D) 4 4   (E) 4 3

14. 9 17 24 30 35 39 42 .... (A) 43 44   (B) 44 46   (C) 44 45   (D) 45 49   (E) 46 50

15. 1 4 9 16 25 36 49 .... (A) 56 64   (B) 60 65   (C) 62 75   (D) 64 80   (E) 64 81

16. 8 12 17 24 28 33 40 .... (A) 47 53   (B) 45 50   (C) 43 49   (D) 48 54   (E) 44 49

17. 28 31 34 37 40 43 46 .... (A) 49 52   (B) 47 49   (C) 50 54   (D) 49 53   (E) 51 55

18. 17 17 24 24 31 31 38 .... (A) 38 39   (B) 38 17   (C) 38 45   (D) 38 44   (E) 39 50

19. 3 12 6 24 12 48 24 .... (A) 96 48   (B) 56 23   (C) 64 12   (D) 52 36   (E) 64 48

20. 87 83 79 75 71 67 63 .... (A) 62 61   (B) 63 59   (C) 60 56   (D) 59 55   (E) 59 54

21. 10 2 8 2 6 2 4 .... (A) 4 4   (B) 2 2   (C) 3 3   (D) 4 2   (E) 5 2

22. 8 9 11 14 18 23 29 .... (A) 35 45   (B) 32 33   (C) 38 48   (D) 34 40   (E) 36 44

23. 11 14 12 15 13 16 14 .... (A) 14 17   (B) 15 16   (C) 16 20   (D) 17 15   (E) 18 13

24. 14 2 12 4 10 6 8 .... (A) 10 12   (B) 6 8   (C) 12 10   (D) 8 6   (E) 10 14

PART D—FOLLOWING ORAL INSTRUCTIONS

DIRECTIONS AND SAMPLE QUESTIONS

Listening to Instructions: When you are ready to try these sample questions, give the following instructions to a friend to read them aloud to you at the rate of 80 words per minute. Do not read them to yourself. Your friend will need a watch with a second hand. Listen carefully and do exactly what your friend tells you to do with the worksheet and answer sheet. Your friend will tell you some things to do with each item on the worksheet. After each set of instructions, your friend will give you time to mark your answer by darkening a circle on the sample answer sheet. Because B and D sound very much alike, your friend will say "B as in baker" when he or she means B, and "D as in dog" when he or she means D.

Before proceeding further, tear out the worksheet on the next page. Then, hand this book to your friend.

To the Person Who Is to Read the Instructions: The instructions are to be read at the rate of 80 words per minute. Do not read aloud the material that is in parentheses. Do not repeat any instructions.

READ ALOUD TO THE CANDIDATE

Look at line 1 on the worksheet. (Pause slightly.) Write a D as in dog in the fourth box. (Pause 2 seconds.) Now, on your answer sheet, find the number in that box and darken space D as in dog for that number. (Pause 5 seconds.)

Look at line 2. The number in each circle is the number of employees in a post office. In the circle holding the largest number of employees, write a B as in baker. (Pause 2 seconds.) Now, on your answer sheet, darken the space for the number-letter combination that is in the circle you just wrote in. (Pause 5 seconds.) Look at line 3 on the worksheet. (Pause slightly.) Write the letter C on the blank next to the right-hand number. (Pause 2 seconds.) Now, on your answer sheet, find the number beside which you just wrote and darken space C. (Pause 5 seconds.)

Look at line 3 again. (Pause slightly.) Write the letter B as in baker on the blank next to the left-hand number. (Pause 2 seconds.) Now, on your answer sheet, find the number beside which you just wrote and darken space B as in baker. (Pause 5 seconds.)

Look at line 4 on your worksheet. (Pause slightly.) Draw a line under every X in the line. (Pause 5 seconds.) Count the number of lines that you have drawn, divide by 2, and write that number at the end of the line. (Pause 5 seconds.) Now, on your answer sheet, find that number and darken space C for that number. (Pause 5 seconds.)

SAMPLE WORKSHEET

> *Directions:* Listening carefully to each set of instructions, mark each item on this worksheet as directed. Then, complete each question by marking the sample answer sheet below as directed. For each answer you will darken the answer for a number-letter combination. Should you fall behind and miss an instruction, don't become excited. Let that one go and listen for the next one. If, when you start to darken a space for a number, you find that you have already darkened another space for that number, either erase the first mark and darken the space for the new combination or let the first mark stay and do not darken a space for the new combination. Write with a pencil that has a clean eraser. When you finish, you should have no more than one space darkened for each number.

1. | 4 __ | | 14 __ | | 11 __ | | 7 __ | | 9 __ |

2. (3 __)   (12 __)   (15 __)   (8 __)   (6 __)

3. 10 _____   2 _____

4. X O X X X X O O X O X O X O X X X O X

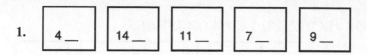

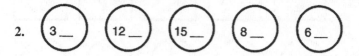

SAMPLE ANSWER SHEET

1. Ⓐ Ⓑ Ⓒ Ⓓ Ⓔ	6. Ⓐ Ⓑ Ⓒ Ⓓ Ⓔ	11. Ⓐ Ⓑ Ⓒ Ⓓ Ⓔ
2. Ⓐ Ⓑ Ⓒ Ⓓ Ⓔ	7. Ⓐ Ⓑ Ⓒ Ⓓ Ⓔ	12. Ⓐ Ⓑ Ⓒ Ⓓ Ⓔ
3. Ⓐ Ⓑ Ⓒ Ⓓ Ⓔ	8. Ⓐ Ⓑ Ⓒ Ⓓ Ⓔ	13. Ⓐ Ⓑ Ⓒ Ⓓ Ⓔ
4. Ⓐ Ⓑ Ⓒ Ⓓ Ⓔ	9. Ⓐ Ⓑ Ⓒ Ⓓ Ⓔ	14. Ⓐ Ⓑ Ⓒ Ⓓ Ⓔ
5. Ⓐ Ⓑ Ⓒ Ⓓ Ⓔ	10. Ⓐ Ⓑ Ⓒ Ⓓ Ⓔ	15. Ⓐ Ⓑ Ⓒ Ⓓ Ⓔ

CORRECTLY FILLED ANSWER SHEET

CORRECT ANSWERS TO SAMPLE QUESTIONS

1. Ⓐ Ⓑ ● Ⓓ Ⓔ   6. Ⓐ Ⓑ Ⓒ Ⓓ Ⓔ   11. Ⓐ Ⓑ Ⓒ Ⓓ Ⓔ
2. Ⓐ Ⓑ ● Ⓓ Ⓔ   7. Ⓐ Ⓑ Ⓒ ● Ⓔ   12. Ⓐ Ⓑ Ⓒ Ⓓ Ⓔ
3. Ⓐ Ⓑ Ⓒ Ⓓ Ⓔ   8. Ⓐ Ⓑ Ⓒ Ⓓ Ⓔ   13. Ⓐ Ⓑ Ⓒ Ⓓ Ⓔ
4. Ⓐ Ⓑ Ⓒ Ⓓ Ⓔ   9. Ⓐ Ⓑ Ⓒ Ⓓ Ⓔ   14. Ⓐ Ⓑ Ⓒ Ⓓ Ⓔ
5. Ⓐ Ⓑ ● Ⓓ Ⓔ   10. Ⓐ ● Ⓒ Ⓓ Ⓔ   15. Ⓐ ● Ⓒ Ⓓ Ⓔ

CORRECTLY FILLED WORKSHEET

1. [4 __]   [14 __]   [11 __]   [7 _D_]   [9 __]

2. (3 __)   (12 __)   (15 _B_)   (8 __)   (6 __)

3. 10 _B_   2 _C_

4. X̲OX̲X̲X̲X̲OOX̲OX̲OX̲X̲OX̲ **5**

FOLLOWING ORAL INSTRUCTIONS
Time: 25 Minutes

LISTENING TO INSTRUCTIONS

> *Directions: When you are ready to try this test of the Model Exam, give the following instructions to a friend and have the friend read them aloud to you at the rate of 80 words per minute. Do not read them to yourself. Your friend will need a watch with a second hand. Listen carefully and do exactly what your friend tells you to do with the worksheet and answer sheet. Your friend will tell you some things to do with each item on the worksheet. After each set of instructions, your friend will give you time to mark your answer by darkening a circle on the sample answer sheet. Because B and D sound very much alike, your friend will say "B as in baker" when he or she means B and "D as in dog" when he or she means D.*

Before proceeding further, tear out the worksheet located after the instructions. Then, hand this book to your friend.

To the Person Who Is to Read the Instructions: The instructions are to be read at the rate of 80 words per minute. Do not read aloud the material that is in parentheses. After you have begun the test itself, do not repeat any instructions. The next three paragraphs consist of approximately 120 words. Read these three paragraphs aloud to the candidate in about one and one-half minutes. You may reread these paragraphs as often as necessary to establish an 80 words per minute reading speed.

READ ALOUD TO THE CANDIDATE

On the job you will have to listen to directions and then do what you have been told to do. In this test, I will read instructions to you. Try to understand them as I read them; I cannot repeat them. After we begin, you may not ask any questions until the end of the test.

On the job you won't have to deal with pictures, numbers, and letters like those in the test, but you will have to listen to instructions and follow them. We are using this test to see how well you can follow instructions.

You are to mark your test booklet according to the instructions that I'll read to you. After each set of instructions, I'll give you time to record your answers on the separate answer sheet.

The actual test begins now.

Look at line 1 on the worksheet. (Pause slightly.) Draw a line under the fourth number in the line. (Pause 2 seconds.) Now, on your answer sheet, find the number under which you just drew the line and darken space A for that number. (Pause 5 seconds.)

Look at the letters in line 2 on the worksheet. (Pause slightly.) Draw a line under the fifth letter in the line. Now, on your answer sheet, find number 59 (Pause 2 seconds.) and darken the space for the letter under which you drew a line. (Pause 5 seconds.)

Look at the letters in line 2 on the worksheet again. (Pause slightly.) Now, draw two lines under the third letter in the line. (Pause 2 seconds.) Now, on your answer sheet, find number 65 (Pause 2 seconds.) and darken the space for the letter under which you drew two lines. (Pause 5 seconds.)

Look at line 3 on the worksheet. (Pause slightly.) Write an E in the last box. (Pause 2 seconds.) Now, on your answer sheet, find the number in that box and darken space E for that number. (Pause 5 seconds.)

Now, look at line 3 again. (Pause slightly.) Write an A in the first box. (Pause 2 seconds.) Now, on your answer sheet, find the number in that box and darken space A for that number. (Pause 5 seconds.)

Look at line 4. (Pause slightly.) The number in each circle is the number of packages in a mail sack. In the circle for the sack holding the largest number of packages, write a B as in baker. (Pause 2 seconds.) Now, on your answer sheet, darken the space for the number-letter combination that is in the circle you just wrote in. (Pause 5 seconds.)

Look at line 4 again. In the circle for the sack holding the smallest number of packages, write an E. (Pause 2 seconds.) Now, on your answer sheet, darken the space for the number-letter combination that is in the circle you just wrote in. (Pause 5 seconds.)

Look at the drawings on line 5 on the worksheet. The four boxes are trucks for carrying mail. (Pause 2 seconds.) The truck with the highest number is to be loaded first. Write a B as in baker on the line beside the highest number. (Pause 2 seconds.) Now, on your answer sheet, darken the space for the number-letter combination that is in the box you just wrote in. (Pause 5 seconds.)

Look at line 6 on the worksheet. (Pause slightly.) Next to the middle number, write the letter D as in dog. (Pause 2 seconds.) Now, on your answer sheet, find the space for the number beside which you wrote and darken space D as in dog.

Look at the five circles in line 7 on the worksheet. Write B as in baker on the blank in the second circle. (Pause 2 seconds.) Now, on your answer sheet, darken the space for the number-letter combination that is in the circle you just wrote in. (Pause 5 seconds.)

Now, take the worksheet again and write C on the blank in the third circle on line 7. (Pause 2 seconds.) Now, on your answer sheet, darken the space for the number-letter combination that is in the circle you just wrote in. (Pause 5 seconds.)

Now, look at line 8 on the worksheet. (Pause slightly.) Write an A on the line next to the right-hand number. (Pause 2 seconds.) Now, on your answer sheet, find the space for the number beside which you wrote and darken space A. (Pause 5 seconds.)

Look at line 9 on the worksheet. (Pause slightly.) Draw a line under every number that is more the 60 but less than 70. (Pause 12 seconds.) Now, on your answer sheet, for each number that you drew a line under, darken space C. (Pause 25 seconds.)

Look at line 10 on the worksheet. (Pause slightly.) Draw a line under every number that is more than 5 and less than 15. (Pause 10 seconds.) Now, on your answer sheet, for each number that you drew a line under, darken space D as in dog. (Pause 25 seconds.)

Look at line 11 on the worksheet. (Pause slightly.) In each circle there is a time when the mail must leave. In the circle for the latest time, write on the line the last two figures of the time. (Pause 5 seconds.) Now, on your answer sheet, darken the space for the number-letter combination that is in the circle you just wrote in. (Pause 5 seconds.)

Look at the five boxes in line 12 on your worksheet. (Pause slightly.) If 6 is less than 3, put an E in the fourth box. (Pause slightly.) If 6 is not less than 3, put a B as in baker in the first box. (Pause 10 seconds.) Now, on your answer sheet, darken the space for the number-letter combination that is in the circle you just wrote in. (Pause 5 seconds.)

Now, look at line 13 on the worksheet. (Pause slightly.) There are five circles. Each circle has a letter. (Pause slightly.) In the second circle, write the answer to this question: Which of the following numbers is smallest: 72, 51, 88, 71, 58? (Pause 10 seconds.) Now, on your answer sheet, darken the space for the number-letter combination that is in the circle you wrote in.

(Pause 5 seconds.) In the third circle on the same line, write 28. (Pause 2 seconds.) Now, on your answer sheet, darken the space for the number-letter combination that is in the circle you just wrote in. (Pause 5 seconds.) In the fourth circle do nothing. In the fifth circle write the answer to this question: How many months are there in a year? (Pause 5 seconds.) Now, on your answer sheet, darken the space for the number-letter combination that is in the circle you just wrote in. (Pause 5 seconds.)

Look at line 14 on your worksheet. (Pause slightly.) There are two circles and two boxes of different sizes with numbers in them. (Pause slightly.) If 2 is smaller than 4, and 7 is less than 3, write A in the larger circle. (Pause slightly.) Otherwise, write B as in baker in the smallest box. (Pause 10 seconds.) Now, on your answer sheet, darken the space for the number-letter combination in the box or circle in which you just wrote. (Pause 5 seconds.)

Look at the boxes and words in line 15 on the worksheet. (Pause slightly.) Write the second letter of the first word in the third box. (Pause 5 seconds.) Write the first letter of the second word in the first box. (Pause 5 seconds.) Write the first letter of the third word in the second box. (Pause 5 seconds.) Now, on your answer sheet, darken the spaces for the number-letter combinations that are in the three boxes you just wrote in. (Pause 15 seconds.)

Look at line 16 on the worksheet. (Pause slightly.) Draw a line under every "O" in the line. (Pause 5 seconds.) Count the number of lines that you have drawn, subtract 2, and write that number at the end of the line. (Pause 5 seconds.) Now, on your answer sheet, find that number and darken space D as in dog for that number. (Pause 5 seconds.)

Look at line 17 on the worksheet. (Pause slightly.) If the number in the left-hand circle is smaller than the number in the right-hand circle, add 2 to the number in the left-hand circle, and change the number in that circle to this number. (Pause 8 seconds.) Then, write B as in baker next to the new number. (Pause slightly.) Next, write E beside the number in the smallest box. (Pause 3 seconds.) Then, on your answer sheet, darken the spaces for the number-letter combinations that are in the box and circle you just wrote in. (Pause 5 seconds.)

Look at line 18 on the worksheet. (Pause slightly.) If in a year October comes before September, write A in the box with the smallest number. (Pause slightly.) If it does not, write C in the box with the largest number. (Pause 10 seconds.) Now, on your answer sheet, darken the space for the number-letter combination that is in the box you just wrote in. (Pause 5 seconds.)

Look at line 19 on the worksheet. (Pause slightly.) On the line beside the second letter, write the highest of these numbers: 12, 56, 42, 39, 8. (Pause 2 seconds.) Now, on your answer sheet, darken the space of the number-letter combination you just wrote. (Pause 5 seconds.)

FOLLOWING ORAL INSTRUCTIONS

WORKSHEET

Directions: *Listening carefully to each set of instructions, mark each item on this worksheet as directed. Then complete each question by marking the sample answer sheet below as directed. For each answer you will darken the answer for a number-letter combination. Should you fall behind and miss an instruction, don't become excited. Let that one go and listen for the next one. If, when you start to darken a space for a number, you find that you have already darkened another space for that number, either erase the first mark and darken the space for the new combination or let the first mark stay and do not darken a space for the new combination. Write with a pencil that has a clean eraser. When you finish, you should have no more than one space darkened for each number. Correct answers begin on page 85.*

1. 13   23   2   19   6

2. E   B   D   E   C   A   B

3. | 30 __ | 18 __ | 5 __ | 14 __ | 7 __ |

4. (26 __) (16 __) (23 __) (22 __) (27 __)

5. | 63 __ | 14 __ | 78 __ | 48 __ |

6. 12 ____   5 ____   22 ____

7. (14 __) (1 __) (36 __) (7 __) (19 __)

8. 26 ____   86 ____

9. 57   63   11   78   90   32   45   70   69

10. 16   30   13   25   10   14   23   26   19

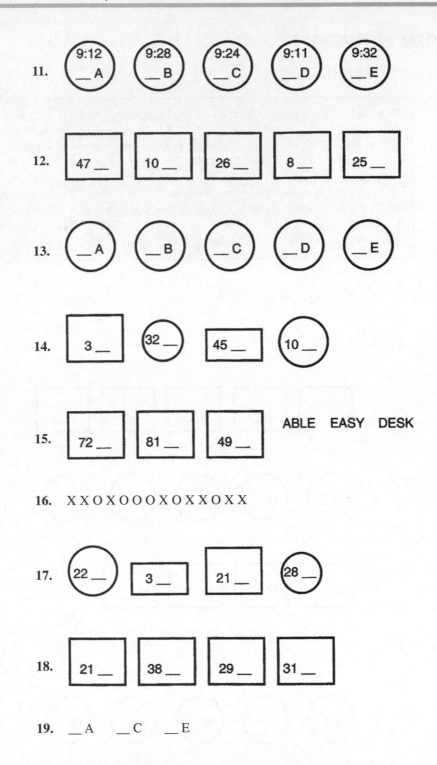

11.
9:12 __A   9:28 __B   9:24 __C   9:11 __D   9:32 __E

12.
47 __   10 __   26 __   8 __   25 __

13.
__A   __B   __C   __D   __E

14.
3 __   32 __   45 __   10 __

15.
72 __   81 __   49 __   ABLE   EASY   DESK

16.   X X O X O O O X O X X O X X

17.   22 __   3 __   21 __   28 __

18.   21 __   38 __   29 __   31 __

19.   __A   __C   __E

END OF EXAMINATION

CORRECT ANSWERS FOR PRELIMINARY EXAM

Part A—Address Checking Answer Key					
1. A	17. D	33. D	49. D	65. A	81. A
2. D	18. A	34. D	50. D	66. D	82. A
3. A	19. A	35. A	51. A	67. D	83. D
4. D	20. D	36. A	52. A	68. D	84. D
5. D	21. D	37. D	53. D	69. A	85. A
6. D	22. D	38. A	54. D	70. D	86. A
7. A	23. D	39. D	55. D	71. A	87. D
8. D	24. A	40. A	56. D	72. D	88. A
9. D	25. A	41. A	57. D	73. A	89. D
10. A	26. D	42. A	58. A	74. D	90. D
11. A	27. D	43. D	59. D	75. D	91. D
12. D	28. A	44. D	60. A	76. D	92. D
13. D	29. D	45. D	61. A	77. D	93. A
14. D	30. D	46. D	62. D	78. D	94. D
15. A	31. D	47. A	63. A	79. D	95. D
16. A	32. D	48. D	64. D	80. D	

ANALYZING YOUR ERRORS

The Address Checking Test of the Preliminary Exam contains 35 addresses that are exactly alike and 60 addresses that are different. The chart below shows what kind of difference occurs in each of the addresses that contains a difference. Check your answers against this chart to see which kind of difference you missed most often. Note also the questions in which you thought you saw a difference but in which there really was none. Becoming aware of your errors will help you eliminate those errors on future model exams and on the actual exam.

Type of Difference	Question Numbers	Number of Questions You Missed
Difference in NUMBERS	2, 12, 13, 22, 26, 31, 39, 44, 49, 53, 54, 67, 68, 70, 72, 76, 79, 89, 91	
Difference in ABBREVIATIONS	4, 9, 14, 20, 21, 23, 27, 30, 32, 33, 46, 55, 59, 62, 74, 75, 78, 84, 87, 95	
Difference in NAMES	5, 6, 8, 17, 29, 34, 37, 43, 45, 48, 50, 56, 57, 64, 66, 77, 80, 83, 90, 92, 94	
No Difference	1, 3, 7, 10, 11, 15, 16, 18, 19, 24, 25, 28, 35, 36, 38, 40, 41, 42, 47, 51, 52, 58, 60, 61, 63, 65, 69, 71, 73, 81, 82, 85, 86, 88, 93	

Part B—Memory for Addresses Answer Keys

PRACTICE I

1. D	14. E	27. E	40. C	53. B	66. C	79. E
2. C	15. D	28. D	41. A	54. E	67. D	80. B
3. C	16. E	29. E	42. B	55. D	68. B	81. B
4. E	17. A	30. D	43. D	56. A	69. E	82. A
5. A	18. D	31. B	44. E	57. C	70. D	83. C
6. B	19. D	32. A	45. E	58. C	71. E	84. B
7. B	20. B	33. C	46. D	59. A	72. D	85. C
8. A	21. A	34. B	47. C	60. A	73. D	86. D
9. B	22. E	35. A	48. B	61. B	74. C	87. A
10. B	23. A	36. C	49. A	62. D	75. A	88. E
11. E	24. A	37. B	50. A	63. E	76. B	
12. B	25. B	38. E	51. D	64. E	77. A	
13. C	26. C	39. C	52. C	65. B	78. E	

PRACTICE II

1. D	14. B	27. B	40. C	53. A	66. E	79. C
2. C	15. E	28. C	41. C	54. B	67. E	80. B
3. B	16. D	29. D	42. A	55. D	68. C	81. B
4. E	17. C	30. D	43. A	56. E	69. D	82. A
5. A	18. A	31. E	44. C	57. A	70. D	83. C
6. E	19. B	32. D	45. D	58. E	71. C	84. C
7. C	20. A	33. B	46. A	59. D	72. B	85. A
8. A	21. B	34. A	47. B	60. B	73. A	86. D
9. D	22. A	35. A	48. B	61. A	74. C	87. E
10. B	23. D	36. C	49. C	62. C	75. C	88. A
11. E	24. C	37. E	50. D	63. A	76. B	
12. A	25. E	38. E	51. E	64. D	77. A	
13. D	26. A	39. B	52. B	65. B	78. E	

PRACTICE III

1. D	14. B	27. A	40. B	53. D	66. D	79. E
2. D	15. B	28. D	41. E	54. A	67. B	80. D
3. D	16. E	29. D	42. C	55. C	68. B	81. E
4. B	17. B	30. E	43. B	56. D	69. A	82. C
5. A	18. D	31. E	44. B	57. E	70. C	83. B
6. E	19. C	32. A	45. E	58. B	71. A	84. C
7. A	20. B	33. B	46. C	59. E	72. A	85. E
8. E	21. C	34. C	47. E	60. C	73. A	86. C
9. A	22. A	35. A	48. E	61. C	74. D	87. E
10. A	23. B	36. B	49. D	62. E	75. D	88. A
11. D	24. B	37. E	50. A	63. A	76. D	
12. C	25. E	38. D	51. D	64. B	77. C	
13. C	26. C	39. C	52. A	65. E	78. B	

Part B—Memory for Addresses—Scored Test Answer Key

1. A	14. E	27. E	40. E	53. A	66. D	79. B
2. B	15. C	28. C	41. D	54. A	67. B	80. B
3. A	16. A	29. C	42. B	55. C	68. D	81. C
4. E	17. B	30. E	43. B	56. E	69. C	82. A
5. E	18. A	31. A	44. C	57. A	70. A	83. E
6. D	19. B	32. E	45. B	58. B	71. C	84. C
7. B	20. D	33. D	46. E	59. E	72. D	85. A
8. D	21. D	34. A	47. D	60. B	73. D	86. E
9. B	22. B	35. D	48. C	61. D	74. B	87. D
10. E	23. D	36. A	49. B	62. D	75. B	88. E
11. C	24. C	37. C	50. A	63. D	76. A	
12. C	25. B	38. E	51. C	64. B	77. E	
13. D	26. B	39. D	52. E	65. E	78. C	

Part C—Number Series Answer Key

1. B	5. E	9. D	13. D	17. A	21. B
2. D	6. E	10. C	14. C	18. C	22. E
3. E	7. D	11. B	15. E	19. A	23. D
4. A	8. A	12. A	16. E	20. D	24. D

EXPLANATIONS FOR PART C

1. **The correct answer is (B).** The series is simply a repetition of the sequence 8 9 10.

2. **The correct answer is (D).** You can feel the rhythm of this series if you read it aloud. Beginning with 4, doubled numbers are progressing upward by +1, separated by the number 3.

3. **The correct answer is (E).** In this series, two 7s separate numbers that are increasing by +1.

4. **The correct answer is (A).** In this series, the numbers are increasing by +1. Every other number is repeated before it increases.

5. **The correct answer is (E).** This series is made up of a number of miniseries. In each miniseries the numbers increase by +4. After each miniseries of three numbers, a new miniseries begins, each time with a number one higher than the beginning number of the previous miniseries.

6. **The correct answer is (E).** This pattern is not as easy to spot as the ones in the previous questions. If you write in the direction and degree of change between each number, you can see that the rule is −3, +7, −3, +7, and so on.

7. **The correct answer is (D).** This series consists of two alternating series. One series begins with 16 and decreases by –1. The alternating series begins with 8 and increases by +1.

8. **The correct answer is (A).** Again, we have alternating series. This time the ascending series consists of two numbers increasing by +1 before being interrupted by one number of the descending series that is decreasing by –1.

9. **The correct answer is (D).** You may see this series as following the rule: +5, –4, +5, –4...or you may see two alternating series, one beginning with 19, the other with 24.

10. **The correct answer is (C).** Repeat, –3, repeat, –3, repeat, –3....

11. **The correct answer is (B).** Each number is reached by adding together the two previous numbers. Thus, 1 + 1 = 2; 1 + 2 = 3; 2 + 3 = 5; 5 + 8 = 13; 8 + 13 = 21; 13 + 21 = 34.

12. **The correct answer is (A).** You might see two alternating series increasing by +1, or you might see a rule: +2, –1, +2, –1.

13. **The correct answer is (D).** In this series, each number appears as often as its name implies: one 1, two 2s, three 3s, four 4s.

14. **The correct answer is (C).** The rule here is: +8, +7, +6, +5, +4, +3, +2....

15. **The correct answer is (E).** The elements of this series are the squares of successive numbers: 1^2, 2^2, 3^2, 4^2, and so on.

16. **The correct answer is (E).** The rule is: +4, +5, +7 and repeat +4, +5, +7....

17. **The correct answer is (A).** This question uses a simple +3 rule.

18. **The correct answer is (C).** Each number repeats itself, then increases by +7.

19. **The correct answer is (A).** You might see this as two alternating parallel series. In each series, the next number is the previous number multiplied by 2.

20. **The correct answer is (D).** Here the rule is: –4.

21. **The correct answer is (B).** The series descends by –2: 10 8 6 4 2. The number 2 appears between terms of the series.

22. **The correct answer is (E).** The rule is: +1, +2, +3, +4, +5, +6, +7, +8.

23. **The correct answer is (D).** Parallel ascending series alternate or the series follows the rule: +3, –2, +3, –2, +3....

24. **The correct answer is (D).** The first series decreases by –2. The alternating series increases by +2.

PART D—FOLLOWING ORAL INSTRUCTIONS

CORRECTLY FILLED ANSWER GRID

1 Ⓐ ● Ⓒ Ⓓ Ⓔ	23 Ⓐ Ⓑ Ⓒ Ⓓ Ⓔ	45 Ⓐ ● Ⓒ Ⓓ Ⓔ	67 Ⓐ Ⓑ Ⓒ Ⓓ Ⓔ
2 Ⓐ Ⓑ Ⓒ Ⓓ Ⓔ	24 Ⓐ ● Ⓒ Ⓓ Ⓔ	46 Ⓐ Ⓑ Ⓒ Ⓓ Ⓔ	68 Ⓐ Ⓑ Ⓒ Ⓓ Ⓔ
3 Ⓐ Ⓑ Ⓒ Ⓓ ●	25 Ⓐ Ⓑ Ⓒ Ⓓ Ⓔ	47 Ⓐ ● Ⓒ Ⓓ Ⓔ	69 Ⓐ Ⓑ ● Ⓓ Ⓔ
4 Ⓐ Ⓑ Ⓒ ● Ⓔ	26 Ⓐ Ⓑ Ⓒ Ⓓ Ⓔ	48 Ⓐ Ⓑ Ⓒ Ⓓ Ⓔ	70 Ⓐ Ⓑ Ⓒ Ⓓ Ⓔ
5 Ⓐ Ⓑ Ⓒ ● Ⓔ	27 Ⓐ ● Ⓒ Ⓓ Ⓔ	49 Ⓐ ● Ⓒ Ⓓ Ⓔ	71 Ⓐ Ⓑ Ⓒ Ⓓ Ⓔ
6 Ⓐ Ⓑ Ⓒ Ⓓ Ⓔ	28 Ⓐ Ⓑ ● Ⓓ Ⓔ	50 Ⓐ Ⓑ Ⓒ Ⓓ Ⓔ	72 Ⓐ Ⓑ Ⓒ Ⓓ ●
7 Ⓐ Ⓑ Ⓒ Ⓓ ●	29 Ⓐ Ⓑ Ⓒ Ⓓ Ⓔ	51 Ⓐ ● Ⓒ Ⓓ Ⓔ	73 Ⓐ Ⓑ Ⓒ Ⓓ Ⓔ
8 Ⓐ Ⓑ Ⓒ Ⓓ Ⓔ	30 ● Ⓑ Ⓒ Ⓓ Ⓔ	52 Ⓐ Ⓑ Ⓒ Ⓓ Ⓔ	74 Ⓐ Ⓑ Ⓒ Ⓓ Ⓔ
9 Ⓐ Ⓑ Ⓒ Ⓓ Ⓔ	31 Ⓐ Ⓑ Ⓒ Ⓓ Ⓔ	53 Ⓐ Ⓑ Ⓒ Ⓓ Ⓔ	75 Ⓐ Ⓑ Ⓒ Ⓓ Ⓔ
10 Ⓐ Ⓑ Ⓒ ● Ⓔ	32 Ⓐ Ⓑ Ⓒ Ⓓ ●	54 Ⓐ Ⓑ Ⓒ Ⓓ Ⓔ	76 Ⓐ Ⓑ Ⓒ Ⓓ Ⓔ
11 Ⓐ Ⓑ Ⓒ Ⓓ Ⓔ	33 Ⓐ Ⓑ Ⓒ Ⓓ Ⓔ	55 Ⓐ Ⓑ Ⓒ Ⓓ Ⓔ	77 Ⓐ Ⓑ Ⓒ Ⓓ Ⓔ
12 Ⓐ Ⓑ Ⓒ Ⓓ ●	34 Ⓐ Ⓑ Ⓒ Ⓓ Ⓔ	56 Ⓐ Ⓑ ● Ⓓ Ⓔ	78 Ⓐ ● Ⓒ Ⓓ Ⓔ
13 Ⓐ Ⓑ Ⓒ ● Ⓔ	35 Ⓐ Ⓑ Ⓒ Ⓓ Ⓔ	57 Ⓐ Ⓑ Ⓒ Ⓓ Ⓔ	79 Ⓐ Ⓑ Ⓒ Ⓓ Ⓔ
14 Ⓐ Ⓑ Ⓒ ● Ⓔ	36 Ⓐ Ⓑ ● Ⓓ Ⓔ	58 Ⓐ Ⓑ Ⓒ Ⓓ Ⓔ	80 Ⓐ Ⓑ Ⓒ Ⓓ Ⓔ
15 Ⓐ Ⓑ Ⓒ Ⓓ Ⓔ	37 Ⓐ Ⓑ Ⓒ Ⓓ Ⓔ	59 Ⓐ Ⓑ ● Ⓓ Ⓔ	81 Ⓐ Ⓑ Ⓒ ● Ⓔ
16 Ⓐ Ⓑ Ⓒ Ⓓ ●	38 Ⓐ Ⓑ ● Ⓓ Ⓔ	60 Ⓐ Ⓑ Ⓒ Ⓓ Ⓔ	82 Ⓐ Ⓑ Ⓒ Ⓓ Ⓔ
17 Ⓐ Ⓑ Ⓒ Ⓓ Ⓔ	39 Ⓐ Ⓑ Ⓒ Ⓓ Ⓔ	61 Ⓐ Ⓑ Ⓒ Ⓓ Ⓔ	83 Ⓐ Ⓑ Ⓒ Ⓓ Ⓔ
18 Ⓐ Ⓑ Ⓒ Ⓓ Ⓔ	40 Ⓐ Ⓑ Ⓒ Ⓓ Ⓔ	62 Ⓐ Ⓑ Ⓒ Ⓓ Ⓔ	84 Ⓐ Ⓑ Ⓒ Ⓓ Ⓔ
19 ● Ⓑ Ⓒ Ⓓ Ⓔ	41 Ⓐ Ⓑ Ⓒ Ⓓ Ⓔ	63 Ⓐ Ⓑ ● Ⓓ Ⓔ	85 Ⓐ Ⓑ Ⓒ Ⓓ Ⓔ
20 Ⓐ Ⓑ Ⓒ Ⓓ Ⓔ	42 Ⓐ Ⓑ Ⓒ Ⓓ Ⓔ	64 Ⓐ Ⓑ Ⓒ Ⓓ Ⓔ	86 ● Ⓑ Ⓒ Ⓓ Ⓔ
21 Ⓐ Ⓑ Ⓒ Ⓓ Ⓔ	43 Ⓐ Ⓑ Ⓒ Ⓓ Ⓔ	65 Ⓐ Ⓑ Ⓒ ● Ⓔ	87 Ⓐ Ⓑ Ⓒ Ⓓ Ⓔ
22 Ⓐ Ⓑ Ⓒ Ⓓ Ⓔ	44 Ⓐ Ⓑ Ⓒ Ⓓ Ⓔ	66 Ⓐ Ⓑ Ⓒ Ⓓ Ⓔ	88 Ⓐ Ⓑ Ⓒ Ⓓ Ⓔ

CORRECTLY FILLED WORKSHEET

1. 13 23 2 <u>19</u> 6

2. E B <u><u>D</u></u> E <u>C</u> A B

3.

30 A	18 __	5 __	14 __	7 E

4. (26 __) (16 E) (23 __) (22 __) (27 B)

5.

63 __	14 __	78 B	48 __

6. 12 ____ 5 D 22 ____

7. (14 __) (1 B) (36 C) (7 __) (19 __)

8. 26 ____ 86 A

9. 57 <u>63</u> 11 78 90 32 45 70 <u>69</u>

10. 16 30 <u>13</u> 25 <u>10</u> <u>14</u> 23 26 19

11. (9:12 __ A) (9:28 __ B) (9:24 __ C) (9:11 __ D) (9:32 32 E)

12.
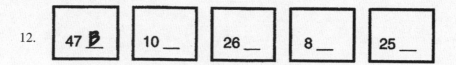

13.

14.

15.

ABLE   EASY   DESK

16.
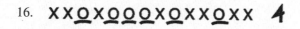

XX**O**X**O**O**O**X**O**XX**O**XX   **4**

17.
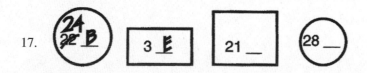

18.

19.   __A   **56**C   __E

CHAPTER 9

Familiarize Yourself with the Tests

Feeling anxious before you take a test is a normal reaction. You've spent many hours studying and preparing for the exam, and you want to get the best score possible. In addition, you probably think (and rightly so) that this test might be just a bit more important than some of those spelling tests you took back in elementary school. This is your career, and you want to prove to yourself and others that you're capable of achieving the highest performance.

Well, you can relax! Although the postal exams are a bit unusual (as compared to other tests), there really is no reason for you to be overly nervous. If you put in the time studying for the exam, use common sense, and don't panic, you'll be well on your way to achieving a good score.

This chapter is designed to help alleviate even more of your pre-test anxiety by introducing you to the format of the tests. Then, as you study the rest of this book, you have plenty of opportunity to practice the various question types. By test day, you still might be a bit nervous, but you shouldn't encounter any surprises.

GET TO KNOW THE TEST

The four-part U.S. Postal Examination is structured as follows:

Question Type	Part Number	Number of Questions	Time Allowed
Address Checking	A	95	6 minutes
Memory for Addresses	B	88	5 minutes*
Number Series	C	24	20 minutes
Following Oral Instructions	D	20–25 (will vary)	25 minutes (approximately)

Does not include the time allowed for memorizing addresses.

The remaining chapters in Part III of this book, as well as the full-length sample exams, will give you the opportunity to practice the various question types.

RULES AND PROCEDURES

Do not underestimate the importance of following all of the rules and procedures required at the test center. This includes following all of the examiner's test-taking instructions and filling in the answer sheets correctly.

Test 470 is used by the Postal Service to evaluate job-related skills. However, it is not a true aptitude test of your abilities. Don't fall into the trap of thinking you must possess certain innate talents to get a high score. On the contrary, preparing for this test will definitely increase your chances for doing well on it. The four question types are extremely coachable and get easier with practice. Use your desire for getting hired as a key motivator throughout the test-preparation process.

TEST-TAKING INSTRUCTIONS

Instructions read by the examiner are intended to ensure that you and all the other applicants have the same fair and objective opportunity to compete in the examination. All applicants are expected to play on a level playing field. Any infraction of the rules is considered cheating. If you cheat, your test paper is not scored, and you are not eligible for appointment.

■   Listen to what the examiner says at all times. Be prepared to immediately act on any exam changes to content, question type, directions, or time limits.

■   Follow all instructions the examiner gives you. If you do not understand any of the examiner's instructions, ask questions.

■   Don't begin working on any part of the test until told to do so.

■   Stop working on any part of the test when told to do so. Stop working as soon as the examiner tells you to do so. Remember that your ability to follow instructions is considered in the hiring process.

■   Review your work for a test part if you finish that test part before time is called. Although you cannot go on or back to any other part of the test, you have the chance to review answers of which you are unsure or guess if guessing is a good strategy for that test part. Use the extra time you have wisely.

■   Don't work on any part of the test other than the one you are told to work on. Be certain to make sure you're working on the correct test part immediately after starting. Although working in the wrong section could be an inadvertent error on your part, it would not leave a favorable impression on the examiner and would probably put you out of the running.

> *You cannot afford to lose precious exam time erasing and reentering incorrectly recorded answers. Therefore, as you answer each question for Parts A–C, look at its number and check that you are marking your answer in the space with the same number. If you cannot do this after each question, then remember to check yourself after every five questions. Either way, plan your strategy and **stick to it.***

FILLING IN ANSWER SHEETS

You are required to fill in required personal information on the sample answer sheet sent to you by the Postal Service to be admitted to the test center. You cannot take the test without doing this. At the center, you are instructed to transfer the personal information you filled in on the sample answer sheet to the actual answer sheet.

HOW TO ENTER YOUR ANSWERS

Because Test 470 is machine scored, you must be careful to fill in your answer sheets clearly and accurately. You are given instructions concerning this in the test kit sent to you by the Postal Service. You are also given ample opportunity to perfect your skills in the practice material in this book.

SCORE DETERMINATION AND REPORTING

When the exam is over, the examiner collects your test booklet and answer sheets. Your answer sheet is then sent to the National Test Administration Center in Merrifield, Virginia, where a machine scans your answers and marks them as either right or wrong. Then, your raw score is calculated according to the steps described on the "Score Sheet" in Chapter 7.

> *Although a total scaled score of 70 is considered passing, it probably won't get you hired. Many candidates prepare rigorously for this test and strive for perfect scores. In fact, most applicants who are hired score between 90–100 percent.*

REPORTING OF SCALED SCORES

Your raw score is not your final score. The Postal Service:

1. Records your raw scores for each test part

2. Combines the raw test scores according to a formula

3. Converts the result to a scaled score, on a scale of 1 to 100

A total scaled score of 70 is a passing score. The names of all people with 70 or more are placed on an eligibility list (called the register) that remains valid for two years. The register is ordered according to score rankings—the names of individuals with the highest scores are at the top of the list. Hiring then takes place from the top of the list as vacancies occur. Note that the entire process of conversion from raw to scaled score is confidential information.

LEARNING HOW YOU DID

The scoring process can take 6 to 10 weeks or even longer. Be patient. The process could take many months, but you remain eligible for employment for two years after taking the test. If you pass the exam, you receive notice of your scaled score. As the hiring process nears your number, you are notified to appear for the four remaining steps of the hiring process:

1. Drug testing

2. Psychological interview

3. Physical performance tests according to the requirements of the position

4. Alpha-numeric typing test

If you fail the exam, you are not informed of your score. You are simply notified that you have failed and are not being considered for postal employment.

It is important to note that as many as 50 percent of applicants fail Test 470. This percentage, of course, varies per exam administration. Use this number as a reality check for setting a serious study schedule. And even though this is a high failure rate, don't let it shake your confidence. Your preparation gives you better odds of getting a higher score than many of the candidates.

GENERAL TEST-TAKING STRATEGIES

KNOW DIRECTIONS FOR EACH QUESTION TYPE

Don't waste time during the test reading directions. You are given the instructions by the Postal Service in your exam kit. Know them inside and out. This book also gives you the most recent directions used on Test 470. Remember, though, to listen to the examiner for an announcement that something has changed.

SKIP QUESTIONS WHEN STUMPED

When you cannot answer a question in Parts A–C, skip the question and come back to it after finishing the other questions in the part of the test. Circle the number of the question in your test booklet to indicate the question skipped and remember to skip the appropriate space on your answer sheet. Whether you should or should not guess is discussed in the following sections.

AVOID PERFECTIONISM

You are not expected to answer every question in Parts A and B. Don't be a perfectionist and waste time on questions you cannot answer. This kind of attitude restricts the number of questions which you attempt to answer, which lowers your score. Come back to the difficult questions if you have extra time to spare.

Use the practice tests in this book to get used to the quick pace of the test and the stringent time limitations for each test part. Adhere to these time limitations without exception. Use a stopwatch or kitchen timer for accurate measurement. This gives you a sense of your optimal pace to apply on the actual test. Not doing this handicaps your chances for a higher score.

KNOW HOW MUCH TIME YOU HAVE

To do well on Test 470, you must work quickly within the time limits allowed. The examiner will probably inform you at periodic intervals of how much time you have left. Check your wristwatch as a backup; however, don't become obsessed by clock watching. Your time is better spent answering the questions.

Keeping track of time does not imply you should rush through a section and answer questions carelessly. You have to be in control of the situation to do your best. This means practicing for the test as much as possible, knowing what to expect, and following the strategies provided in this book.

BUILD A TEST-SMART ATTITUDE

By practicing as much as possible for Test 470, you gain confidence in yourself, which in turn helps you succeed on the actual test. Having a test-smart attitude helps build your competitive spirit, an essential factor in doing well on this highly competitive examination.

USE THE TEST BOOKLET AS SCRAP PAPER

You may find it helpful to make notes or draw lines or arrows in the test booklet in pencil to help solve certain test questions. This can focus your thoughts and channel your energy to solve the question. However, don't spend too much time doing this. If it doesn't help you, stop, and go on to the next question.

ELIMINATE OBVIOUSLY INCORRECT ANSWERS

This common test-taking strategy can be used to different degrees on each test part except Part A, which only has two answer choices. To use this strategy, you must usually read all the answer choices listed to eliminate incorrect answers before choosing the correct answer. This prevents your picking a deliberately misleading answer choice as the answer.

CHAPTER 10

Score Higher: Address Checking

ADDRESS CHECKING STRATEGIES

Of all the questions on Test 470, the address checking questions are probably the easiest. However, you should realize that these questions also carry the highest penalties for guessing. So, you should treat this question type as you would any other question—with the highest degree of speed and accuracy you can muster.

Take a look at the following address checking quiz, and don't worry about timing yourself. In fact, go through this quiz at your own pace, taking time to become familiar with the question type. When you're done, check your answers against the answer key provided after the quiz.

PRACTICE QUIZ

When you are finished with the quiz, take time to review the questions you missed. If you can spot your errors, you learn to avoid them in the future.

Directions: *For each question, compare the address in the left column with the address in the right column. If the two addresses are ALIKE in every way, write A next to the question number. If the two addresses are DIFFERENT in any way, write D next to the question number.*

1	...197 Apple Ridge Dr NW	197 Apple Ridge Dr NW
2	...243 S Calumet Ave	234 S Calumet Ave
3	...4300 Las Pillas Rd	4300 Las Pillas Rd
4	...5551 N Summit Ave	5551 N Summit St
5	...Walden CO 80480	Waldon CO 80480
6	...2200 E Beach St	2200 E Beech St
7	...2700 Helena Way	2700 Helena Way
8	...3968 S Kingsberry Ave	3698 S Kingsbury Ave
9	...14011 Costilla Ave NE	14011 Costilla Ave SE
10	...1899 N Dearborn Dr	1899 N Dearborn Dr
11	...8911 Scranton Way	8911 Scranton Way
12	...3653 Hummingbird St	3563 Hummingbird St

13	...1397 Lewiston Pl	1297 Lewiston Pl
14	...4588 Crystal Way	4588 Crystal Rd
15	...Muscle Shoals AL 35660	Muscle Shoals AL 35660
16	...988 Larkin Johnson Ave SE	988 Larkin Johnson Ave SE
17	...5501 Greenville Blvd NE	5501 Greenview Blvd NE
18	...7133 N Baranmor Pky	7133 N Baranmor Pky
19	...10500 Montana Rd	10500 Montana Rd
20	...4769 E Fox Hollow Dr	4769 E Fox Hollow Cir
21	...Daytona Beach Fla 32016	Daytona Beach FL 32016
22	...2227 W 94th Ave	2272 W 94th Ave
23	...6399 E Ponce De Leon St	6399 E Ponce De Leon Ct
24	...20800 N Rainbow Pl	20800 N Rainbow Pl
25	...Hammond GA 31785	Hammond GA 31785

Answer Key				
1. A	6. D	11. A	16. A	21. D
2. D	7. A	12. D	17. D	22. D
3. A	8. D	13. D	18. A	23. D
4. D	9. D	14. D	19. A	24. A
5. D	10. A	15. A	20. D	25. A

STRATEGIES TO SCORE HIGHER

How did you do on the quiz? Remember to take time to review the questions you answered incorrectly.

Although everyone responds to the tests differently, you can use the following tips and guidelines to assist you in answering these questions. In fact, you might read through the following sections, and then try the quiz above again. Does your score improve?

■ **Read for *differences* only.** When you spot a difference between the two given addresses, mark your answer sheet with a "D" and go immediately to the next question.

■ **Vocalize your reading.** This doesn't mean simply "reading out loud," but rather reading *exactly* what is listed. For example, if you see "St." don't read it as "Street" but as "ess t." This helps you to focus on the exact details.

■ **Use your hands.** Don't be afraid to use your index finger under or alongside the addresses being compared. This helps you keep your place and to focus on just one line at a time.

■ **Take the question apart.** Try to break the addresses into parts; for example, first compare the street name, then the ZIP code, and so on of each of the items to be compared. This helps to make the comparison more manageable.

> *There is a severe penalty for guessing on this question type. The total number of wrong answers is subtracted from the total number of correct answers. If you start to run out of time, don't panic and start filling in answers at random. Instead, relax and try and remember the tips and guidelines in the rest of this chapter—you might find you have more time to finish than you thought!*

■ **Read from right to left.** It might be very difficult for some people (remember, English speakers read left to right, so this might take some practice if English—or another left-to-right language—is your natural tongue!) You might be surprised how this forces your brain to focus on the details and not, for all practical purposes, "extraneous" information (the extraneous part being the parts of the two items that are the same).

■ **Play the numbers game.** You can expect to find many differences in numbers, so keep a close eye on this when you make your comparison. Questions with two items that are not alike often have differences in the number of digits as well as differences in the order of digits.

■ **Watch for differences in abbreviations.** Similar to differences in numbers, you'll find many different types of standard abbreviations; you'll also find that it's very easy to misread these, especially when comparing two items.

■ **Try to work as quickly and as accurately as possible.** Avoid guessing if you start to run out of time (instead, rely on the tips above). Remember—you aren't expected to answer all the questions in the time given.

KNOW YOUR STATE AND TERRITORY ABBREVIATIONS

You should be familiar with conventional abbreviations as well as the two-letter capitalized abbreviations used with ZIP codes. Don't worry about memorizing this list. The point of having it included here is to demonstrate how easy it is to mistake one abbreviation for another. If you vocalize what you see, you should "hear" the differences. And remember: your task is not to read for meaning, but to spot differences.

State	Conventional Abbreviation	Two-Letter Abbreviation
Alabama	Ala.	AL
Alaska	n/a	AK
American Samoa	Amer. Samoa	AS
Arizona	Ariz.	AZ
Arkansas	Ark.	AR
California	Calif.	CA
Colorado	Colo.	CO
Connecticut	Conn.	CT
Delaware	Del.	DE
District of Columbia	D.C.	DC
Florida	Fla.	FL
Georgia	Ga.	GA
Guam	n/a	GU
Hawaii	n/a	HI
Idaho	n/a	ID
Illinois	Ill.	IL
Indiana	Ind.	IN
Iowa	n/a	IA
Kansas	Kans.	KS
Kentucky	Ky.	KY
Louisiana	La.	LA
Maine	n/a	ME
Maryland	Md.	MD
Massachusetts	Mass.	MA
Michigan	Mich.	MI
Minnesota	Minn.	MN
Missouri	Mo.	MO

continued

continued

Montana	Mont.	MT
Nebraska	Nebr.	NE
Nevada	Nev.	NV
New Hampshire	N.H.	NH
New Jersey	N.J.	NJ
New Mexico	N. Mex.	NM
New York	N.Y.	NY
North Carolina	N.C.	NC
North Dakota	N.Dak.	ND
Ohio	n/a	OH
Oklahoma	Okla.	OK
Oregon	Oreg.	OR
Pennsylvania	Pa.	PA
Puerto Rico	P.R.	PR
Rhode Island	R.I.	RI
South Carolina	S.C.	SC
South Dakota	S.Dak.	SD
Tennessee	Tenn.	TN
Texas	Tex.	TX
Utah	n/a	UT
Vermont	Vt.	VT
Virginia	Va.	VA
Virgin Islands	V.I.	VI
Washington	Wash.	WA
West Virginia	W.Va.	WV
Wisconsin	Wis.	WI
Wyoming	Wyo.	WY

PRACTICE EXERCISES

Use the following practice exercises to try out the tips and techniques listed in the previous bulleted list to score the highest on Address Checking questions.

VOCALIZING TECHNIQUES

Try sounding out the following abbreviations and numbers:

NY	VA	MT	TX	10001	Pkw
CA	AL	MA	68919	3694	Cir
OR	HA	IL	828	Ct	

INDEX FINGER AS RULER OR POINTER

Try using your index finger or pointer and compare the following addresses. Are they alike (A) or different (D)?

1	...5115 Colchester Rd	5115 Calchester Rd
2	...4611 N Randall Pl	4611 N Randall Pl
3	...17045 Pascack Cir	17045 Pascack Cir
4	...3349 Palma del Mar Blvd	3346 Palma del Mar Blvd
5	...13211 E 182nd Ave	13211 E 182nd Ave
6	...Francisco WY 82636	Francisco WI 82636

7	...6198 N Albritton Rd	6198 N Albretton Rd
8	...11230 Twinflower Cir	11230 Twintower Cir
9	...6191 MacDonald Station Rd	6191 MacDonald Station Rd
10	...1587 Vanderbilt Dr N	1587 Vanderbilt Dr S

Answer Key				
1. D	3. A	5. A	7. D	9. A
2. A	4. D	6. D	8. D	10. D

BREAK THE ADDRESS INTO PARTS

Try this technique on the following addresses. Are they alike (A) or different (D)?

1	...3993 S Freemont Ter	3993 S Freemount Ter
2	...3654 S Urbane Dr	3564 S Urbane Cir
3	...1408 Oklahoma Ave NE	1408 Oklahoma Ave NE
4	...6201 Meadowland Ln	6201 Meadowlawn Ln
5	...5799 S Rockaway Ln	15799 S Rockaway Ln
6	...3782 SE Verrazanno Bay	37872 SE Verrazanno Bay
7	...2766 N Thunderbird Ct	2766 N Thunderbird Ct
8	...2166 N Elmmorado Ct	2166 N Eldorado Ct
9	...10538 Innsbruck Ln	10538 Innsbruck Ln
10	...888 Powerville Rd	883 Powerville Rd

Answer Key				
1. D	3. A	5. D	7. A	9. A
2. D	4. D	6. D	8. D	10. D

READ FROM RIGHT TO LEFT

Compare the following addresses using this technique. Are they alike (A) or different (D)?

1	...4202 N Bainbridge Rd	4202 N Bainbridge Rd
2	...300 E Roberta Ave	3000 E Roberta Ave
3	...Quenemo KS 66528	Quenemo KS 66528
4	...13845 Donahoo St	13345 Donahoo St
5	...10466 Gertrude NE	10466 Gertrude NE
6	...2733 N 105th Ave	2773 N 105th Ave

7	...3100 N Wyandotte Cir	3100 N Wyandottte Ave
8	...11796 Summerville Dr	11769 Summerville Dr
9	...Wilburnum Miss 65566	Vilburnum Miss 65566
10	...9334 Kindleberger Rd	9334 Kindleberger Rd

Answer Key				
1. A	3. A	5. A	7. D	9. D
2. D	4. D	6. D	8. D	10. A

DIFFERENCES IN NUMBERS

Select choice (A) if the two numbers are exactly alike or choice (D) if the two numbers are different in any way.

1.	2003	2003
2.	75864	75864
3.	7300	730
4.	50105	5016
5.	2184	2184
6.	8789	8789
7.	36001	3601
8.	1112	1112
9.	89900	8990
10.	07035	07035

Answer Key				
1. A	3. D	5. A	7. D	9. D
2. A	4. D	6. A	8. A	10. A

THE REAL THING: A PRACTICE EXAM

Use the following practice exam to try out the techniques you learned in this chapter, as well as give you a good idea of how it will feel on test day to confront this number of address checking questions. Go through the practice at a steady pace. When you're finished check your answers.

> **Directions:** *For each question, compare the address in the left column with the address in the right column. If the two addresses are ALIKE in every way, write A next to the question number. If the two addresses are DIFFERENT in any way, write D next to the question number.*

1	...8690 W 134th St	8960 W 134th St
2	...1912 Berkshire Rd	1912 Berkshire Wy
3	...5331 W Professor St	5331 W Proffesor St
4	...Philadelphia PA 19124	Philadelphia PN 19124
5	...7450 Gaguenay St	7450 Saguenay St
6	...8650 Christy St	8650 Christey St
7	...Lumberville PA 18933	Lumberville PA 1998333
8	...114 Alabama Ave NW	114 Alabama Av NW
9	...1756 Waterford St	1756 Waterville St
10	...2214 Wister Wy	2214 Wister Wy
11	...2974 Repplier Rd	2974 Repplier Dr
12	...Essex CT 06426	Essex CT 06426
13	...7676 N Bourbon St	7616 N Bourbon St
14	...2762 Rosengarten Wy	2762 Rosengarden Wy
15	...239 Windell Ave	239 Windell Ave
16	...4667 Edgeworth Rd	4677 Edgeworth Rd
17	...2661 Kennel St Se	2661 Kennel St Sw
18	...Alamo TX 78516	Alamo TX 78516
19	...3709 Columbine St	3709 Columbine St
20	...9699 W 14th St	9699 W 14th Rd
21	...2207 Markland Ave	2207 Markham Ave
22	...Los Angeles CA 90013	Los Angeles CA 90018
23	...4608 N Warnock St	4806 N Warnock St
24	...7718 S Summer St	7718 S Sumner St
25	...New York NY 10016	New York NY 10016

26	...4514 Ft Hamilton Pk	4514 Ft Hamilton Pk
27	...5701 Kosciusko St	5701 Koscusko St
28	...5422 Evergreen St	4522 Evergreen St
29	...Gainsville FL 43611	Gainsville FL 32611
30	...5018 Church St	5018 Church Ave
31	...1079 N Blake St	1097 N Blake St
32	...8072 W 20th Rd	80702 W 20th Dr
33	...Onoro ME 04473	Orono ME 04473
34	...2175 Kimbell Rd	2175 Kimball Rd
35	...1243 Mermaid St	1243 Mermaid St
36	...4904 SW 134th St	4904 SW 134th St
37	...1094 Hancock St	1049 Hancock St
38	...Des Moines IA 50311	Des Moines IA 50311
39	...4832 S Rinaldi Rd	48323 S rinaldo Rd
40	...2015 Dorchester Rd	2015 Dorchester Rd
41	...5216 Woodbine St	5216 Woodburn St
42	...Boulder CO 80302	Boulder CA 80302
43	...4739 N Marion St	479 N Marion St
44	...3720 Nautilus Wy	3270 Nautilus Way
45	...3636 Gramercy Pk	3636 Gramercy Pk
46	...757 Johnson Ave	757 Johnston Ave
47	...3045 Brighton 12th St	3045 Brighton 12th St
48	...237 Ovington Ave	237 Ovington Ave
49	...Kalamazoo MI 49007	Kalamazoo MI 49007
50	...Lissoula MT 59812	Missoula MS59812
51	...Stillwater OK 74704	Stillwater OK 47404
52	...47446 Empire Blvd	4746 Empire Bldg
53	...6321 St Johns Pl	6321 St Johns Pl
54	...2242 Vanderbilt Ave	2242 Vanderbilt Ave
55	...542 Ditmas Blvd	542 Ditmars Blvd
56	...4603 W Argyle Rd	4603 W Argyle Rd
57	...653 Knickerbocker Ave NE	653 Knickerbocker Ave NE

58	...3651 Midwood Terr	3651 Midwood Terr
59	...Chapel Hill NC 27514	Chaple Hill NC 27514
60	...3217 Vernon Pl NW	3217 Vernon Dr NW
61	...1094 Rednor Pkwy	1049 Rednor Pkwy
62	...986 S Doughty Blvd	986 S Douty Blvd
63	...Lincoln NE 68508	Lincoln NE 65808
64	...1517 LaSalle Ave	1517 LaSalle Ave
65	...3857 S Morris St	3857 S Morriss St
66	...6104 Saunders Expy	614 Saunders Expy
67	...2541 Appleton St	2541 Appleton Rd
68	...Washington DC 20052	Washington DC 20052
69	...6439 Kessler Blvd S	6439 Kessler Blvd S
70	...4786 Catalina Dr	4786 Catalana Dr
71	...132 E Hampton Pkwy	1322 E Hampton Pkwy
72	...1066 Goethe Sq S	1066 Geothe Sq S
73	...1118 Jerriman Wy	1218 Jerriman Wy
74	...5798 Grand Central Pkwy	57998 Grand Central Pkwy
75	...Delaware OH 43015	Delaware OK 43015
76	...Corvallis OR 97331	Corvallis OR 97331
77	...4231 Keating Ave N	4231 Keating Av N
78	...5689 Central Pk Pl	5869 Central Pk Pl
79	...1108 Lyndhurst Dr	1108 Lyndhurst Dr
80	...842 Chambers Ct	842 Chamber Ct
81	...Athens OH 45701	Athens GA 45701
82	...Tulsa OK 74171	Tulsa OK 71471
83	...6892 Beech Grove Ave	6892 Beech Grove Ave
84	...2939 E Division St	2929 W Division St
85	...1554 Pitkin Ave	1554 Pitkin Ave
86	...905 St Edwards Plz	950 St Edwards Plz
87	...1906 W 152nd St	1906 W 152nd St
88	...3466 Glenmore Ave	3466 Glenville Ave
89	...Middlebury VT 05753	Middleberry VT 05753

90	...Evanston IL 60201	Evanston IN 60201
91	...9401 W McDonald Ave	9401 W MacDonald Ave
92	...55527 Albermarle Rd	5527 Albermarle Rd
93	...9055 Carter Dr	9055 Carter Dr
94	...Greenvale NY 11548	Greenvale NY 11458
95	...1149 Cherry Gr S	1149 Cherry Gr S

Answer Key

1. D	20. D	39. D	58. A	77. D
2. D	21. D	40. A	59. D	78. D
3. D	22. D	41. D	60. D	79. A
4. D	23. D	42. D	61. D	80. D
5. D	24. D	43. D	62. D	81. D
6. D	25. A	44. D	63. D	82. D
7. D	26. A	45. A	64. A	83. A
8. D	27. D	46. D	65. D	84. D
9. D	28. D	47. A	66. D	85. A
10. A	29. D	48. A	67. D	86. D
11. D	30. D	49. A	68. A	87. A
12. A	31. D	50. D	69. A	88. D
13. D	32. D	51. D	70. D	89. D
14. D	33. D	52. D	71. D	90. D
15. A	34. D	53. A	72. D	91. D
16. D	35. A	54. A	73. D	92. D
17. D	36. A	55. D	74. D	93. A
18. A	37. D	56. A	75. D	94. D
19. A	38. A	57. A	76. A	95. A

CHAPTER 11

SCORE HIGHER: MEMORY FOR ADDRESSES

MEMORY STRATEGIES

Compared to address checking questions, "Memory for Addresses" are often considered one of the hardest types of questions on the exam. However, as with most exam questions on standardized tests, the questions *look* harder than they really are.

This chapter introduces you to some techniques that help you score higher on this question type. To begin, take the following quiz (which consists of an official set of sample questions). Take your time, become familiar with the question type and what it asks of you.

PRACTICE QUIZ

Directions: The five boxes below are labeled A, B, C, D, and E. In each box are five addresses: three are street addresses with number ranges and two are unnumbered place names. The position of an address within a box is not important. You need only remember the letter of the box in which the address is found. After memorizing the addresses, cover up the boxes and answer the questions. Take as much time as you need to answer the questions.

A	B	C	D	E
4700–5599 Table	6800–6999 Table	5600–6499 Table	6500–6799 Table	4400–4699 Table
Lismore	Kelford	Joel	Tatum	Ruskin
5600–6499 West	6500–6799 West	6800–6999 West	4400–4699 West	4700–5599 West
Hesper	Musella	Sardis	Porter	Nathan
4400–4699 Blake	5600–6499 Blake	6500–6799 Blake	4700–5599 Blake	6800–6999 Blake

Directions: For each of the following addresses, select the letter of the box in which each addresses is found. Write in the letter next to the question number.

1. Sardis
2. 4700–5599 Table
3. 4700–5599 Blake
4. Porter
5. 4400–4699 West
6. Tatum
7. Hesper
8. Musella
9. 6500–6799 West
10. Ruskin

Answer Key				
1. C	3. D	5. D	7. A	9. B
2. A	4. D	6. D	8. B	10. E

TIPS AND TECHNIQUES

Did you find this quiz difficult? If you did, don't worry. Even though some people have great visual memory (that is, they can look at a page and remember what the information said, as well as how it looked), most of us don't have this skill (at least not to a prodigy-like degree).

The actual test requires you to answer up to 88 questions in 5 minutes without referring back to the original boxes. You are, however, given an extensive unscored pretest practice with these boxes (like the one you saw in the sample quiz) to help you memorize what's in each box.

This extensive pretest practice, while perhaps daunting at first glance, can really pay off. It gives you time to memorize the information you need. If you can use the techniques described in this chapter to help you during this "practice time," you can turn a very difficult section of the test into one that is, perhaps, a little more manageable. Read through the tips and techniques listed in this chapter to help you improve your memory techniques.

- **Memorize single names first.** First, take a good look at the five boxes. You should notice that in each box there are two single names and three sets of number spans with names. Single names usually are easier to memorize than the name/number combinations, so memorize these single names first.

- **Combine name pairs into keywords.** This is a good way of memorizing large chunks of information, as you "combine" information into one single piece. For example, if one of the boxes had the names "Tatum" and "Porter" (let's say box "C"), you could combine this into "TaP." Hopefully, this combination of words triggers the association to "Tatum" and "Porter" in your mind when you need to recall the information.

- **Use word associations.** In the example above, we combine "Tatum" and "Porter" into "TaP." Don't just leave it at that—go ahead and associate "TaP" with "Tap Dancing" or "Tap Water"—the point is to make your word combination as useful as possible, so your mind can better associate it with the original information you are attempting to memorize.

- **Use the information to make up sentences or phrases.** Again, drawing on our "Tatum" and "Porter" example, it might be easier for you to simply combine the information to make a sentence (this might prove much more useful if you are struggling with short word combinations). For example, you might end up an associative sentence like, "Porter found the Tatum Hotel very nice."

- **Focus on number spans.** If you look again at the five sample lettered boxes used in the practice quiz, you will find five different number spans paired with three street names. In other words, each street name has the same five number spans.

Table	4400–4699, 4700–5599, 5600–6499, 6500–6799, 6800–6999
West	4400–4699, 4700–5599, 5600–6499, 6500–6799, 6800–6999
Blake	4400–4699, 4700–5599, 5600–6499, 6500–6799, 6800–6999

Remember, though, that you have 15 different addresses to remember, not 5, because each number span is paired with three different names in three different locations.

- **Shorten the numbers.** If you look at the number spans listed above, you'll see they all begin with "00" as the final two digits and end with "99" as the last two digits. So, you can save some precious "memory space" by not worrying about the "00" and "99"; instead, focus on just the beginning two digits.

THE REAL THING: A PRACTICE EXAM

Complete the following two practice sets. For Set 1, you can refer back to the boxes. You must answer Set 2 solely from memory. Write your answer next to the question number.

A	B	C	D	E
32 Apple	10 Apple	35 Apple	22 Apple	29 Apple
35 Hills	22 Hills	32 Hills	29 Hills	10 Hills
29 Leaf	32 Leaf	10 Leaf	35 Leaf	22 Leaf
Gray	Trace	Arden	Stewart	Inman
Book	Fish	Paris	Narrows	Hard

> **Directions:** *Now do the two practice sets. For the first practice exercise, you can refer back to the boxes. The second set must be answered solely from memory. Indicate your answers by writing in your answer next to the question number.*

SET 1

1.	2200–2899 Hills	23.	2200–2899 Apple	45.	3500–3599 Hills
2.	3500–3599 Leaf	24.	Fish	46.	1000–2199 Apple
3.	Stewart	25.	Book	47.	Fish
4.	3200–3499 Apple	26.	2900–3199 Apple	48.	Book
5.	3200–3499 Hills	27.	2900–3199 Hills	49.	3200–3499 Leaf
6.	2200–2899 Apple	28.	1000–2199 Leaf	50.	2200–2899 Apple
7.	Inman	29.	2200–2899 Hills	51.	3200–3499 Hills
8.	Gray	30.	3200–3499 Apple	52.	2900–3199 Apple
9.	3500–3599 Hills	31.	Gray	53.	2200–2899 Leaf
10.	2200–2899 Leaf	32.	Trace	54.	Gray
11.	2900–3199 Leaf	33.	Arden	55.	Narrows
12.	Trace	34.	3200–3499 Hills	56.	Hard
13.	Hard	35.	Narrows	57.	3200–3499 Apple
14.	Arden	36.	Hard	58.	1000–2199 Hills
15.	2200–2899 Hills	37.	2900–3199 Leaf	59.	1000–2199 Leaf
16.	1000–2199 Hills	38.	2200–2899 Hills	60.	Inman
17.	1000–2199 Apple	39.	3500–3599 Apple	61.	Book
18.	Narrows	40.	2900–3199 Hills	62.	3500–3599 Hills
19.	3200–3499 Leaf	41.	2200–2899 Leaf	63.	2900–3199 Hills
20.	Paris	42.	Inman	64.	3500–3599 Apple
21.	3500–3599 Leaf	43.	Stewart	65.	3500–3599 Leaf
22.	3500–3599 Apple	44.	Paris	66.	Trace

67. Paris
68. 2200–2899 Apple
69. 2900–3199 Leaf
70. Narrows
71. 2900–3199 Apple
72. 1000–2199 Apple
73. Fish
74. Gray

75. 2200–2899 Leaf
76. 3500–3599 Apple
77. 2200–2899 Hills
78. Stewart
79. Hard
80. 3500–3599 Hills
81. 2200–2899 Apple
82. Paris

83. 3500–3599 Leaf
84. 2900–3199 Leaf
85. Gray
86. 2900–3199 Hills
87. Inman
88. 3500–3599 Apple

SET 2

1. 2200–2899 Leaf
2. Narrows
3. 3200–3499 Hills
4. Fish
5. 3200–3499 Apple
6. 2900–3199 Leaf
7. Trace
8. Stewart
9. 2900–3199 Apple
10. 3500–3599 Apple
11. 1000–2199 Leaf
12. Hard
13. 1000–2199 Hills
14. 3500–3599 Leaf
15. 1000–2199 Apple
16. Gray
17. Arden
18. 2200–2899 Hills
19. 3200–3499 Hills
20. Paris
21. Book
22. 3500–3599 Hills
23. 3500–3599 Apple
24. Inman

25. 2200–2899 Apple
26. 2900–3199 Leaf
27. 2900–3199 Apple
28. 3200–3499 Hills
29. Arden
30. Gray
31. 1000–2199 Apple
32. 3500–3599 Leaf
33. 2200–2899 Leaf
34. 3500–3599 Apple
35. Trace
36. Stewart
37. Inman
38. 3500–3599 Hills
39. 2900–3199 Hills
40. 2200–2899 Hills
41. 2200–2899 Apple
42. Hard
43. Fish
44. 3500–3599 Leaf
45. 3200–3499 Hills
46. 3200–3499 Apple
47. 3200–3499 Leaf
48. Narrows

49. Paris
50. 1000–2199 Apple
51. 2900–3199 Hills
52. 3500–3599 Leaf
53. 2200–2899 Apple
54. Book
55. Stewart
56. 3500–3599 Hills
57. 2900–3199 Leaf
58. 1000–2199 Hills
59. 1000–2199 Leaf
60. Fish
61. Hard
62. 3200–3499 Hills
63. 3200–3499 Leaf
64. 2200–2899 Leaf
65. Arden
66. Inman
67. 2900–3199 Apple
68. 1000–2199 Apple
69. 2900–3199 Hills
70. 3500–3599 Hills
71. 2900–3199 Leaf
72. Paris

73.	Book	79.	2200–2899 Hills	85.	Book
74.	Hard	80.	Stewart	86.	Trace
75.	Gray	81.	Fish	87.	3500–3599 Leaf
76.	3200–3499 Leaf	82.	2200–2899 Apple	88.	2900–3199 Apple
77.	3200–3499 Apple	83.	2900–3199 Leaf		
78.	1000–2199 Hills	84.	2900–3199 Hills		

Answer Key

SET 1

1.	B	14.	C	27.	D	40.	D	53.	E	66.	B	79.	E
2.	D	15.	B	28.	C	41.	E	54.	A	67.	C	80.	A
3.	D	16.	E	29.	B	42.	E	55.	D	68.	D	81.	D
4.	A	17.	B	30.	A	43.	D	56.	E	69.	A	82.	C
5.	C	18.	D	31.	A	44.	C	57.	A	70.	D	83.	D
6.	D	19.	B	32.	B	45.	A	58.	E	71.	E	84.	A
7.	E	20.	C	33.	C	46.	B	59.	C	72.	B	85.	A
8.	A	21.	D	34.	C	47.	B	60.	E	73.	B	86.	D
9.	A	22.	C	35.	D	48.	A	61.	A	74.	A	87.	E
10.	E	23.	D	36.	E	49.	B	62.	A	75.	E	88.	C
11.	A	24.	B	37.	A	50.	D	63.	D	76.	C		
12.	B	25.	A	38.	B	51.	C	64.	C	77.	B		
13.	E	26.	E	39.	C	52.	E	65.	D	78.	D		

SET 2

1.	E	14.	D	27.	E	40.	B	53.	D	66.	E	79.	B
2.	D	15.	B	28.	C	41.	D	54.	A	67.	E	80.	D
3.	C	16.	A	29.	C	42.	E	55.	D	68.	B	81.	B
4.	B	17.	C	30.	A	43.	B	56.	A	69.	D	82.	D
5.	A	18.	B	31.	B	44.	D	57.	A	70.	A	83.	A
6.	A	19.	C	32.	D	45.	C	58.	E	71.	A	84.	D
7.	B	20.	C	33.	E	46.	A	59.	C	72.	C	85.	A
8.	D	21.	A	34.	C	47.	B	60.	B	73.	A	86.	B
9.	E	22.	A	35.	B	48.	D	61.	E	74.	E	87.	D
10.	C	23.	C	36.	D	49.	C	62.	C	75.	A	88.	E
11.	C	24.	E	37.	E	50.	B	63.	B	76.	B		
12.	E	25.	D	38.	A	51.	D	64.	E	77.	A		
13.	E	26.	A	39.	D	52.	D	65.	C	78.	E		

CHAPTER 12

Score Higher: Number Series

NUMBER SERIES STRATEGIES

Don't be nervous about these types of questions (especially if you don't have very advanced math skills). You're not going to be asked to do algebra, but rather simple addition, subtraction, multiplication, and division. Best of all, you can solve most of these questions quickly, and there is no penalty for guessing.

Let's get started with the usual practice quiz. The following 10-question test will familiarize you with the question type. The questions are all at varying levels of difficulty—just like they are on the actual test. Again, take your time with this, so you can get used to the type of question that is being asked.

PRACTICE QUIZ

> **Directions:** *For each question below, there is at the left a series of numbers that follows some definite order and at the right five sets of two numbers each. You are to look at the numbers in the series at the left and find out what order they follow. Then, decide what the next two numbers in the series would be if the same order were continued. Circle the letter of the correct answer.*

1. 21 21 19 17 17 15 13 .. (A) 11 11   (B) 13 11   (C) 11 9   (D) 9 7   (E) 13 13

2. 23 22 20 19 16 15 11 .. (A) 6 5   (B) 10 9   (C) 6 1   (D) 10 6   (E) 10 5

3. 5 6 8 9 11 12 14 .... (A) 15 16   (B) 16 17   (C) 15 17   (D) 16 18   (E) 17 19

4. 7 10 8 13 16 8 19 .... (A) 22 8   (B) 8 22   (C) 20 21   (D) 22 25   (E) 8 25

5. 1 35 2 34 3 33 4 .... (A) 4 5   (B) 32 31   (C) 32 5   (D) 5 32   (E) 31 6

6. 75 75 72 72 69 69 66 .. (A) 66 66   (B) 66 68   (C) 63 63   (D) 66 63   (E) 63 60

7. 12 16 21 27 31 36 42 .. (A) 48 56   (B) 44 48   (C) 48 52   (D) 46 52   (E) 46 51

Here's a good tip on guessing—if you must guess, make all your guesses the same letter. By the law of averages, this gives you a better chance of hitting the right answer.

8. 22 24 12 26 28 12 30 .. (A) 12 32   (B) 32 34   (C) 32 12   (D) 12 12   (E) 32 36

9. 5 70 10 68 15 66 20 .... (A) 25 64   (B) 64 25   (C) 24 63   (D) 25 30   (E) 64 62

10. 13 22 32 43 55 68 82 .. (A) 97 113   (B) 100 115   (C) 96 110   (D) 95 105   (E) 99 112

Answer Key				
1. B	3. C	5. C	7. E	9. B
2. E	4. A	6. D	8. C	10. A

EXPLANATIONS

1. **The correct answer is (B).** The pattern of this series is: repeat the number, then subtract 2 and subtract 2 again; repeat the number, then subtract 2 and subtract 2 again, and so on. Following the pattern, the series should continue with choice (B), 13 and 11, and then go on 9 9 7 5 5 3 1 1.

2. **The correct answer is (E).** The pattern is: –1, –2, –1, –3, –1, –4, –1, –5, and so on. Fitting the pattern to the remaining numbers, it is apparent that choice (E) is the correct answer because 11 – 1 = 10 and 10 – 5 = 5.

3. **The correct answer is (C).** The pattern here is: +1, +2; +1, +2; +1, +2 and so on. The correct answer is (C) because 14 + 1 = 15 and 15 + 2 = 17.

4. **The correct answer is (A).** You first must notice that the number 8 is repeated after each two numbers. If you disregard the 8s, you can see that the series is increasing by a factor of +3. With this information, you can choose choice (A) as the correct answer because 19 + 3 = 22, and the two numbers, 19 and 22, are then followed by 8.

5. **The correct answer is (C).** This series is, in reality, two alternating series. One series, beginning with 1, increases at the rate of +1. The other series alternates with the first. It begins with 35 and decreases by –1. The correct answer is choice (C) because the next number in the decreasing series is 32 and the next number in the increasing series is 5.

6. **The correct answer is (D).** The pattern established in this series is: repeat the number, –3; repeat the number, –3, and so on. To continue the series, repeat 66, then subtract 3.

7. **The correct answer is (E).** The pattern is: +4, +5, +6; +4, +5, +6; +4, +5, +6. Continuing the series: 42 + 4 = 46 + 5 = 51.

8. **The correct answer is (C).** In this series the basic pattern is +2. The series maybe read: 22 24 26 28 30 32. After each two numbers of the series we find the number 12, which serves no function except for repetition. To continue the series, add 2 to 30 to get 32. After 30 and 32, you must put in the number 12.

9. **The correct answer is (B).** In this problem there are two distinct series alternating with one another. The first series is ascending by a factor of +5. It reads: 10 15 20. The alternating series is descending by a factor of –2. It reads: 70 68 66. At the point where you must continue the series, the next number must be a member of the descending series, so it must be 64. Following that number must come the next number of the ascending series, which is 25.

10. **The correct answer is (A).** The numbers are large but the progression is simple between each number in the series: +9, +10, +11, +12, +13, +14. Continuing the series: 82 + 15 = 97 + 16 = 113.

Remember, take time to review your answers carefully and spend a little extra time on any that you missed.

STRATEGIES FOR WORKING WITH NUMBER SERIES QUESTIONS

Okay, so you're a bit anxious about working with numbers. Well, put your fears aside and remember that the test isn't going to ask you to break out the calculus (or even a simple calculator, for that matter). You need to work—as usual—with as much speed and efficiency as you can muster. However, if you try to remember the following tips, you might find that this type of question isn't as frightening as you thought!

■ **In number series with one pattern, look for the following number arrangements:**

1. simple ascending (increasing) or descending (decreasing) numbers where the same number is added to or subtracted from each number in a series

2. alternating ascending or descending numbers where two different numbers are alternately added to or subtracted from each number in a series

3. simple or alternating multiplication or division

4. simple repetition where one or more numbers in the series is repeated immediately before or after addition or subtraction or other arithmetic operation

5. repetition of a number pattern by itself

6. unusual pattern

■ **In number series with two or more patterns, look for the following kinds of patterns:**

1. random number (not one of the numbers in the series)

2. introduced and repeated number in a one-pattern series

3. two or more alternating series of two or more distinct patterns

4. two or more alternating series of patterns plus repetitive or random numbers

5. two or more alternating patterns that include simple multiplication and division

6. unusual alternating or combination arrangements

■ **Solve at a glance.** Look for simple number series that "jump out" at you, like 1 2 3 1 2 3. Also, be on the lookout for patterns that are either adding or subtracting to get the next number, such 20 21 22 23 or 35 34 33 32.

■ **Vocalize for meaning.** With all those numbers flying around, it might easy for your eye (and thus, your brain) to get confused, mistakenly reading a number for something else. That's why it sometimes helps to vocalize (or, say quietly to yourself) what you are reading. You might be able to "hear" a pattern more quickly—and more accurately— than if you had just looked at it.

■ **When you spot a difference, mark it down!** By "difference" we mean that you should immediately mark any change in the number series that you find. For example, if you're reading and you notice that the series is increasing by 2 (for example, 2 4 6 8), write down that difference in the numbers of the series (again, in this case 2). Remember, most series are either ascending, descending or a combination of the two. If you can't figure it out with addition and subtraction, try multiplication and division. Number series that use multiplication and division are fairly rare. However, you shouldn't discount this possibility entirely (just remember to try addition and subtraction first).

■ **Know how to spot repeating and random numbers**. Repeating and random numbers might not be so obvious. Be sure and mark up the question in your test booklet—this helps you spot these types of numbers more easily than if you simply try to "see" them in your brain.

PRACTICE I

You should be able to answer the following questions based on your work so far. Take the quiz at your own pace using all of the techniques you learned in this chapter. When you're finished, check your answers against the answer key and explanations.

> **Directions:** *For each question below, there is at the left a series of numbers that follows some definite order and at the right five sets of two numbers each. You are to look at the numbers in the series at the left and find out what order they follow. Then, decide what the next two numbers in the series would be if the same order were continued. Circle the letter of the correct answer.*

1. 8 9 10 8 9 10 8 .... (A) 8 9   (B) 9 10   (C) 9 8   (D) 10 8   (E) 8 10

2. 16 16 15 15 14 14 13 .... (A) 12 13   (B) 14 13   (C) 12 11   (D) 12 10   (E) 13 12

3. 2 6 10 2 7 11 15 .... (A) 12 16   (B) 15 19   (C) 15 16   (D) 12 13   (E) 2 19

4. 30 28 27 25 24 22 21 .... (A) 21 20   (B) 19 18   (C) 20 19   (D) 20 18   (E) 21 21

5. 25 25 22 22 19 19 16 .... (A) 18 18   (B) 16 16   (C) 16 13   (D) 15 15   (E) 15 13

6. 9 17 24 30 35 39 42 .... (A) 43 44   (B) 44 46   (C) 44 45   (D) 45 49   (E) 46 50

7. 28 31 34 37 40 43 46 .... (A) 49 52   (B) 47 49   (C) 50 54   (D) 49 53   (E) 51 55

8. 17 17 24 24 31 31 38 .... (A) 38 39   (B) 38 17   (C) 38 45   (D) 38 44   (E) 39 50

9. 87 83 79 75 71 67 63 .... (A) 62 61   (B) 63 59   (C) 60 56   (D) 59 55   (E) 59 54

10. 8 9 11 14 18 23 29 .... (A) 35 45   (B) 32 33   (C) 38 48   (D) 34 40   (E) 36 44

11. 4 8 12 16 20 24 .... (A) 26 28   (B) 28 30   (C) 28 30   (D) 28 32   (E) 28 29

12. 3 4 1 3 4 1 3 .... (A) 4 1   (B) 4 5   (C) 4 3   (D) 1 2   (E) 4 4

Answer Key				
1. B	3. E	5. C	7. A	9. D	11. D
2. E	4. B	6. C	8. C	10. E	12. A

EXPLANATIONS

1. **The correct answer is (B).** The series is simply a repetition of the sequence 8 9 10.

2. **The correct answer is (E).** This series is a simple descending series combined with repetition. Each number is first repeated and then decreased by 1.

3. **The correct answer is (E).** This pattern is +4, then repeat the number 2.

4. **The correct answer is (B).** This pattern is not as easy to spot as the ones in the previous questions. If you write in the direction and degree of change between each number, you can see that this an alternating descending series with the pattern –2, –1, –2, –1, etc.

5. **The correct answer is (C).** Repeat, –3, repeat, –3, repeat, –3.

6. **The correct answer is (C).** The rule here is: +8, +7, +6, +5, +4, +3, +2.

7. **The correct answer is (A).** A simple +3 rule.

8. **The correct answer is (C).** Each number repeats itself, and then increases by +7.

9. **The correct answer is (D).** Here the rule is –4.

10. **The correct answer is (E).** The rule is: +1, +2, +3, +4, +5, +6, +7, +8.

11. **The correct answer is (D).** This is a simple ascending series where each number increases by 4.

12. **The correct answer is (A).** A simple +1 series with the number 1 repeated after each step of the series.

PRACTICE II

Answer every question to the best of your ability. Write next to each question which technique you used. After you have finished every question, then check your answers against the answer key and explanations that follow.

> **Directions:** *For each question below, there is at the left a series of numbers that follows some definite order and at the right five sets of two numbers each. You are to look at the numbers in the series at the left and find out what order they follow. Then, decide what the next two numbers in the series would be if the same order were continued. Circle the letter of the correct answer.*

1. 12 26 15 26 18 26 21 .... (A) 21 24 (B) 24 26 (C) 21 26 (D) 26 24 (E) 26 25

2. 72 67 69 64 66 61 63 .... (A) 58 60 (B) 65 62 (C) 60 58 (D) 65 60 (E) 60 65

3. 81 10 29 81 10 29 81 .... (A) 29 10 (B) 81 29 (C) 10 29 (D) 81 10 (E) 29 81

4. 91 91 90 88 85 81 76 .... (A) 71 66 (B) 70 64 (C) 75 74 (D) 70 65 (E) 70 63

5. 22 44 29 37 36 30 43 .... (A) 50 23 (B) 23 50 (C) 53 40 (D) 40 53 (E) 50 57

6. 0 1 1 0 2 2 0 .... (A) 0 0 (B) 0 3 (C) 3 3 (D) 3 4 (E) 2 3

7. 32 34 36 34 36 38 36 .... (A) 34 32 (B) 36 34 (C) 36 38 (D) 38 40 (E) 38 36

8. 26 36 36 46 46 56 56 .... (A) 66 66 (B) 56 66 (C) 57 57 (D) 46 56 (E) 26 66

9. 64 63 61 58 57 55 52 .... (A) 51 50 (B) 52 49 (C) 50 58 (D) 50 47 (E) 51 49

10. 4 6 8 7 6 8 10 9 8 .... (A) 7 9   (B) 11 12   (C) 12 14   (D) 7 10   (E) 10 12

11. 57 57 52 47 47 42 37 .... (A) 32 32   (B) 37 32   (C) 37 37   (D) 32 27   (E) 27 27

12. 13 26 14 25 16 23 19 .... (A) 20 21   (B) 20 22   (C) 20 23   (D) 20 24   (E) 22 25

13. 15 27 39 51 63 75 87 .... (A) 97 112   (B) 99 111   (C) 88 99   (D) 89 99   (E) 90 99

14. 2 0 2 2 2 4 2 6 2 8 .... (A) 2 2   (B) 2 8   (C) 2 10   (D) 2 12   (E) 2 16

15. 19 18 18 17 17 17 16 .... (A) 16 16   (B) 16 15   (C) 15 15   (D) 15 14   (E) 16 17

16. 55 53 44 51 49 44 47 .... (A) 45 43   (B) 46 45   (C) 46 44   (D) 44 44   (E) 45 44

17. 100 81 64 49 36 25 16 ..... (A) 8 4   (B) 8 2   (C) 9 5   (D) 9 4   (E) 9 3

18. 2 2 4 6 8 18 16 .... (A) 32 64   (B) 32 28   (C) 54 32   (D) 32 54   (E) 54 30

19. 47 43 52 48 57 53 62 .... (A) 58 54   (B) 67 58   (C) 71 67   (D) 58 67   (E) 49 58

20. 38 38 53 48 48 63 58 .... (A) 58 58   (B) 58 73   (C) 73 73   (D) 58 68   (E) 73 83

21. 12 14 16 13 15 17 14 .... (A) 17 15   (B) 15 18   (C) 17 19   (D) 15 16   (E) 16 18

22. 30 30 30 37 37 37 30 .... (A) 30 30   (B) 30 37   (C) 37 37   (D) 37 30   (E) 31 31

23. 75 52 69 56 63 59 57 .... (A) 58 62   (B) 55 65   (C) 51 61   (D) 61 51   (E) 63 55

24. 176 88 88 44 44 22 22 ..... (A) 22 11   (B) 11 11   (C) 11 10   (D) 11 5   (E) 22 10

Answer Key					
1. D	5. B	9. E	13. B	17. D	21. E
2. A	6. C	10. E	14. C	18. C	22. A
3. C	7. D	11. B	15. A	19. D	23. D
4. E	8. A	12. C	16. E	20. B	24. B

EXPLANATIONS

1. **The correct answer is (D).** A +3 series with the number 26 between terms.

   12^{+3} ㉖ 15^{+3} ㉖ 18^{+3} ㉖ 21^{+3} ㉖ 24

2. **The correct answer is (A).** You may read this as a −5, +2 series:

   72^{-5} 67^{+2} 69^{-5} 64^{+2} 66^{-5} 61^{+2} 63^{-5} 58^{+2} 60

   Or as two alternating −3 series:

   $$72 \quad 67 \quad 69 \quad 64 \quad 66 \quad 61 \quad 63 \quad 58 \quad 60$$

   with −3 linking 72→69→66→63→60 and 67→64→61→58

3. **The correct answer is (C).** You should see by inspection that the sequence 81 10 29 repeats itself over and over.

4. **The correct answer is (E).** Write in the numbers for this one:

    91^{-0} 91^{-1} 90^{-2} 88^{-3} 85^{-4} 81^{-5} 76^{-6} 70^{-7} 63

5. **The correct answer is (B).** Here we have two distinct alternating series:

6. **The correct answer is (C).** The digit 0 intervenes after each repeating number of a simple +1 and repeat series.

7. **The correct answer is (D).** Group the numbers into threes. Each succeeding group of three begins with a number two higher than the first number of the preceding group of three. Within each group the pattern is +2, +2.

8. **The correct answer is (A).** The pattern is +10, repeat(r) the number, +10, repeat the number.

    26^{+10} 36^{r} 36^{+10} 46^{r} 46^{+10} 56^{r} 56^{+10} 66^{r} 66

9. **The correct answer is (E).** The pattern is –1, –2, –3; –1, –2, –3 and so on. If you can't see it, write it in for yourself.

10. **The correct answer is (E).** Here the pattern is +2, +2, –1, –1; +2, +2, –1, –1.

    4^{+2} 6^{+2} 8^{-1} 7^{-1} 6^{+2} 8^{+2} 10^{-1} 9^{-1} 8^{+2} 10^{+2} 12

    The series that is given to you is a little bit longer than most to better assist you in establishing this extra long pattern.

11. **The correct answer is (B).** This is a –5 pattern with every other term repeated(r).

    57^{r} 57^{-5} 52^{-5} 47^{r} 47^{-5} 42^{-5} 37^{r} 37^{-5} 32

12. **The correct answer is (C).** This series consists of two alternating series.

13. **The correct answer is (B).** This is a simple +12 series.

14. **The correct answer is (C).** Even with the extra length, you might have trouble with this one. You might have to change your approach a couple of times to figure it out.

    $2^{\times 0}$ 0; $2^{\times 1}$ 2; $2^{\times 2}$ 4; $2^{\times 3}$ 6; $2^{\times 4}$ 8; $2^{\times 5}$ 10

15. **The correct answer is (A).** Each number is repeated one time more than the number before it. Nineteen appears only once, 18 twice, 17 three times and, if the series were extended beyond the question, 16 would appear four times.

16. **The correct answer is (E).** This is a –2 series with the number 44 appearing after every two numbers of the series. You probably can see this now without writing it out.

17. **The correct answer is (D).** The series consists of the squares of the numbers from 2 to 10 in descending order.

18. **The correct answer is (C).** This is a tricky alternating series question.

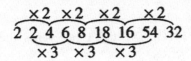

19. **The correct answer is (D).** The progress of this series is –4, +9; –4, +9.

20. **The correct answer is (B).** This series is not really difficult, but you might have to write it out to see it.

$38^r\ 38^{+15}\ 53^{-5}\ 48^r\ 48^{+15}\ 63^{-5}\ 58^r\ 58^{+15}\ 73$

You might also see this as two alternating +10 series with the numbers ending in 8 repeated.

21. **The correct answer is (E).** Group into groups of three numbers. Each +2 group begins one step up from the previous group.

22. **The correct answer is (A).** By inspection, you can see that this series is nothing more than the number 30 repeated three times and the number 37 repeated three times. Because you have no further clues, you must assume that the series continues with the number 30 repeated three times.

23. **The correct answer is (D).** Here are two alternating series:

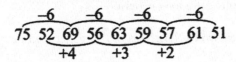

24. **The correct answer is (B).** The pattern is +2 and repeat(r) the number, +2 and repeat the number.

$176^{+2}\ 88^r\ 88^{+2}\ 44^r\ 44^{+2}\ 22^r\ 22^{+2}\ 11^r\ 11$

CHAPTER 13

Score Higher: Following Oral Instructions

TIPS FOR ORAL INSTRUCTION QUESTIONS

Due to the nature of these questions, we're going to dismiss with the "warm-up questions" that have been at the opening of each of these strategy chapters and start with a list of strategies. Later on in this chapter, you have a chance to try out everything you've learned.

It always pays to be a good listener, and oral instruction questions are no exception. Unlike other types of questions you encounter, oral instruction questions require you to focus your attention on another individual (or more precisely, the sound of his or her voice) rather than simply the test booklet. However, like all questions on the exam, you'll score your highest if you concentrate, relax, and are well prepared. The information in this chapter helps you to do just that.

Use the following tips and techniques to tackle the oral instruction questions:

- **Pay attention to the instructions.** We've stressed in previous chapters that concentration is important. Well, with oral instruction questions, attention is paramount! Unlike other questions, if you "space out" during this portion of the exam, you can't simply "reread" the question in your booklet. Try to stay focused!

- **Mark your answer sheet as instructed.** Unlike other questions, you do not answer the oral instruction questions in sequential order on your answer sheet. In fact, you skip around the page, filling in answers in the order specified. (Actually, you do not use all the answer spaces provided to you!)

- **Work from left to right.** If the instructions say to mark the "fourth letter", it is the fourth letter from the left, no exceptions. Of course, if the instructions tell you differently (for example, if they say, "Please put a circle around the fifth letter from the right"), then you obviously need to make an exception from reading left to right. Again, listen closely!

- **Don't waste time changing answers.** If you are about to enter a choice on your answer sheet and suddenly realize you've already filled in that choice (for example, you've made that choice from another question), don't make a change. Wait for the next set of instructions, and move on. If you find that you've blackened two answer spaces for the same question, erase one of them only if you have time, and if you won't get distracted and fall behind in the instructions.

PRACTICE WITH ORAL INSTRUCTIONS QUESTIONS

For this section, you need to find a friend who can read through the instructions to you. As you work through the sample test, try your best to relax, concentrate, and remember the tips listed previously. Good luck!

PRACTICE EXAM 1

ANSWER SHEET

1. Ⓐ Ⓑ Ⓒ Ⓓ Ⓔ	23. Ⓐ Ⓑ Ⓒ Ⓓ Ⓔ	45. Ⓐ Ⓑ Ⓒ Ⓓ Ⓔ	67. Ⓐ Ⓑ Ⓒ Ⓓ Ⓔ
2. Ⓐ Ⓑ Ⓒ Ⓓ Ⓔ	24. Ⓐ Ⓑ Ⓒ Ⓓ Ⓔ	46. Ⓐ Ⓑ Ⓒ Ⓓ Ⓔ	68. Ⓐ Ⓑ Ⓒ Ⓓ Ⓔ
3. Ⓐ Ⓑ Ⓒ Ⓓ Ⓔ	25. Ⓐ Ⓑ Ⓒ Ⓓ Ⓔ	47. Ⓐ Ⓑ Ⓒ Ⓓ Ⓔ	69. Ⓐ Ⓑ Ⓒ Ⓓ Ⓔ
4. Ⓐ Ⓑ Ⓒ Ⓓ Ⓔ	26. Ⓐ Ⓑ Ⓒ Ⓓ Ⓔ	48. Ⓐ Ⓑ Ⓒ Ⓓ Ⓔ	70. Ⓐ Ⓑ Ⓒ Ⓓ Ⓔ
5. Ⓐ Ⓑ Ⓒ Ⓓ Ⓔ	27. Ⓐ Ⓑ Ⓒ Ⓓ Ⓔ	49. Ⓐ Ⓑ Ⓒ Ⓓ Ⓔ	71. Ⓐ Ⓑ Ⓒ Ⓓ Ⓔ
6. Ⓐ Ⓑ Ⓒ Ⓓ Ⓔ	28. Ⓐ Ⓑ Ⓒ Ⓓ Ⓔ	50. Ⓐ Ⓑ Ⓒ Ⓓ Ⓔ	72. Ⓐ Ⓑ Ⓒ Ⓓ Ⓔ
7. Ⓐ Ⓑ Ⓒ Ⓓ Ⓔ	29. Ⓐ Ⓑ Ⓒ Ⓓ Ⓔ	51. Ⓐ Ⓑ Ⓒ Ⓓ Ⓔ	73. Ⓐ Ⓑ Ⓒ Ⓓ Ⓔ
8. Ⓐ Ⓑ Ⓒ Ⓓ Ⓔ	30. Ⓐ Ⓑ Ⓒ Ⓓ Ⓔ	52. Ⓐ Ⓑ Ⓒ Ⓓ Ⓔ	74. Ⓐ Ⓑ Ⓒ Ⓓ Ⓔ
9. Ⓐ Ⓑ Ⓒ Ⓓ Ⓔ	31. Ⓐ Ⓑ Ⓒ Ⓓ Ⓔ	53. Ⓐ Ⓑ Ⓒ Ⓓ Ⓔ	75. Ⓐ Ⓑ Ⓒ Ⓓ Ⓔ
10. Ⓐ Ⓑ Ⓒ Ⓓ Ⓔ	32. Ⓐ Ⓑ Ⓒ Ⓓ Ⓔ	54. Ⓐ Ⓑ Ⓒ Ⓓ Ⓔ	76. Ⓐ Ⓑ Ⓒ Ⓓ Ⓔ
11. Ⓐ Ⓑ Ⓒ Ⓓ Ⓔ	33. Ⓐ Ⓑ Ⓒ Ⓓ Ⓔ	55. Ⓐ Ⓑ Ⓒ Ⓓ Ⓔ	77. Ⓐ Ⓑ Ⓒ Ⓓ Ⓔ
12. Ⓐ Ⓑ Ⓒ Ⓓ Ⓔ	34. Ⓐ Ⓑ Ⓒ Ⓓ Ⓔ	56. Ⓐ Ⓑ Ⓒ Ⓓ Ⓔ	78. Ⓐ Ⓑ Ⓒ Ⓓ Ⓔ
13. Ⓐ Ⓑ Ⓒ Ⓓ Ⓔ	35. Ⓐ Ⓑ Ⓒ Ⓓ Ⓔ	57. Ⓐ Ⓑ Ⓒ Ⓓ Ⓔ	79. Ⓐ Ⓑ Ⓒ Ⓓ Ⓔ
14. Ⓐ Ⓑ Ⓒ Ⓓ Ⓔ	36. Ⓐ Ⓑ Ⓒ Ⓓ Ⓔ	58. Ⓐ Ⓑ Ⓒ Ⓓ Ⓔ	80. Ⓐ Ⓑ Ⓒ Ⓓ Ⓔ
15. Ⓐ Ⓑ Ⓒ Ⓓ Ⓔ	37. Ⓐ Ⓑ Ⓒ Ⓓ Ⓔ	59. Ⓐ Ⓑ Ⓒ Ⓓ Ⓔ	81. Ⓐ Ⓑ Ⓒ Ⓓ Ⓔ
16. Ⓐ Ⓑ Ⓒ Ⓓ Ⓔ	38. Ⓐ Ⓑ Ⓒ Ⓓ Ⓔ	60. Ⓐ Ⓑ Ⓒ Ⓓ Ⓔ	82. Ⓐ Ⓑ Ⓒ Ⓓ Ⓔ
17. Ⓐ Ⓑ Ⓒ Ⓓ Ⓔ	39. Ⓐ Ⓑ Ⓒ Ⓓ Ⓔ	61. Ⓐ Ⓑ Ⓒ Ⓓ Ⓔ	83. Ⓐ Ⓑ Ⓒ Ⓓ Ⓔ
18. Ⓐ Ⓑ Ⓒ Ⓓ Ⓔ	40. Ⓐ Ⓑ Ⓒ Ⓓ Ⓔ	62. Ⓐ Ⓑ Ⓒ Ⓓ Ⓔ	84. Ⓐ Ⓑ Ⓒ Ⓓ Ⓔ
19. Ⓐ Ⓑ Ⓒ Ⓓ Ⓔ	41. Ⓐ Ⓑ Ⓒ Ⓓ Ⓔ	63. Ⓐ Ⓑ Ⓒ Ⓓ Ⓔ	85. Ⓐ Ⓑ Ⓒ Ⓓ Ⓔ
20. Ⓐ Ⓑ Ⓒ Ⓓ Ⓔ	42. Ⓐ Ⓑ Ⓒ Ⓓ Ⓔ	64. Ⓐ Ⓑ Ⓒ Ⓓ Ⓔ	86. Ⓐ Ⓑ Ⓒ Ⓓ Ⓔ
21. Ⓐ Ⓑ Ⓒ Ⓓ Ⓔ	43. Ⓐ Ⓑ Ⓒ Ⓓ Ⓔ	65. Ⓐ Ⓑ Ⓒ Ⓓ Ⓔ	87. Ⓐ Ⓑ Ⓒ Ⓓ Ⓔ
22. Ⓐ Ⓑ Ⓒ Ⓓ Ⓔ	44. Ⓐ Ⓑ Ⓒ Ⓓ Ⓔ	66. Ⓐ Ⓑ Ⓒ Ⓓ Ⓔ	88. Ⓐ Ⓑ Ⓒ Ⓓ Ⓔ

WORKSHEET

> **Directions:** *Listen carefully to the instructions read to you, and mark each item on this worksheet as directed. Then, complete each question by marking the answer sheet as directed. For each answer, you will darken the answer sheet for a number-letter combination.*

1. 13   23   2   19   6

2. E   B   D   E   C   A   B

3. [30 __] [18 __] [5 __] [14 __] [7 __]

4. (26 __) (16 __) (23 __) (23 __) (27 __)

5. [63 __] [16 __] [78 __] [48 __]

6. 12 ____   5 ____   22 ____

7. (14 __) (1 __) (36 __) (7 __) (19 __)

8. 26 ____   86 ____

9. 57   63   11   78   90   32   45   70   69

10. 16   30   13   25   10   14   23   26   19

11. (9:12 __ A) (9:28 __ B) (9:24 __ C) (9:11 __ D) (9:32 __ E)

12. [47 __] [10 __] [26 __] [8 __] [25 __]

13.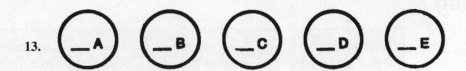

14. 3 __   32 __   45 __   10 __

15. 72 __   81 __   49 __   ABLE   EASY

16. X X O X O O O X O X X O X X

17. 22 __   3 __   21 __   28 __

18. 21 __   38 __   29 __   31 __

19. __ A   __ C   __ E

ORAL INSTRUCTIONS

> *Here are the instructions to be read aloud. Do **not** read the words in parentheses aloud.*

On the job you will have to listen to directions and then do what you have been told to do. In this test, I will read instructions to you. Try to understand them as I read them; I cannot repeat them. Once we begin, you may not ask any questions until the end of the test.

On the job you won't have to deal with pictures, numbers, and letters like those in the test, but you will have to listen to instructions and follow them. We are using this test to see how well you can follow instructions.

You are to mark your test booklet according to the instructions that I'll read to you. After each set of instructions, I'll give you time to record your answers on the separate answer sheet.

The actual test begins now.

Look at line 1 on the worksheet. (Pause slightly.) Draw a line under the fourth number in the line. (Pause 2 seconds.) Now, on your answer sheet, find the number under which you just drew the line and darken space A for that number. (Pause 5 seconds.)

Look at the letters in line 2 on the worksheet. (Pause slightly.) Draw a line under the fifth letter in the line. Now, on your answer sheet, find number 59 (Pause 2 seconds.) and darken the space for the letter under which you drew a line. (Pause 5 seconds.)

Look at the letters in line 2 on the worksheet again. (Pause slightly.) Now draw two lines under the third letter in the line. (Pause 2 seconds.) Now, on your answer sheet, find number 65 (Pause 2 seconds.) and darken the space for the letter under which you drew two lines. (Pause 5 seconds.)

Look at line 3 on the worksheet. (Pause slightly.) Write an E in the last box. (Pause 2 seconds.) Now, on your answer sheet, find the number in that box and darken space E for that number. (Pause 5 seconds.)

Now, look at line 3 again. (Pause slightly.) Write an A in the first box. (Pause 2 seconds.) Now, on your answer sheet, find the number in that box and darken space A for that number. (Pause 5 seconds.)

Look at line 4. The number in each circle is the number of packages in a mail sack. In the circle for the sack holding the largest number of packages, write a B as in baker. (Pause 2 seconds.) Now, on your answer sheet, darken the space for the number-letter combination that is in the circle in which you just wrote. (Pause 5 seconds.)

Look at line 4 again. In the circle for the sack holding the smallest number of packages, write an E. (Pause 2 seconds.) Now, on your answer sheet, darken the space for the number-letter combination that is in the circle in which you just wrote. (Pause 5 seconds.)

Look at the drawings on line 5 on the worksheet. The four boxes are trucks for carrying mail. (Pause slightly.) The truck with the highest number is to be loaded first. Write B as in baker on the line beside the highest number. (Pause 2 seconds.) Now, on your answer sheet, darken the space for the number-letter combination that is in the box in which you just wrote. (Pause 5 seconds.)

Look at line 6 on the worksheet. (Pause slightly.) Next to the middle number write the letter D as in dog. (Pause 2 seconds.) Now, on your answer sheet, find the space for the number beside which you wrote and darken space D as in dog. (Pause 5 seconds.)

Look at the five circles in line 7 on the worksheet. Write B as in baker on the blank in the second circle. (Pause 2 seconds.) Now, on your answer sheet, darken the space for the number-letter combination that is in the circle in which you just wrote. (Pause 5 seconds.)

Now, take the worksheet again and write C on the blank in the third circle on line 7. (Pause 2 seconds.) Now, on your answer sheet, darken the space for the number-letter combination that is in the circle in which you just wrote. (Pause 5 seconds.)

Now, look at line 8 on the worksheet. (Pause slightly.) Write an A on the line next to the right-hand number. (Pause 2 seconds.) Now, on your answer sheet, find the space for the number beside which you wrote and darken box A. (Pause 5 seconds.)

Look at line 9 on the worksheet. (Pause slightly.) Draw a line under every number that is more than 60 but less than 70. (Pause 12 seconds.) Now, on your answer sheet, for each number that you drew a line under, darken space C. (Pause 25 seconds.)

Look at line 10 on the worksheet. (Pause slightly.) Draw a line under every number that is more than 5 and less than 15. (Pause 10 seconds.) Now, on your answer sheet, for each number that you drew a line under, darken space D as in dog. (Pause 25 seconds.)

Look at line 11 on the worksheet. (Pause slightly.) In each circle, there is a time when the mail must leave. In the circle for the latest time, write on the line the last two figures of the time. (Pause 5 seconds.) Now, on your answer sheet, darken the space for the number-letter combination that is in the circle in which you just wrote. (Pause 5 seconds.)

Look at the five boxes in line 12 on your worksheet. (Pause slightly.) If 6 is less than 3, put an E in the fourth box. (Pause slightly.) If 6 is not less than 3, put a B as in baker in the first box. (Pause 10 seconds.) Now, on your answer sheet, darken the space for the number-letter combination that is in the box in which you just wrote. (Pause 5 seconds.)

Now, look at line 13 on the worksheet. (Pause slightly.) There are five circles. Each circle has a letter. (Pause slightly.) In the second circle, write the answer to this question: Which of the following numbers is smallest: 72, 51, 88, 71, 58? (Pause 10 seconds.) Now, on your answer sheet, darken the space for the number-letter combination that is in the circle you just wrote in. (Pause 5 seconds.) In the third circle on the same line, write 28. (Pause 2 seconds.) Now, on your answer sheet, darken the space for the number-letter combination that is in the circle you just wrote in. (Pause 5 seconds.) In the fourth circle do nothing. In the fifth circle write the answer to this question: How many months are there in a year? (Pause 5 seconds.) Now, on your answer sheet, darken the space for the number-letter combination that is in the circle in which you just wrote. (Pause 5 seconds.)

Look at line 14 on your worksheet. (Pause slightly.) There are two circles and two boxes of different sizes with numbers in them. (Pause slightly.) If 2 is smaller than 4 and if 7 is less than 3, write A in the larger circle. (Pause slightly.) Otherwise, write B as in baker in the smaller box. (Pause 10 seconds.) Now, on your answer sheet, darken the space for the number-letter combination in the box or circle in which you just wrote. (Pause 5 seconds.)

Look at the boxes and words in line 15 on the worksheet. (Pause slightly.) Write the second letter of the first word in the third box. (Pause 5 seconds.) Write the first letter of the second word in the first box. (Pause 5 seconds.) Write the first letter of the third word in the second box. (Pause 5 seconds.) Now, on your answer sheet, darken the spaces for the number-letter combinations that are in the three boxes in which you just wrote. (Pause 15 seconds.)

Look at line 16 on the worksheet. (Pause slightly.) Draw a line under every "0" in the line. (Pause 5 seconds.) Count the number of lines that you have drawn, subtract 2, and write that number at the end of the line. (Pause 5 seconds.) Now, on your answer sheet, find that number and darken space D as in dog for that number. (Pause 5 seconds.)

Look at line 17 on the worksheet. (Pause slightly.) If the number in the left-hand circle is smaller than the number in the right-hand circle, add 2 to the number in the left-hand circle, and change the number in that circle to this number. (Pause 8 seconds.) Then write B as in baker next to the new number. (Pause slightly.) Next, write E beside the number in the smaller box. (Pause 3 seconds.) Then, on your answer sheet, darken the spaces for the number-letter combinations that are in the box and circle in which you just wrote. (Pause 5 seconds.)

Look at line 18 on the worksheet. (Pause slightly.) If in a year October comes before September, write A in the box with the smallest number. (Pause slightly.) If it does not, write C in the box with the largest number. (Pause 10 seconds.) Now, on your answer sheet, darken the space for the number-letter combination that is in the box in which you just wrote. (Pause 5 seconds.)

Look at line 19 on the worksheet. (Pause slightly.) On the line beside the second letter, write the highest of these numbers: 12, 56, 42, 39, 8. (Pause 2 seconds.) Now, on your answer sheet, darken the space of the number-letter combination you just wrote. (Pause 5 seconds.)

ANSWERS TO PRACTICE EXAM I

1. A ● C D E	23. A B C D E	45. A ● C D E	67. A B C D E
2. A B C D E	24. A ● C D E	46. A B C D E	68. A B C D E
3. A B C D ●	25. A B C D E	47. A ● C D E	69. A B ● D E
4. A B C ● E	26. A B C D E	48. A B C D E	70. A B C D E
5. A B C ● E	27. A ● C D E	49. A ● C D E	71. A B C D E
6. A B C D E	28. A B ● D E	50. A B C D E	72. A B C D ●
7. A B C D ●	29. A B C D E	51. A ● C D E	73. A B C D E
8. A B C D E	30. ● B C D E	52. A B C D E	74. A B C D E
9. A B C D E	31. A B C D E	53. A B C D E	75. A B C D E
10. A B C ● E	32. A B C D ●	54. A B C D E	76. A B C D E
11. A B C D E	33. A B C D E	55. A B C D E	77. A B C D E
12. A B C D ●	34. A B C D E	56. A B ● D E	78. A ● C D E
13. A B C ● E	35. A B C D E	57. A B C D E	79. A B C D E
14. A B C ● E	36. A B ● D E	58. A B C D E	80. A B C D E
15. A B C D E	37. A B C D E	59. A B ● D E	81. A B C ● E
16. A B C D ●	38. A B ● D E	60. A B C D E	82. A B C D E
17. A B C D E	39. A B C D E	61. A B C D E	83. A B C D E
18. A B C D E	40. A B C D E	62. A B C D E	84. A B C D E
19. ● B C D E	41. A B C D E	63. A B ● D E	85. A B C D E
20. A B C D E	42. A B C D E	64. A B C D E	86. ● B C D E
21. A B C D E	43. A B C D E	65. A B C ● E	87. A B C D E
22. A B C D E	44. A B C D E	66. A B C D E	88. A B C D E

1. **13   23   2   <u>19</u>   6**

2. **E   B   <u>D</u>   E   <u>C</u>   A   B**

3. | 30 <u>A</u> | 18 __ | 5 __ | 14 __ | 7 <u>E</u> |

4. (26 __) (16 <u>E</u>) (23 __) (23 __) (27 <u>B</u>)

5. | 63 __ | 16 __ | 78 <u>B</u> | 48 __ |

6. **12 ___   5 <u>d</u>   22 ___**

7. (14 __) (1 <u>B</u>) (36 <u>C</u>) (7 __) (19 __)

8. **26 ___   86 <u>A</u>**

9. **57   <u>63</u>   11   78   90   32   45   70   <u>69</u>**

10. **16   30   <u>13</u>   25   <u>10</u>   <u>14</u>   23   26   19**

11. (9:12 __ A) (9:28 __ B) (9:24 __ C) (9:11 __ D) (9:32 <u>32</u> E)

12. | 47 <u>B</u> | 10 __ | 26 __ | 8 __ | 25 __ |

13. (__ A) (<u>51</u> B) (<u>28</u> C) (__ D) (<u>12</u> E)

14.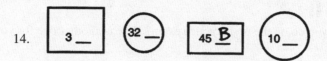

3 __   (32 __)   45 B   (10 __)

15. 72 E   81 D   49 B   ABLE   EASY   DESK

16. X X O X O O O X O X X O X X **4**

17. (24 22 B)   3 E   21 __   (28 __)

18. 21 __   38 C   29 __   31 __

19. __ A   56 C   __ E

PRACTICE EXAM II

How did you do on the first practice exam? Here is another one for you to try.

ANSWER SHEET

1. Ⓐ Ⓑ Ⓒ Ⓓ Ⓔ	23. Ⓐ Ⓑ Ⓒ Ⓓ Ⓔ	45. Ⓐ Ⓑ Ⓒ Ⓓ Ⓔ	67. Ⓐ Ⓑ Ⓒ Ⓓ Ⓔ
2. Ⓐ Ⓑ Ⓒ Ⓓ Ⓔ	24. Ⓐ Ⓑ Ⓒ Ⓓ Ⓔ	46. Ⓐ Ⓑ Ⓒ Ⓓ Ⓔ	68. Ⓐ Ⓑ Ⓒ Ⓓ Ⓔ
3. Ⓐ Ⓑ Ⓒ Ⓓ Ⓔ	25. Ⓐ Ⓑ Ⓒ Ⓓ Ⓔ	47. Ⓐ Ⓑ Ⓒ Ⓓ Ⓔ	69. Ⓐ Ⓑ Ⓒ Ⓓ Ⓔ
4. Ⓐ Ⓑ Ⓒ Ⓓ Ⓔ	26. Ⓐ Ⓑ Ⓒ Ⓓ Ⓔ	48. Ⓐ Ⓑ Ⓒ Ⓓ Ⓔ	70. Ⓐ Ⓑ Ⓒ Ⓓ Ⓔ
5. Ⓐ Ⓑ Ⓒ Ⓓ Ⓔ	27. Ⓐ Ⓑ Ⓒ Ⓓ Ⓔ	49. Ⓐ Ⓑ Ⓒ Ⓓ Ⓔ	71. Ⓐ Ⓑ Ⓒ Ⓓ Ⓔ
6. Ⓐ Ⓑ Ⓒ Ⓓ Ⓔ	28. Ⓐ Ⓑ Ⓒ Ⓓ Ⓔ	50. Ⓐ Ⓑ Ⓒ Ⓓ Ⓔ	72. Ⓐ Ⓑ Ⓒ Ⓓ Ⓔ
7. Ⓐ Ⓑ Ⓒ Ⓓ Ⓔ	29. Ⓐ Ⓑ Ⓒ Ⓓ Ⓔ	51. Ⓐ Ⓑ Ⓒ Ⓓ Ⓔ	73. Ⓐ Ⓑ Ⓒ Ⓓ Ⓔ
8. Ⓐ Ⓑ Ⓒ Ⓓ Ⓔ	30. Ⓐ Ⓑ Ⓒ Ⓓ Ⓔ	52. Ⓐ Ⓑ Ⓒ Ⓓ Ⓔ	74. Ⓐ Ⓑ Ⓒ Ⓓ Ⓔ
9. Ⓐ Ⓑ Ⓒ Ⓓ Ⓔ	31. Ⓐ Ⓑ Ⓒ Ⓓ Ⓔ	53. Ⓐ Ⓑ Ⓒ Ⓓ Ⓔ	75. Ⓐ Ⓑ Ⓒ Ⓓ Ⓔ
10. Ⓐ Ⓑ Ⓒ Ⓓ Ⓔ	32. Ⓐ Ⓑ Ⓒ Ⓓ Ⓔ	54. Ⓐ Ⓑ Ⓒ Ⓓ Ⓔ	76. Ⓐ Ⓑ Ⓒ Ⓓ Ⓔ
11. Ⓐ Ⓑ Ⓒ Ⓓ Ⓔ	33. Ⓐ Ⓑ Ⓒ Ⓓ Ⓔ	55. Ⓐ Ⓑ Ⓒ Ⓓ Ⓔ	77. Ⓐ Ⓑ Ⓒ Ⓓ Ⓔ
12. Ⓐ Ⓑ Ⓒ Ⓓ Ⓔ	34. Ⓐ Ⓑ Ⓒ Ⓓ Ⓔ	56. Ⓐ Ⓑ Ⓒ Ⓓ Ⓔ	78. Ⓐ Ⓑ Ⓒ Ⓓ Ⓔ
13. Ⓐ Ⓑ Ⓒ Ⓓ Ⓔ	35. Ⓐ Ⓑ Ⓒ Ⓓ Ⓔ	57. Ⓐ Ⓑ Ⓒ Ⓓ Ⓔ	79. Ⓐ Ⓑ Ⓒ Ⓓ Ⓔ
14. Ⓐ Ⓑ Ⓒ Ⓓ Ⓔ	36. Ⓐ Ⓑ Ⓒ Ⓓ Ⓔ	58. Ⓐ Ⓑ Ⓒ Ⓓ Ⓔ	80. Ⓐ Ⓑ Ⓒ Ⓓ Ⓔ
15. Ⓐ Ⓑ Ⓒ Ⓓ Ⓔ	37. Ⓐ Ⓑ Ⓒ Ⓓ Ⓔ	59. Ⓐ Ⓑ Ⓒ Ⓓ Ⓔ	81. Ⓐ Ⓑ Ⓒ Ⓓ Ⓔ
16. Ⓐ Ⓑ Ⓒ Ⓓ Ⓔ	38. Ⓐ Ⓑ Ⓒ Ⓓ Ⓔ	60. Ⓐ Ⓑ Ⓒ Ⓓ Ⓔ	82. Ⓐ Ⓑ Ⓒ Ⓓ Ⓔ
17. Ⓐ Ⓑ Ⓒ Ⓓ Ⓔ	39. Ⓐ Ⓑ Ⓒ Ⓓ Ⓔ	61. Ⓐ Ⓑ Ⓒ Ⓓ Ⓔ	83. Ⓐ Ⓑ Ⓒ Ⓓ Ⓔ
18. Ⓐ Ⓑ Ⓒ Ⓓ Ⓔ	40. Ⓐ Ⓑ Ⓒ Ⓓ Ⓔ	62. Ⓐ Ⓑ Ⓒ Ⓓ Ⓔ	84. Ⓐ Ⓑ Ⓒ Ⓓ Ⓔ
19. Ⓐ Ⓑ Ⓒ Ⓓ Ⓔ	41. Ⓐ Ⓑ Ⓒ Ⓓ Ⓔ	63. Ⓐ Ⓑ Ⓒ Ⓓ Ⓔ	85. Ⓐ Ⓑ Ⓒ Ⓓ Ⓔ
20. Ⓐ Ⓑ Ⓒ Ⓓ Ⓔ	42. Ⓐ Ⓑ Ⓒ Ⓓ Ⓔ	64. Ⓐ Ⓑ Ⓒ Ⓓ Ⓔ	86. Ⓐ Ⓑ Ⓒ Ⓓ Ⓔ
21. Ⓐ Ⓑ Ⓒ Ⓓ Ⓔ	43. Ⓐ Ⓑ Ⓒ Ⓓ Ⓔ	65. Ⓐ Ⓑ Ⓒ Ⓓ Ⓔ	87. Ⓐ Ⓑ Ⓒ Ⓓ Ⓔ
22. Ⓐ Ⓑ Ⓒ Ⓓ Ⓔ	44. Ⓐ Ⓑ Ⓒ Ⓓ Ⓔ	66. Ⓐ Ⓑ Ⓒ Ⓓ Ⓔ	88. Ⓐ Ⓑ Ⓒ Ⓓ Ⓔ

WORKSHEET

> **Directions:** *Listen carefully to the instructions read to you, and mark each item on this worksheet as directed. Then, complete each question by marking the answer sheet as directed. For each answer, you will darken the answer sheet for a number-letter combination.*

1. A B   B   D   C   D   E   D

2. 24   12   17   11   14   20

3.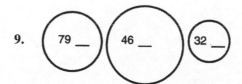

     41 __   62 __   18 __   27 __   73 __   10 __

4. ___B ___D ___C ___E ___A

5. 76   14   67   46   11   74

6.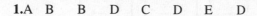

     ___A   ___E   ___B   ___C   ___D

7. 9 __   46 __   34 __   LETTER   PARCEL

8. G   G   G   G   G   G   G   G

9. 79 __   46 __   32 __

10.

     4:45 ___B   5:20 ___C   4:53 ___E   5:11 ___A   4:59 ___D

11.

37	84	65
SAN FRANCISCO	MILWAUKEE	SPRINGFIELD
LOS ANGELES	GREEN BAY	CHICAGO
_____	_____	_____

12. E   M   R   B   C   A

13.   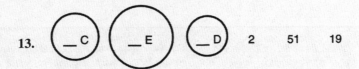   2   51   19

14.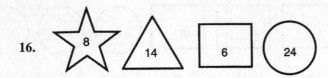

15.   42   68   87   20   12   36

16.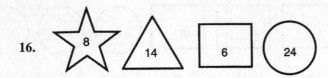

17.   J   J   J   L   L   L   J   L   J   J

18.   41   38   62   59   44   40   54

19.   __C   __A   __D

ORAL INSTRUCTIONS

On the job you will have to listen to instructions and then do what you have been told to do. In this test, I will read instructions to you. Try to understand them as I read them; I cannot repeat them. Once we begin, you may not ask any questions until the end of the test.

On the job you won't have to deal with pictures, numbers, and letters like those on the test, but you will have to listen to instructions and follow them. We are using this test to see how well you can follow instructions.

You are to mark your worksheet according to the instruction that I'll read to you. After each set of instructions, I'll give you time to record your answers on the separate answer sheet.

The actual test begins now.

Look at line 1 on your worksheet. (Pause slightly.) Circle the seventh letter on line 1. (Pause 5 seconds.) Now, on your answer sheet, find number 83 and for number 83 darken the space for the letter you just circled. (Pause 5 seconds.)

Look at line 2 on your worksheet. (Pause slightly.) Draw a line under all the odd numbers between 12 and 20. (Pause 5 seconds.) Now, on your answer sheet, darken space B as in baker for all the numbers under which you drew a line. (Pause 5 seconds.)

Look at line 2 again. (Pause slightly.) Find the number that is two times another number on line 2 and circle it. (Pause 5 seconds.) Now, on your answer sheet, darken space A for the number you just circled. (Pause 5 seconds.)

Look at line 3 on your worksheet. (Pause slightly.) Write the letter C in the middle box. (Pause 2 seconds.) Now, on your answer sheet, darken the space for the number-letter combination in the figure in which you just wrote. (Pause 5 seconds.)

Look at line 3 again. (Pause slightly.) Write the letter D as in dog in the left-hand circle. (Pause 2 seconds.) Now, on your answer sheet, darken the space for the number-letter combination in the figure in which you just wrote. (Pause 5 seconds.)

Look at line 4 on your worksheet. (Pause slightly.) If first class mail costs more than bulk rate mail, write the number 22 on the third line; if not, write the number 19 on the fourth line. (Pause 5 seconds.) Now, on your answer sheet, darken the space for the number-letter combination on the line on which you just wrote. (Pause 5 seconds.)

Look at line 4 again. (Pause slightly.) Write the number 31 on the second line from the left. (Pause 2 seconds.) Now, on your answer sheet, darken the space for the number-letter combination on the line on which you just wrote. (Pause 5 seconds.)

Look at line 5 on your worksheet. (Pause slightly.) Find the highest number on line 5 and draw a line under the number. (Pause 2 seconds.) Now, on your answer sheet, find the number under which you just drew a line and darken space E for that number. (Pause 5 seconds.)

Look at line 5 again. (Pause slightly.) Find the lowest number on line 5 and draw two lines under the number. (Pause 2 seconds.) Now, on your answer sheet, find the number under which you just drew two lines and darken space A for that number. (Pause 5 seconds.)

Look at line 6 on your worksheet. (Pause slightly.) Write the number 57 in the figure that does not belong on line 6. (Pause 2 seconds.) Now, on your answer sheet, darken the number-letter combination that is in the figure in which you just wrote. (Pause 5 seconds.)

Look at line 7 on your worksheet. (Pause slightly.) Write the second letter of the second word in the first box. (Pause 5 seconds.) Write the fifth letter of the first word in the third box. (Pause 5 seconds.)

Write the fourth letter of the second word in the second box. (Pause 5 seconds.) Now, on your answer sheet, darken the number-letter combinations in all three boxes. (Pause 15 seconds.)

Look at line 8 on your worksheet. (Pause slightly.) Count the number of Gs on line 8 and divide the number of Gs by 2. Write that number at the end of the line. (Pause 5 seconds.) Now, on your answer sheet, darken space D as in dog for the number you wrote at the end of line 8. (Pause 5 seconds.)

Look at line 9 on your worksheet. (Pause slightly.) Write the letter B as in baker in the middle-sized circle. (Pause 2 seconds.) Now, on your answer sheet, darken the space for the number-letter combination in the circle in which you just wrote. (Pause 5 seconds.)

Look at line 10 on your worksheet. (Pause slightly.) The time in each circle represents the last scheduled pickup of the day from a street letterbox. Find the circle with the earliest pickup time and write the last two figures of that time on the line in the circle. (Pause 10 seconds.) Now, on your answer sheet, darken the space for the number-letter combination in the circle in which you just wrote. (Pause 5 seconds.)

Look at line 10 again. (Pause slightly.) Find the circle with the latest pickup time and write the last two figures of that time on the line in the circle. (Pause 10 seconds.) Now, on your answer sheet, darken the space for the number-letter combination in the circle in which you just wrote. (Pause 5 seconds.)

Look at line 11 on your worksheet. (Pause slightly.) Mail directed for San Francisco and Los Angeles is to be placed in box 37; mail for Milwaukee and Green Bay in box 84; mail for Springfield and Chicago in box 65. Find the box for mail being sent to Green Bay and write the letter A in the box. (Pause 2 seconds.) Now, on your answer sheet, darken the number-letter combination for the box in which you just wrote. (Pause 5 seconds.)

Look at line 11 again. (Pause slightly.) Mr. Green lives in Springfield. Find the box in which to put Mr. Green's mail and write E on the line. (Pause 2 seconds.) Now, on your answer sheet, darken the space for the number-letter combination in the box in which you just wrote. (Pause 5 seconds.)

Look at line 12 on your worksheet. (Pause slightly.) Find the letter on line 12 that is not in the word CREAM and draw a line under the letter. (Pause 2 seconds.) Now, on your answer sheet, find number 38 and darken the space for the letter under which you just drew a line. (Pause 5 seconds.)

Look at line 13 on your worksheet. (Pause slightly.) Write the smallest number in the largest circle. (Pause 2 seconds.) Write the largest number in the left-hand circle. (Pause 2 seconds.) Now, on your answer sheet, darken the number-letter combinations that are in the circles in which you just wrote. (Pause 10 seconds.)

Look at line 14 on your worksheet. (Pause slightly.) If there are 36 inches in a foot, write B as in baker in the first box; if not, write D as in dog in the third box. (Pause 5 seconds.) Now, on your answer sheet, darken the number-letter combination that is in the box in which you just wrote. (Pause 5 seconds.)

Look at line 14 again. (Pause slightly.) Find the box that contains a number in the teens and write B as in baker in that box. (Pause 2 seconds.) Now, on your answer sheet, darken the number-letter combination that is in the box in which you just wrote. (Pause 5 seconds.)

Look at line 15 on your worksheet. (Pause slightly.) Circle the only number on line 15 that is not divisible by 2. (Pause 2 seconds.) Now, on your answer sheet, darken space A for the number you circled. (Pause 5 seconds.)

Look at line 16 on your worksheet. (Pause slightly.) If the number in the circle is greater than the number in the box, write the letter E in the box; if not, write the letter E in the circle. (Pause 5 seconds.) Now, on your answer sheet, darken the number-letter combination that is in the figure in which you just wrote. (Pause 5 seconds.)

Look at line 16 again. (Pause slightly.) If the number in the triangle is smaller than the number in the figure directly to its left, write the letter A in the triangle; if not, write the letter C in the triangle. (Pause 5 seconds.) Now, on your answer sheet, darken the number-letter combination that is in the figure in which you just wrote. (Pause 5 seconds.)

Look at line 17 on your worksheet. (Pause slightly.) Count the number of Js on line 17, multiply the number of Js by 5, and write that number at the end of the line. (Pause 5 seconds.) Now, on your answer sheet, find the number you just wrote at the end of the line and darken space C for that number. (Pause 5 seconds.)

Look at line 18 on your worksheet. (Pause slightly.) Draw one line under the number that is at the middle of line 18. (Pause 5 seconds.) Now, on your answer sheet, darken space B as in baker for the number under which you just drew a line. (Pause 5 seconds.)

Look at line 18 again. (Pause slightly.) Draw two lines under each odd number that falls between 35 and 45. (Pause 10 seconds.) Now, on your answer sheet, darken space D as in dog for each number under which you drew two lines. (Pause 5 seconds.)

Look at line 19 on your worksheet. (Pause slightly.) Next to the last letter on line 19, write the first number you hear: 53, 18, 6, 75. (Pause 2 seconds.) Now, on your answer sheet, darken the space for the number-letter combination you just wrote. (Pause 5 seconds.)

ANSWERS TO PRACTICE EXAM II

1. Ⓐ Ⓑ Ⓒ Ⓓ Ⓔ	23. Ⓐ Ⓑ Ⓒ Ⓓ Ⓔ	45. Ⓐ ● Ⓒ Ⓓ Ⓔ	67. Ⓐ Ⓑ Ⓒ Ⓓ Ⓔ
2. Ⓐ Ⓑ Ⓒ Ⓓ ●	24. ● Ⓑ Ⓒ Ⓓ Ⓔ	46. Ⓐ Ⓑ ● Ⓓ Ⓔ	68. Ⓐ Ⓑ Ⓒ Ⓓ Ⓔ
3. Ⓐ Ⓑ Ⓒ Ⓓ Ⓔ	25. Ⓐ Ⓑ Ⓒ Ⓓ Ⓔ	47. Ⓐ Ⓑ Ⓒ Ⓓ Ⓔ	69. Ⓐ Ⓑ Ⓒ Ⓓ Ⓔ
4. Ⓐ Ⓑ Ⓒ ● Ⓔ	26. Ⓐ Ⓑ Ⓒ Ⓓ Ⓔ	48. Ⓐ Ⓑ Ⓒ Ⓓ Ⓔ	70. Ⓐ Ⓑ Ⓒ Ⓓ Ⓔ
5. Ⓐ Ⓑ Ⓒ Ⓓ Ⓔ	27. Ⓐ Ⓑ Ⓒ ● Ⓔ	49. Ⓐ Ⓑ Ⓒ Ⓓ Ⓔ	71. Ⓐ Ⓑ Ⓒ ● Ⓔ
6. Ⓐ Ⓑ Ⓒ Ⓓ ●	28. Ⓐ Ⓑ Ⓒ Ⓓ Ⓔ	50. Ⓐ Ⓑ Ⓒ Ⓓ Ⓔ	72. Ⓐ Ⓑ Ⓒ Ⓓ Ⓔ
7. Ⓐ Ⓑ Ⓒ Ⓓ Ⓔ	29. Ⓐ Ⓑ Ⓒ Ⓓ Ⓔ	51. Ⓐ Ⓑ ● Ⓓ Ⓔ	73. Ⓐ Ⓑ Ⓒ Ⓓ Ⓔ
8. Ⓐ Ⓑ Ⓒ Ⓓ Ⓔ	30. Ⓐ Ⓑ ● Ⓓ Ⓔ	52. Ⓐ Ⓑ Ⓒ Ⓓ Ⓔ	74. Ⓐ Ⓑ Ⓒ Ⓓ Ⓔ
9. ● Ⓑ Ⓒ Ⓓ Ⓔ	31. Ⓐ Ⓑ Ⓒ ● Ⓔ	53. Ⓐ Ⓑ Ⓒ ● Ⓔ	75. Ⓐ Ⓑ Ⓒ Ⓓ Ⓔ
10. Ⓐ Ⓑ Ⓒ Ⓓ Ⓔ	32. Ⓐ Ⓑ Ⓒ Ⓓ Ⓔ	54. Ⓐ Ⓑ Ⓒ Ⓓ Ⓔ	76. Ⓐ Ⓑ Ⓒ Ⓓ ●
11. ● Ⓑ Ⓒ Ⓓ Ⓔ	33. Ⓐ Ⓑ Ⓒ Ⓓ Ⓔ	55. Ⓐ Ⓑ Ⓒ Ⓓ Ⓔ	77. Ⓐ Ⓑ Ⓒ Ⓓ Ⓔ
12. Ⓐ Ⓑ Ⓒ Ⓓ Ⓔ	34. Ⓐ Ⓑ Ⓒ Ⓓ ●	56. Ⓐ Ⓑ Ⓒ Ⓓ Ⓔ	78. Ⓐ Ⓑ Ⓒ Ⓓ Ⓔ
13. Ⓐ Ⓑ Ⓒ Ⓓ Ⓔ	35. Ⓐ Ⓑ Ⓒ Ⓓ Ⓔ	57. Ⓐ ● Ⓒ Ⓓ Ⓔ	79. Ⓐ ● Ⓒ Ⓓ Ⓔ
14. Ⓐ Ⓑ ● Ⓓ Ⓔ	36. Ⓐ Ⓑ Ⓒ Ⓓ Ⓔ	58. Ⓐ Ⓑ Ⓒ Ⓓ Ⓔ	80. Ⓐ Ⓑ Ⓒ Ⓓ Ⓔ
15. Ⓐ Ⓑ Ⓒ Ⓓ Ⓔ	37. Ⓐ Ⓑ Ⓒ Ⓓ Ⓔ	59. Ⓐ ● Ⓒ Ⓓ Ⓔ	81. Ⓐ Ⓑ Ⓒ Ⓓ Ⓔ
16. Ⓐ Ⓑ Ⓒ Ⓓ Ⓔ	38. Ⓐ ● Ⓒ Ⓓ Ⓔ	60. Ⓐ Ⓑ Ⓒ Ⓓ Ⓔ	82. Ⓐ Ⓑ Ⓒ Ⓓ Ⓔ
17. Ⓐ ● Ⓒ Ⓓ Ⓔ	39. Ⓐ Ⓑ Ⓒ Ⓓ Ⓔ	61. Ⓐ Ⓑ Ⓒ Ⓓ Ⓔ	83. Ⓐ Ⓑ Ⓒ Ⓓ ●
18. Ⓐ ● Ⓒ Ⓓ Ⓔ	40. Ⓐ Ⓑ Ⓒ Ⓓ Ⓔ	62. Ⓐ Ⓑ ● Ⓓ Ⓔ	84. ● Ⓑ Ⓒ Ⓓ Ⓔ
19. Ⓐ Ⓑ Ⓒ Ⓓ Ⓔ	41. Ⓐ Ⓑ Ⓒ ● Ⓔ	63. Ⓐ Ⓑ Ⓒ Ⓓ Ⓔ	85. Ⓐ Ⓑ Ⓒ Ⓓ Ⓔ
20. Ⓐ Ⓑ ● Ⓓ Ⓔ	42. Ⓐ Ⓑ Ⓒ Ⓓ Ⓔ	64. Ⓐ Ⓑ Ⓒ Ⓓ Ⓔ	86. Ⓐ Ⓑ Ⓒ Ⓓ Ⓔ
21. Ⓐ Ⓑ Ⓒ Ⓓ Ⓔ	43. Ⓐ Ⓑ Ⓒ Ⓓ Ⓔ	65. Ⓐ Ⓑ Ⓒ Ⓓ ●	87. ● Ⓑ Ⓒ Ⓓ Ⓔ
22. Ⓐ Ⓑ ● Ⓓ Ⓔ	44. Ⓐ Ⓑ Ⓒ Ⓓ Ⓔ	66. Ⓐ Ⓑ Ⓒ Ⓓ Ⓔ	88. Ⓐ Ⓑ Ⓒ Ⓓ Ⓔ

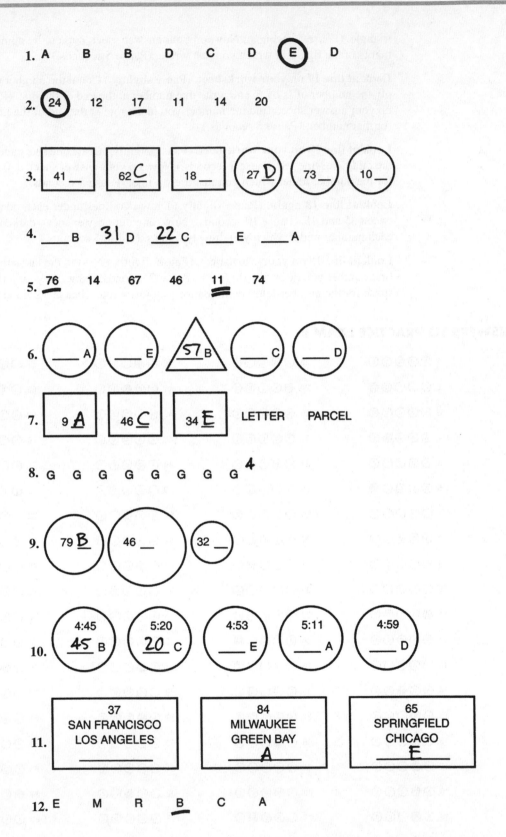

1. A   B   B   D   C   D   (E)   D

2. (24)   12   17   11   14   20

3. | 41 __ | 62 C | 18 __ | 27 D | 73 __ | 10 __ |

4. ___ B   31 D   22 C   ___ E   ___ A

5. 76   14   67   46   11   74

6. ___ A   ___ E   57 B   ___ C   ___ D

7. 9 A   46 C   34 E   LETTER   PARCEL

8. G   G   G   G   G   G   G   G   4

9. 79 B   46 __   32 __

10. 4:45 45 B   5:20 20 C   4:53 ___ E   5:11 ___ A   4:59 ___ D

11.
| 37 SAN FRANCISCO LOS ANGELES _____ | 84 MILWAUKEE GREEN BAY A | 65 SPRINGFIELD CHICAGO E |

12. E   M   R   B   C   A

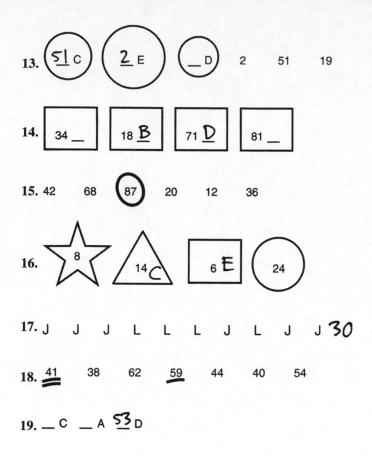

13. 51 C   2 E   ___ D   2   51   19

14. 34 ___   18 B   71 D   81 ___

15. 42   68   87   20   12   36

16. 8   14 C   6 E   24

17. J J J L L L J L J J 30

18. 41   38   62   59   44   40   54

19. ___ C   ___ A   53 D

PART IV

Practice Tests and Full-Length Practice Exams

CHAPTER 14

ADDRESS CHECKING PRACTICE TESTS

TAKING THE TIMED PRACTICE TESTS

This is your first real chance to answer Address Checking questions under the time constraints of the actual test. To get the most benefits from this practice, proceed as follows:

1. Choose a workspace that is quiet, well lit, clean, and uncluttered.

2. Use a stopwatch or kitchen timer to accurately time each test.

3. Start the first test at a convenient time and stop exactly when your 6 minutes are up.

4. Give yourself at least a 5-minute breather between each test. You can use this non-test time to skim through review material in earlier chapters.

5. After you complete all three tests, check your answers against the answer keys provided. Circle all wrong answers in red so that you can easily locate them.

6. Calculate your raw score for each test as instructed.

7. Check to see where your scores fall on the self-evaluation chart.

8. If you receive less than an excellent score on a test, go back and review the appropriate study chapters in this book.

9. Retake the test to see your improvement.

Remember not to become discouraged if you cannot answer all 95 questions in 6 minutes. You are not expected to. Work quickly but strive for accuracy using all of the techniques you have learned so far.

PRACTICE TEST I

Time: 6 Minutes • 95 Questions

> **Directions:** *For each question, compare the address in the left column with the address in the right column. If the two addresses are ALIKE in every way, write A next to the question number. If the two addresses are DIFFERENT in any way, write D next to the question number.*

1	...1897 Smicksburg Rd	1897 Smithsburg Rd
2	...3609 E Paseo Aldeano	3909 E Paseo Aldeano
3	...11787 Ornamental Ln	1787 Ornamental Ln
4	...1096 Camino Grande E	1096 Camino Grande E
5	...2544 E Radcliff Ave	2544 E Redcliff Ave
6	...5796 E Narragansett Dr	5796 E Narragasett Dr
7	...12475 Ebbtide Way W	12475 Ebbtide Way W
8	...14396 N Via Armando	14396 S Via Armando
9	...2155 S Del Giorgio Rd	2155 S Del Giorgio Rd
10	...16550 Bainbridge Cir	16505 Bainbridge Cir
11	...1826 Milneburg Rd	1826 Milneburg St
12	...Eureka KS 67045	Eureka KY 67045
13	...4010 Glenaddie Ave	4010 Glenaddie Ave
14	...13501 Stratford Rd	13501 Standford Rd
15	...3296 W 64th St	3296 E 64th St
16	...2201 Tennessee Cir	2201 Tennessee Cir
17	...1502 Avenue M NE	1502 Avenue N NE
18	...1096 SE Longrone Dr	1096 SE Longrone Dr
19	...1267 Darthmouth Ct	1267 Darthmont Ct
20	...825 Ophanage Rd	825 Ophanage Rd
21	...1754 Golden Springs Rd	1754 Golden Springs Road
22	...1015 Tallwoods Ln	1015 Tallwoods Ln
23	...1097 Lambada Dr	1097 Lambadd Dr
24	...Vredenburgh AL 36481	Verdenburgh AL 36481

25	...1800 Monticello Ave	1800 Monticello Ave
26	...1723 Yellowbird Ln	1723 Yellowbird Ct
27	...700 Valca Materials Rd	700 Valca Materials Rd
28	...1569 Ladywood Ln N	1569 Ladywood Ln W
29	...3256 Interurban Dr	3256 Interurban Dr
30	...1507 Haughton Cir	1507 Haughton Ct
31	...8971 Robertson Ave	8971 Robinson Ave
32	...3801 NE 49th Street	3801 NW 49th Street
33	...4102 Chalkville Rd	4102 Chalkview Rd
34	...1709 Ingersoll Cir	1709 Ingersoll Cir
35	...6800 N Nantucket Ln	6800 N Nantucket Ln
36	...12401 Tarrymore Dr	12401 Terrymore Dr
37	...1097 Huntsville Ave	1097 Huntsville Ave
38	...3566 Lornaridge Pl	3566 Lornaridge Pl
39	...2039 Klondike Ave SW	2039 Klondie Ave SW
40	...3267 Mayland Ln	3267 Maryland Ln
41	...12956 Strawberry Ln	12596 Strawberry Ln
42	...De Armanville AL 36257	De Armanville AL 36257
43	...6015 Anniston Dr	6015 Anneston Dr
44	...1525 E 90th St	1525 E 90th St
45	...1299 Chappaque Rd	1266 Chappaque Rd
46	...2156 Juliette Dr	2156 Juliaetta Dr
47	...999 N Hollingsworth St	999 S Hollingsworth St
48	...16901 Odum Crest Ln	19601 Odum Crest Ln
49	...9787 Zellmark Dr	9787 Zealmark Dr
50	...11103 NE Feasell Ave	11103 NE Feasell Ave
51	...51121 N Mattison Rd	51121 S Mattison Rd
52	...8326 Blackjack Ln	8326 Blackjack Blvd
53	...18765 Lagarde Ave	18765 Lagrande Ave

54	...11297 Gallatin Ln	11297 Gallatin Ln
55	...Wormleysburg PA 17043	Wormleysburg PA 17043
56	...22371 N Sprague Ave	22371 S Sprague Ave
57	...15014 Warrior River Rd	15014 Warrior River Rd
58	...45721 Hueytown Plaza	45721 Hueytowne Plaza
59	...8973 Tedescki Dr	8793 Tedescki Dr
60	...12995 Raimond Muscoda Pl	12995 Raimont Muscoda Pl
61	...Phippsburg CO 80469	Phippsburg CA 80469
62	...52003 W 49th Ave	52003 W 46th Ave
63	...17201 Zenobia Cir	17210 Zenobia Cir
64	...4800 Garrison Cir	4800 Garrison Dr
65	...Los Angeles CA 90070	Los Angeles CA 90076
66	...14798 W 62nd Ave	14198 W 62nd Ave
67	...7191 E Eldridge Way	7191 E Eldridge Way
68	...1279 S Quintard Dr	1279 S Guintard Dr
69	...21899 Dellwood Ave	21899 Dillwood Ave
70	...7191 Zenophone Cir	7191 Zenohone Cir
71	...4301 Los Encinos Way	4301 Los Encinas Way
72	...19700 Ostronic Dr NW	19700 Ostronic Dr NE
73	...23291 Van Velsire Dr	23219 Van Velsire Dr
74	...547 Paradise Valley Rd	547 Paradise Valley Ct
75	...23167 Saltillo Ave	23167 Santillo Ave
76	...43001 Mourning Dove Way	43001 Mourning Dove Way
77	...21183 Declaration Ave	21183 Declaration Ave
78	...10799 Via Sierra Ramal Ave	10799 Via Sierra Ramel Ave
79	...16567 Hermosillia Ct	16597 Hermosillia Ct
80	...Villamont VA 24178	Villamont VA 24178
81	...18794 Villaboso Ave	18794 Villeboso Ave
82	...24136 Ranthom Ave	24136 Ranthon Ave
83	...13489 Golondrina Pl	13489 Golondrina St

84	...6598 Adamsville Ave	6598 Adamsville Ave
85	...12641 Indals Pl NE	12641 Indals Pl NW
86	...19701 SE 2nd Avenue	19701 NE 2nd Avenue
87	...22754 Cachalote Ln	22754 Cachalott Ln
88	...12341 Kingfisher Rd	12341 Kingsfisher Rd
89	...24168 Lorenzana Dr	24168 Lorenzano Dr
90	...32480 Blackfriar Rd	32480 Blackfriar Rd
91	...16355 Wheeler Dr	16355 Wheelen Dr
92	...5100 Magna Carta Rd	5100 Magna Certa Rd
93	...2341 N Federalist Pl	2341 N Federalist Pl
94	...22200 Timpangos Rd	22200 Timpangos Rd
95	...19704 Calderon Rd	19704 Calderon Rd

PRACTICE TEST II

Time: 6 Minutes • 95 Questions

> **Directions:** *For each question, compare the address in the left column with the address in the right column. If the two addresses are ALIKE in every way, write A next to the question number. If the two addresses are DIFFERENT in any way, write D next to the question number.*

1	...4623 Grand Concourse	4623 Grand Concourse
2	...6179 Ridgecroft Rd	6719 Ridgecroft Rd
3	...5291 Hanover Cir	5291 Hangover Cir
4	...2333 Palmer Ave	233 Palmer Ave
5	...1859 SE 148th St	1859 SE 148th St
6	...Dowagiac MI 49047	Dowagiac MI 49047
7	...4147 Wykagyl Terr	4147 Wykagyl Terr
8	...1504 N 10th Ave	1504 N 10th St
9	...2967 Montross Ave	2967 Montrose Ave
10	...Chicago IL 60601	Chicago IL 60601
11	...2073 Defoe Ct	2073 Defoe Ct
12	...2433 Westchester Plz	2343 Westchester Plz

13	...6094 Carpenter Ave	6094 Charpenter Ave
14	...5677 Bolman Twrs	5677 Bolman Twrs
15	...Chappaqua NY 10514	Chappaqua NY 10541
16	...3428 Constantine Ave	3248 Constantine Ave
17	...847 S 147th Rd	847 S 147th Rd
18	...6676 Harwood Ct	6676 Hardwood Ct
19	...3486 Mosholu Pky	3486 Mosholu Pkwy
20	...Mindenmines MO 64769	Mindenmines MO 64679
21	...816 Oscawana Lake Rd	816 Ocsawana Lake Rd
22	...9159 Battle Hill Rd	9195 Battle Hill Rd
23	...7558 Winston Ln	7558 Winston Ln
24	...3856 W 385th St	3856 W 386th St
25	...3679 W Alpine Pl	3679 W Alpine Pl
26	...Hartford CT 06115	Hartford CN 06115
27	...6103 Locust Hill Wy	6013 Locust Hill Wy
28	...4941 Annrock Dr	4941 Annrock Dr
29	...2018 N St Andrews Pl	2018 N St Andrews Pl
30	...8111 Drewville Rd	8111 Drewsville Rd
31	...463 Peaceable Hill Rd	463 Peaceable Hill Rd
32	...Biloxi MS 39532	Biloxi MS 39532
33	...3743 Point Dr S	3734 Point Dr S
34	...5665 Barnington Rd	5665 Barnington Rd
35	...2246 E Sheldrake Ave	2246 W Sheldrake Ave
36	...1443 Bloomingdale Rd	1443 Bloomingdales Rd
37	...2064 Chalford Ln	2064 Chalford Ln
38	...McMinnville OR 97128	McMinville OR 97128
39	...6160 Shadybrook Ln	6160 Shadybrook Ln
40	...2947 E Lake Blvd	2947 E Lake Blvd
41	...3907 Evergreen Row	3907 Evergreen Row
42	...2192 SE Hotel Dr	2192 SE Hotel Dr

43	...8844 Fremont St	8844 Fremont Rd
44	...8487 Wolfshead Rd	8487 Wolfshead Rd
45	...Anamosa IA 52205	Anamoosa IA 52205
46	...4055 Katonah Ave	4055 Katonah Ave
47	...1977 Buckingham Apts	1979 Buckingham Apts
48	...983 W 139th Way	983 W 139th Wy
49	...7822 Bayliss Ln	7822 Bayliss Ln
50	...8937 Banksville Rd	8937 Banksville Rd
51	...4759 Strathmore Rd	4579 Strathmore Rd
52	...2221 E Main St	221 E Main St
53	...South Orange NJ 07079	South Orange NJ 07079
54	...4586 Sylvia Wy	4586 Sylvan Wy
55	...6335 Soundview Ave	6335 SoundView Ave
56	...3743 Popham Rd	3743 Poppam Rd
57	...2845 Brookfield Dr	2485 Brookfield Dr
58	...3845 Fort Slocum Rd	3845 Fort Slocum St
59	...9268 Jochum Ave	9268 Jochum Ave
60	...Bloomington MN 55437	Bloomington MN 54537
61	...6903 S 184th St	6903 S 184th St
62	...7486 Rossmor Rd	7486 Rosemor Rd
63	...4176 Whitlockville Rd	4176 Whitlockville Wy
64	...4286 Megquire Ln	4286 Megquire Ln
65	...6270 Tamarock Rd	6270 Tammarock Rd
66	...3630 Bulkley Mnr	3630 Bulkley Mnr
67	...7158 Scarswold Apts	7185 Scarswold Apts
68	...Brooklyn NY 11218	Brooklyn NY 11128
69	...9598 Prince Edward Rd	9598 Prince Edward Rd
70	...8439 S 145th St	8439 S 154th St
71	...9795 Shady Glen Ct	9795 Shady Grove Ct
72	...7614 Ganung St	7614 Ganung St

73	...Teaneck NJ 07666	Teaneck NH 07666
74	...6359 Dempster Rd	6359 Dumpster Rd
75	...1065 Colchester Hl	1065 Colchester Hl
76	...5381 Phillipse Pl	5381 Philipse Pl
77	...6484 Rochester Terr	6484 Rochester Terr
78	...2956 Quinin St	2956 Quinin St
79	...Tarzana CA 91356	Tarzana CA 91536
80	...7558 Winston Ln	7558 Whinston Ln
81	...1862 W 293rd St	1862 W 393rd St
82	...8534 S Huntington Ave	8534 N Huntington Ave
83	...9070 Wild Oaks Vlg	9070 Wild Oakes Vlg
84	...4860 Smadbeck Ave	4680 Smadbeck Ave
85	...8596 E Commonwealth Ave	8596 E Commonwealth Ave
86	...Ridgefield NJ 07657	Ridgefield NJ 07657
87	...1478 Charter Cir	1478 W Charter Cir
88	...3963 Priscilla Ave	3963 Pricsilla Ave
89	...4897 Winding Ln	4897 Winding Ln
90	...847 Windmill Terr	847 Windmill Terr
91	...1662 Wixon St W	1662 Wixon St W
92	...West Hartford CT 06107	West Hartford CT 06107
93	...6494 Rochelle Terr	9464 Rochelle Terr
94	...4228 Pocantico Rd	4228 Pocantico Rd
95	...1783 S 486th Ave	1783 S 486th Ave

PRACTICE TEST III

Time: 6 Minutes • 95 Questions

> **Directions:** *For each question, compare the address in the left column with the address in the right column. If the two addresses are ALIKE in every way, write A next to the question number. If the two addresses are DIFFERENT in any way, write D next to the question number.*

1	...1038 Nutgrove St	1038 Nutgrove St
2	...4830 Schroeder Ave	4380 Schroeder Ave
3	...2343 Martine Ave	2343 Martini Ave

4	...Winkelman AZ 85292	Winkelman AZ 85292
5	...298 Chatterton Pky	298 Chatterton Pky
6	...3798 Hillandale Ave	3798 Hillanddale Ave
7	...7683 Fountain Pl	7863 Fountain Pl
8	...1862 W 164th St	1864 W 164th St
9	...Scarborough NY 10510	Scarbourough NY 10510
10	...1734 N Highland Ave	1734 W Highland Ave
11	...1385 Queens Blvd	1385 Queens Blvd
12	...6742 Mendota Ave	6742 Mendota Ave
13	...8496 E 245th St	8496 E 254th St
14	...2010 Wyndcliff Rd	2010 Wyndecliff Rd
15	...4098 Gramatan Ave	4098 Gramatan Ave
16	...Denver CO 80236	Denver CO 80236
17	...3778 N Broadway	3778 N Broadway
18	...532 Broadhollow Rd	532 Broadhollow Rd
19	...1386 Carriage House Ln	1386 Carriage House Ln
20	...3284 S 10th St	2384 S 10th St
21	...2666 Dunwoodie Rd	266 Dunwoodie Rd
22	...Pontiac MI 48054	Pontiac MI 48054
23	...1080 Nine Acres Ln	1080 Nine Acres Ln
24	...2699 Quaker Church Rd	2669 Quaker Church Rd
25	...7232 S 45th Ave	7232 S 45th Ave
26	...1588 Grand Boulevard	1588 Grand Boulevard
27	...2093 S Waverly Rd	2093 S Waverley Rd
28	...Las Vegas NV 89112	Las Vegas NM 89112
29	...116 Cottage Pl Gdns	116 Cottage Pl Gdns
30	...1203 E Lakeview Ave	1203 E Lakeside Ave
31	...3446 E Westchester Ave	3446 E Westchester Ave
32	...7482 Horseshoe Hill Rd	7482 Horseshoe Hill Rd
33	...Waimanalo HI 96795	Waimanale HI 96795
34	...9138 McGuire Ave	9138 MacGuire Ave

35	...7438 Meadway	7348 Meadway
36	...2510 Maryland Ave NW	2510 Maryland Ave NW
37	...1085 S 83rd Rd	1085 S 83rd Rd
38	...5232 Maplewood Wy	523 Maplewood Wy
39	...Kansas City MO 64108	Kansas City MO 61408
40	...1063 Valentine Ln	1063 Valentine Ln
41	...1066 Furnace Dock Rd	1606 Furnace Dock Rd
42	...2121 Rosedale Rd	2121 Rosedale Rd
43	...1396 Orawapum St	1396 Orawampum St
44	...3004 Palisade Ave	3004 Palisades Ave
45	...1776 Independence St	1776 Independence St
46	...Canton OH 44707	Canton OH 44707
47	...1515 Geoga Cir	1515 Geogia Cir
48	...1583 Central Ave	1583 Central Ave
49	...4096 Valley Terr	4096 Valley Terr
50	...2075 Boston Post Rd	2075 Boston Post Rd
51	...1016 Frost Ln	1016 Frost La
52	...2186 Ashford Ave	2186 Ashford Ave
53	...Battle Mountain NV 89820	Battle Mountain NV 89820
54	...6634 Weber Pl	6634 Webber Pl
55	...6832 Halcyon Terr	6832 Halcyon Terr
56	...198 Gedney Esplnde	198 Gedney Esplnde
57	...8954 Horsechestnut Rd	8954 Horsechestnut Rd
58	...1926 S 283rd Wy	1926 S 283rd Wy
59	...Hartsdale NY 10530	Hartsdale NY 15030
60	...1569 Ritchy Pl	1569 Ritchy Pl
61	...423 S Columbia Ave	423 S Colombia Ave
62	...2466 Linette Ct	2466 Linnette Ct
63	...2970 Rockledge Ave	2970 Rockridge Ave
64	...5764 Guion Blvd	5764 Guion Blvd
65	...6976 SW 5th Ave	6976 SE 5th Ave

66	...Milwaukie OR 97222	Milwaukee OR 97222
67	...2243 Hudson View Ests	2234 Hudson View Ests
68	...7743 S 3rd Ave	7743 S 3rd Ave
69	...2869 Romaine Ave	2869 Romaine Ave
70	...2943 Windermere Dr	2943 Windemere Dr
71	...5117 Balmoral Crsnt	5117 Balmoral Crsnt
72	...3797 Wappanocca Ave	3797 Wappannocca Ave
73	...Arkabutla MS 38602	Arkabutla MS 38602
74	...2275 Greenway Terr	2275 Greenaway Terr
75	...7153 Taymil Rd	7153 Taymil Rd
76	...3864 W 248th St	3864 W 284th St
77	...2032 Central Park S	2023 Central Park S
78	...1803 Pinewood Rd	1803 Pineywood Rd
79	...New York NY 10023	New York NY 10023
80	...1555 E 19th St	1555 E 19th St
81	...3402 Comer Cir	3402 Comer Ct
82	...9416 Lakeshore Dr	9416 Lakeshore Dr
83	...1576 Kimball Ave	1576 Kimbell Ave
84	...2015 W 51st Ln	2015 W 51st Ln
85	...Silver Springs NV 89429	Silver Springs NV 89429
86	...2354 N Washington St	2354 N Washington St
87	...8528 Convent Pl	8258 Convent Pl
88	...1911 Downer Ave	1911 Downer Ave
89	...6108 Woodstock Rd	6108 Woodstock St
90	...Akron OH 44308	Akron OK 44308
91	...4548 College Pt Ave	4548 College Pk Ave
92	...8194 Great Oak Ln	8194 Great Oak Ln
93	...280 SW Collins Ave	280 SW Collins Ave
94	...8276 Abbott Mews	8726 Abbott Mews
95	...4717 Deerfield Blvd	4717 Deerfield Blvd

PRACTICE TEST ANSWERS

Practice Test I Answer Key						
1. D	15. D	29. A	43. D	57. A	71. D	85. D
2. D	16. A	30. D	44. A	58. D	72. D	86. D
3. D	17. D	31. D	45. D	59. D	73. D	87. D
4. A	18. A	32. D	46. D	60. D	74. D	88. D
5. D	19. D	33. D	47. D	61. D	75. D	89. D
6. D	20. A	34. A	48. D	62. D	76. A	90. A
7. A	21. D	35. A	49. D	63. D	77. A	91. D
8. D	22. A	36. D	50. A	64. D	78. D	92. D
9. A	23. D	37. A	51. D	65. D	79. D	93. A
10. D	24. D	38. A	52. D	66. D	80. A	94. A
11. D	25. A	39. D	53. D	67. A	81. D	95. A
12. D	26. D	40. D	54. A	68. D	82. D	
13. A	27. A	41. D	55. A	69. D	83. D	
14. D	28. D	42. A	56. D	70. D	84. A	

DETERMINE YOUR RAW SCORE

Practice Test I: Your score on Address Checking is based upon the number of questions you answered correctly minus the number of questions you answered incorrectly:

1. Enter number of right answers   _____

2. Enter number of wrong answers   _____

3. Subtract number wrong from right   _____

   Raw Score =   _____

Practice Test II Answer Key						
1. A	15. D	29. A	43. D	57. D	71. D	85. A
2. D	16. D	30. D	44. A	58. D	72. A	86. A
3. D	17. A	31. A	45. D	59. A	73. D	87. D
4. D	18. D	32. A	46. A	60. D	74. D	88. D
5. A	19. D	33. D	47. D	61. A	75. A	89. A
6. A	20. D	34. A	48. D	62. D	76. D	90. A
7. A	21. D	35. D	49. A	63. D	77. A	91. A
8. D	22. D	36. D	50. A	64. A	78. A	92. A
9. D	23. A	37. A	51. D	65. D	79. D	93. D
10. A	24. D	38. D	52. D	66. A	80. D	94. A
11. A	25. A	39. A	53. A	67. D	81. D	95. A
12. D	26. D	40. A	54. D	68. D	82. D	
13. D	27. D	41. A	55. D	69. A	83. D	
14. A	28. A	42. A	56. D	70. D	84. D	

DETERMINE YOUR RAW SCORE

Practice Test II: Your score on Address Checking is based upon the number of questions you answered correctly minus the number of questions you answered incorrectly:

1. Enter number of right answers _____

2. Enter number of wrong answers _____

3. Subtract number wrong from right _____

Raw Score = _____

Practice Test III Answer Key

1. A	15. A	29. A	43. D	57. A	71. A	85. A
2. D	16. A	30. D	44. D	58. A	72. D	86. A
3. D	17. A	31. A	45. A	59. D	73. A	87. D
4. A	18. A	32. A	46. A	60. A	74. D	88. A
5. A	19. A	33. D	47. D	61. D	75. A	89. D
6. D	20. D	34. D	48. A	62. D	76. D	90. D
7. D	21. D	35. D	49. A	63. D	77. D	91. D
8. D	22. A	36. A	50. A	64. A	78. D	92. A
9. D	23. A	37. A	51. D	65. D	79. A	93. A
10. D	24. D	38. D	52. D	66. D	80. A	94. D
11. A	25. A	39. D	53. A	67. D	81. D	95. A
12. A	26. A	40. A	54. D	68. A	82. A	
13. D	27. D	41. D	55. D	69. A	83. D	
14. D	28. D	42. A	56. A	70. D	84. A	

DETERMINE YOUR RAW SCORE

Practice Test III: Your score on Address Checking is based upon the number of questions you answered correctly minus the number of questions you answered incorrectly:

1. Enter number of right answers _____

2. Enter number of wrong answers _____

3. Subtract number wrong from right _____

Raw Score = _____

SELF-EVALUATION CHART

For each practice test, see how your raw score falls on the following scale. You should not be satisfied with less than excellent. Review all appropriate study material, and then retake the test(s) where you need improvement.

IF your raw score was between	THEN your work was
80–95	**Excellent**
65–79	**Good**
50–64	**Average**
35–49	**Fair**
1–34	**Poor**

CHAPTER 15

Memory for Addresses Practice Tests

TAKING THE TIMED TEST

> *Do not write down your memorization techniques during the time allowed for memorizing addresses. Do whatever it takes to stay focused. Remember, you must do it all in your head on the actual test.*

This is your first real chance to answer Memory for Addresses questions under the time constraints of the actual test. To benefit the most from this practice, proceed as follows:

1. Choose a workspace that is quiet, well lit, clean, and uncluttered.

2. Use a stopwatch or kitchen timer to accurately time each test.

3. Start the first test at a convenient time, and stop exactly when your 6 minutes are up.

4. Give yourself at least a 5-minute breather between each test. You can use this non-test time to skim through review material in earlier chapters.

5. After you complete all four practice tests, check your answers against the answer keys provided. Circle all wrong answers in red so that you can easily locate them.

6. Calculate your raw score for the timed Memory for Addresses test as instructed.

7. Check to see where your score falls on the self-evaluation chart.

8. If you receive less than an "Excellent" score on a test, go back and review the appropriate study chapters in this book.

9. Retake the test to see your improvement.

Remember that you are not expected to answer all the questions. So don't get discouraged if you cannot finish the test. Guess if you can use the process of elimination to weed out one or more incorrect answers.

TIMED PRACTICE TESTS

This exercise is in the same format as the actual test. It includes:

- Sample questions
- Practice I
- Practice II
- Practice III
- Memory for Addresses

SAMPLE QUESTIONS

You will have to memorize the locations (A, B, C, D, and E) of the 25 addresses in the five lettered boxes below. Indicate your answers by writing in your answer (letter) next to the question number.

You now have 5 minutes to study the locations of the addresses. Then, cover the boxes and answer the questions. You may look back at the boxes if you cannot yet mark the address locations from memory.

A	B	C	D	E
2600–3899 Hart	1400–2099 Hart	3900–4199 Hart	4200–5399 Hart	2100–2599 Hart
Linda	Ashley	Farmer	Monroe	Nolan
4200–5399 Dorp	3900–4199 Dorp	2600–3899 Dorp	2100–2599 Dorp	1400–2099 Dorp
Croft	Walton	Brendan	Orton	Gould
2100–2599 Noon	2600–3899 Noon	1400–2099 Noon	3900–4199 Noon	4200–5399 Noon

1. 3900–4199 Noon
2. 4200–5399 Dorp
3. Nolan
4. Farmer
5. 1400–2099 Hart
6. 2100–2599 Hart
7. 1400–2099 Noon
8. Monroe
9. Ashley
10. 2100–2599 Dorp
11. 2600–3899 Hart
12. 2100–2599 Noon
13. Orton
14. 2600–3899 Dorp

Answer Key						
1. D	3. E	5. B	7. C	9. B	11. A	13. D
2. A	4. C	6. E	8. D	10. D	12. A	14. C

Directions: *The five boxes below are labeled A, B, C, D, and E. In each box are five addresses: three are street addresses with number ranges and two are unnumbered place names. You have 3 minutes to memorize the box location of each address. The position of an address within a box is not important. You need only remember the letter of the box in which the address is found. You will use these addresses to answer three sets of practice questions that are NOT scored and one actual test that IS scored.*

A	B	C	D	E
2600–3899 Hart	1400–2099 Hart	3900–4199 Hart	4200–5399 Hart	2100–2599 Hart
Linda	Ashley	Farmer	Monroe	Nolan
4200–5399 Dorp	3900–4199 Dorp	2600–3899 Dorp	2100–2599 Dorp	1400–2099 Dorp
Croft	Walton	Brendan	Orton	Gould
2100–2599 Noon	2600–3899 Noon	1400–2099 Noon	3900–4199 Noon	4200–5399 Noon

PRACTICE I

> *Directions:* You have 3 minutes to write the letters of the boxes in which each of the following addresses is found. Indicate your answers by writing your answer (letter) next to the question number. Try to do this without looking at the boxes. However, if you get stuck, you may refer to the boxes during this practice exercise. If you must look at the boxes, try to memorize as you do so. This test is for practice only. It will not be scored.

1. 4200–5399 Dorp
2. 3900–4199 Hart
3. 4200–5399 Noon
4. Walton
5. Monroe
6. 2100–2599 Noon
7. 1400–2199 Hart
8. Gould
9. 1400–2099 Dorp
10. 2100–2599 Dorp
11. 1400–2099 Noon
12. Linda
13. Croft
14. Brendan
15. 3900–4199 Dorp
16. 2600–3899 Noon
17. 2100–2599 Hart
18. 2600–3899 Hart
19. 1400–2099 Dorp
20. Farmer
21. Ashley
22. 3900–4199 Noon
23. 2100–2599 Dorp
24. 2100–2599 Noon
25. Nolan
26. Croft
27. 4200–5399 Dorp
28. 1400–2099 Noon
29. 4200–5399 Hart
30. Monroe

31. Gould
32. 1400–2099 Hart
33. 2600–3899 Dorp
34. 2600–3899 Noon
35. Linda
36. Walton
37. Orton
38. 3900–4199 Dorp
39. 4200–5399 Noon
40. 3900–4199 Hart
41. Brendan
42. 1400–2099 Dorp
43. 2600–3899 Noon
44. Ashley
45. 4200–5399 Hart
46. 2600–3899 Hart
47. 3900–4199 Dorp
48. Orton
49. Monroe
50. 3900–4199 Noon
51. 2100–2599 Hart
52. 4200–5399 Noon
53. 2100–2599 Noon
54. Walton
55. Farmer
56. 2600–3899 Dorp
57. 3900–4199 Hart
58. 2100–2599 Dorp
59. Gould
60. Brendan

61. 1400–2099 Hart
62. 2600–3899 Noon
63. Ashley
64. 1400–2099 Dorp
65. 4200–5399 Dorp
66. 4200–5399 Hart
67. Linda
68. Croft
69. Nolan
70. 1400–2099 Noon
71. 3900–4199 Hart
72. 2100–2599 Dorp
73. 2600–3899 Noon
74. Walton
75. 2600–3899 Dorp
76. 2600–3899 Hart
77. 4200–5399 Noon
78. Monroe
79. Ashley
80. 2100–2599 Noon
81. 2100–2599 Hart
82. 3900–4199 Hart
83. Brendan
84. Nolan
85. Croft
86. 3900–4199 Dorp
87. 2100–2599 Dorp
88. 1400–2099 Noon

Practice I Answer Key

1. A	14. C	27. A	40. C	53. A	66. D	79. B
2. C	15. B	28. C	41. C	54. B	67. A	80. A
3. E	16. B	29. D	42. E	55. C	68. A	81. E
4. B	17. E	30. D	43. B	56. C	69. E	82. C
5. D	18. A	31. E	44. B	57. C	70. C	83. C
6. A	19. E	32. B	45. D	58. D	71. C	84. E
7. B	20. C	33. C	46. A	59. E	72. D	85. A
8. E	21. B	34. B	47. B	60. C	73. B	86. B
9. E	22. D	35. A	48. D	61. B	74. B	87. D
10. D	23. D	36. B	49. D	62. B	75. C	88. C
11. C	24. A	37. D	50. D	63. B	76. A	
12. A	25. E	38. B	51. E	64. E	77. E	
13. A	26. A	39. E	52. E	65. A	78. D	

PRACTICE II

Directions: *The next 88 questions are for practice. Indicate your answers by writing your answer (letter) next to the question number. Your time limit is 3 minutes. This time, however, you must NOT look at the boxes while answering the questions. You must rely on memory in marking the box location of each item. This practice test will not be scored.*

1. 3900–4199 Hart	17. 2600–3899 Dorp	33. 2600–3899 Hart
2. 3900–4199 Dorp	18. 2100–2599 Dorp	34. 3900–4199 Dorp
3. 2100–2599 Noon	19. 2100–2599 Hart	35. 1400–2099 Noon
4. Nolan	20. Monroe	36. Nolan
5. Orton	21. 4200–5399 Hart	37. Farmer
6. 4200–5399 Noon	22. Linda	38. 4200–5399 Noon
7. 4200–5399 Hart	23. 2600–3899 Noon	39. 2100–2599 Dorp
8. 1400–2099 Noon	24. 3900–4199 Noon	40. 1400–2099 Hart
9. Croft	25. Walton	41. Croft
10. Ashley	26. Monroe	42. Walton
11. 2600–3899 Hart	27. Ashley	43. 2100–2599 Hart
12. 4200–5399 Dorp	28. 1400–2099 Dorp	44. 2600–3899 Noon
13. 1400–2099 Dorp	29. 3900–4199 Hart	45. 2600–3899 Dorp
14. 1400–2099 Hart	30. 2100–2599 Noon	46. Gould
15. Farmer	31. Brendan	47. Orton
16. Brendan	32. Linda	48. 3900–4199 Noon

49. 4200–5399 Dorp
50. 4200–5399 Hart
51. 2600–3899 Dorp
52. Linda
53. 2100–2599 Noon
54. Ashley
55. Gould
56. 4200–5399 Noon
57. 3900–4199 Noon
58. 3900–4199 Dorp
59. Nolan
60. Croft
61. 2600–3899 Hart
62. 2100–2599 Dorp

63. 3900–4199 Hart
64. Farmer
65. Orton
66. 4200–5399 Dorp
67. 1400–2099 Dorp
68. 1400–2099 Hart
69. Brendan
70. Linda
71. 1400–2099 Noon
72. 2600–3899 Noon
73. 4200–5399 Hart
74. Walton
75. Monroe
76. 3900–4199 Dorp

77. 2100–2599 Hart
78. 2100–2599 Noon
79. Ashley
80. Gould
81. Orton
82. 2600–3899 Noon
83. 1400–2099 Hart
84. 2600–3899 Dorp
85. 3900–4199 Noon
86. 2600–3899 Hart
87. Brendan
88. Croft

Practice II Answer Key

1. C	14. B	27. B	40. B	53. A	66. A	79. B
2. B	15. C	28. E	41. A	54. B	67. E	80. E
3. A	16. C	29. C	42. B	55. E	68. B	81. D
4. E	17. C	30. A	43. E	56. E	69. C	82. B
5. D	18. D	31. C	44. B	57. D	70. A	83. B
6. E	19. E	32. A	45. C	58. B	71. C	84. C
7. D	20. D	33. A	46. E	59. E	72. B	85. D
8. C	21. D	34. B	47. D	60. A	73. D	86. A
9. A	22. A	35. C	48. D	61. A	74. B	87. C
10. B	23. B	36. E	49. A	62. D	75. D	88. A
11. A	24. D	37. C	50. D	63. C	76. B	
12. A	25. B	38. E	51. C	64. C	77. E	
13. E	26. D	39. D	52. A	65. D	78. A	

PRACTICE III

> **Directions:** *The same addresses from the previous sets are repeated in the box below. Each address is in the same box as the original set. You now have 3 minutes to study the locations again. Do your best to memorize the letter of the box in which each address is located. This is your last chance to see the boxes. This is your last practice set. Mark the location of each of the 88 addresses by writing the answer (letter) next to the question number. Your time limit is 5 minutes. Do NOT look back at the boxes. This practice test will not be scored.*

A	B	C	D	E
2600–3899 Hart	1400–2099 Hart	3900–4199 Hart	4200–5399 Hart	2100–2599 Hart
Linda	Ashley	Farmer	Monroe	Nolan
4200–5399 Dorp	3900–4199 Dorp	2600–3899 Dorp	2100–2599 Dorp	1400–2099 Dorp
Croft	Walton	Brendan	Orton	Gould
2100–2599 Noon	2600–3899 Noon	1400–2099 Noon	3900–4199 Noon	4200–5399 Noon

1. 2600–3899 Hart
2. 2600–3899 Dorp
3. 2600–3899 Noon
4. Walton
5. Nolan
6. 4200–5399 Noon
7. 2100–2599 Dorp
8. 1400–2099 Noon
9. Gould
10. Monroe
11. 3900–4199 Hart
12. 2100–2599 Hart
13. 3900–4199 Dorp
14. Brendan
15. Ashley
16. 1400–2099 Hart
17. 1400–2099 Dorp
18. 4200–5399 Dorp
19. Farmer
20. Monroe
21. Linda

22. 2100–2599 Noon
23. 3900–4199 Hart
24. 4200–5399 Hart
25. Croft
26. Ashley
27. 3900–4199 Dorp
28. 2600–3899 Noon
29. 2600–3899 Hart
30. Nolan
31. 2100–2599 Dorp
32. 4200–5399 Hart
33. 2600–3899 Noon
34. Monroe
35. Farmer
36. 3900–4199 Noon
37. 3900–4199 Dorp
38. 2600–3899 Hart
39. Nolan
40. Walton
41. 4200–5399 Dorp
42. 4200–5399 Noon

43. 1400–2099 Hart
44. Linda
45. Gould
46. 2100–2599 Hart
47. 3900–4199 Hart
48. 2600–3899 Dorp
49. Ashley
50. Croft
51. 1400–2099 Dorp
52. 1400–2099 Noon
53. 2100–2599 Noon
54. Orton
55. Brendan
56. 2600–3899 Hart
57. 3900–4199 Dorp
58. 4200–5399 Noon
59. 3900–4199 Hart
60. 1400–2099 Noon
61. Ashley
62. Brendan
63. Monroe

64. 1400–2099 Hart

65. 3900–4199 Noon

66. 4200–5399 Hart

67. 3900–4199 Dorp

68. Nolan

69. Walton

70. 4200–5399 Dorp

71. 1400–2099 Dorp

72. 1400–2099 Noon

73. 3900–4199 Hart

74. 2100–2599 Hart

75. Gould

76. Linda

77. Farmer

78. 2600–3899 Hart

79. 2600–3899 Noon

80. 4200–5399 Noon

81. 2600–3899 Dorp

82. 2100–2599 Dorp

83. Croft

84. Orton

85. 2100–2599 Noon

86. 3900–4199 Hart

87. 1400–2099 Dorp

88. 4200–5399 Noon

Practice III Answer Key

1. A	14. C	27. B	40. B	53. A	66. D	79. B
2. C	15. B	28. B	41. A	54. D	67. B	80. E
3. B	16. B	29. A	42. E	55. C	68. E	81. C
4. B	17. E	30. E	43. B	56. A	69. B	82. D
5. E	18. A	31. D	44. A	57. B	70. A	83. A
6. E	19. C	32. D	45. E	58. E	71. E	84. D
7. D	20. D	33. B	46. E	59. C	72. C	85. A
8. C	21. A	34. D	47. C	60. C	73. C	86. C
9. E	22. A	35. C	48. C	61. B	74. E	87. E
10. D	23. C	36. D	49. B	62. C	75. E	88. E
11. C	24. D	37. B	50. A	63. D	76. A	
12. E	25. A	38. A	51. E	64. B	77. C	
13. B	26. B	39. E	52. C	65. D	78. A	

MEMORY FOR ADDRESSES—SCORED TEST

Time: 5 Minutes • 88 Questions

> **Directions:** *Indicate the location (A, B, C, D, or E) of each of the 88 addresses below by writing the answer (letter) next to the question number. You are NOT permitted to look at the boxes. Work from memory as quickly and as accurately as you can.*

1.	Monroe	31.	1400–3899 Noon	60.	Croft		
2.	Walton	32.	Brendan	61.	4200–5399 Dorp		
3.	2600–3899 Dorp	33.	Ashley	62.	1400–2099 Noon		
4.	2100–2599 Noon	34.	2600–3899 Hart	63.	2600–3899 Noon		
5.	2100–2599 Hart	35.	2100–2599 Noon	64.	Monroe		
6.	Linda	36.	1400–2099 Dorp	65.	Ashley		
7.	Gould	37.	2100–2599 Dorp	66.	3900–4199 Hart		
8.	4200–5399 Noon	38.	4200–5399 Noon	67.	4200–5399 Hart		
9.	1400–2099 Dorp	39.	Orton	68.	Orton		
10.	2600–3899 Hart	40.	Croft	69.	Walton		
11.	Ashley	41.	4200–5399 Hart	70.	2100–2599 Hart		
12.	Orton	42.	2600–3899 Noon	71.	4200–5399 Dorp		
13.	3900–4199 Hart	43.	4200–5399 Dorp	72.	3900–4199 Noon		
14.	1400–2099 Noon	44.	Gould	73.	2100–2599 Noon		
15.	4200–5399 Dorp	45.	3900–4199 Noon	74.	2600–3899 Dorp		
16.	4200–5399 Hart	46.	2600–3899 Dorp	75.	3900–4199 Hart		
17.	2600–3899 Noon	47.	1400–2099 Hart	76.	Croft		
18.	2100–2599 Dorp	48.	Linda	77.	Farmer		
19.	Croft	49.	Gould	78.	2100–2599 Hart		
20.	Brendan	50.	2100–2599 Hart	79.	4200–5399 Noon		
21.	Nolan	51.	2100–2599 Dorp	80.	4200–5399 Dorp		
22.	Farmer	52.	3900–4199 Dorp	81.	Brendan		
23.	3900–4199 Dorp	53.	2100–2599 Noon	82.	Monroe		
24.	3900–4199 Noon	54.	Brendan	83.	1400–2099 Noon		
25.	1400–3899 Hart	55.	Farmer	84.	3900–4199 Dorp		
26.	Linda	56.	2600–3899 Hart	85.	4200–5399 Hart		
27.	2100–2599 Hart	57.	4200–5399 Noon	86.	Linda		
28.	3900–4199 Hart	58.	1400–2099 Dorp	87.	Ashley		
29.	Monroe	59.	Nolan	88.	1400–2099 Dorp		
30.	2600–3899 Dorp						

Memory for Addresses—Scored Test Answer Key

1. D	14. C	27. E	40. A	53. A	66. C	79. E
2. B	15. A	28. C	41. D	54. C	67. D	80. A
3. C	16. D	29. D	42. B	55. C	68. D	81. C
4. A	17. B	30. C	43. A	56. A	69. B	82. D
5. E	18. D	31. C	44. E	57. E	70. E	83. C
6. A	19. A	32. C	45. D	58. E	71. A	84. B
7. E	20. C	33. B	46. C	59. E	72. D	85. D
8. E	21. E	34. A	47. B	60. A	73. A	86. A
9. E	22. C	35. A	48. A	61. A	74. C	87. B
10. A	23. B	36. E	49. E	62. C	75. C	88. E
11. B	24. D	37. D	50. E	63. B	76. A	
12. D	25. B	38. E	51. D	64. D	77. C	
13. C	26. A	39. D	52. B	65. B	78. E	

DETERMINE YOUR RAW SCORE

Memory for Addresses—Scored Test: Your score on Memory for Addresses is based on the number of questions you answered correctly minus one-fourth of the questions you answered incorrectly (number wrong divided by four):

1. Number of right answers   _____

2. Number of wrong answers   _____

3. Divide number wrong by 4   _____

4. Subtract answer from number right   _____

Raw Score =   _____

SELF-EVALUATION CHART

For the timed test, see how your raw score falls on the following scale. You should not be satisfied with less than "Excellent." Review all appropriate study material, then retake the test, if necessary.

IF your raw score was between	THEN your work was
75–88	Excellent
60–74	Good
45–59	Average
30–44	Fair
1–29	Poor

CHAPTER 16

NUMBER SERIES PRACTICE TESTS

TAKING THE TIMED TEST

This is your first real chance to answer Number Series questions under the time constraints of the actual test. To benefit the most from this practice, proceed as follows:

1. Choose a workspace that is quiet, well lit, clean, and uncluttered.

2. Use a stopwatch or kitchen timer to accurately time each test.

3. Start the first test at a convenient time and stop exactly when your 6 minutes are up.

4. Give yourself at least a 5-minute breather between each test. You can use this non-test time to skim through review material in earlier chapters.

5. After you complete all three tests, check your answers against the answer keys provided. Circle all wrong answers in red so that you can easily locate them.

6. Calculate your raw score for each test as instructed.

7. Check to see where your scores fall on the self-evaluation chart.

8. If you receive less than an "Excellent" score on a test, go back and review the appropriate study chapters in this book.

9. Retake the test to see your improvement.

Note that there is no guessing penalty on Part C. With this in mind, remember to guess if you are truly stumped or cannot finish the test in the time allowed.

TIMES PRACTICE TESTS

PRACTICE TEST I
Time: 20 Minutes • 24 Questions

> *Directions: For each question below, there is at the left a series of numbers that follows some definite order and at the right five sets of two numbers each. You are to look at the numbers in the series at the left and find out what order they follow. Then decide what the next two numbers in the series would be if the series were continued. Circle the letter of the correct answer.*

1. 19 18 12 17 16 13 15 ..... (A) 16 12   (B) 14 14   (C) 12 14   (D) 14 12   (E) 12 16

2. 7 15 12 8 16 13 9 .... (A) 17 14   (B) 17 10   (C) 14 10   (D) 14 17   (E) 10 14

3. 18 15 6 16 14 6 14 .... (A) 12 6   (B) 14 13   (C) 6 12   (D) 13 12   (E) 33 6

4. 6 6 5 8 8 7 10 10 .... (A) 8 12   (B) 9 12   (C) 22 12   (D) 12 9   (E) 9 9

5. 17 20 23 26 29 32 35 ..... (A) 37 40   (B) 41 44   (C) 38 41   (D) 38 42   (E) 36 39

6. 15 5 7 16 9 11 17 .... (A) 18 13   (B) 15 17   (C) 12 19   (D) 13 15   (E) 12 13

7. 19 17 16 16 13 15 10 ..... (A) 14 7   (B) 12 9   (C) 14 9   (D) 7 12   (E) 10 14

8. 11 1 16 10 6 21 9 .... (A) 12 26   (B) 26 8   (C) 11 26   (D) 11 8   (E) 8 11

9. 15 22 19 26 23 30 27 ..... (A) 28 34   (B) 27 35   (C) 31 34   (D) 29 33   (E) 34 31

10. 99 9 88 8 77 7 66 .... (A) 55 5   (B) 6 55   (C) 66 5   (D) 55 6   (E) 55 44

11. 25 29 29 33 37 37 41 ..... (A) 41 41   (B) 41 45   (C) 45 49   (D) 45 45   (E) 49 49

12. 81 71 61 52 43 35 27 ..... (A) 27 20   (B) 21 14   (C) 20 14   (D) 21 15   (E) 20 13

13. 12 14 16 48 50 52 156 ... (A) 468 470   (B) 158 316   (C) 158 474   (D) 158 160   (E) 158 158

14. 47 42 38 35 30 26 23 ..... (A) 18 14   (B) 21 19   (C) 23 18   (D) 19 14   (E) 19 13

15. 84 84 91 91 97 97 102 ... (A) 102 102   (B) 102 104   (C) 104 106   (D) 106 106   (E) 102 106

16. 66 13 62 21 58 29 54 ..... (A) 50 48   (B) 62 66   (C) 34 42   (D) 37 50   (E) 58 21

17. 14 12 10 10 20 18 16 16   (A) 32 32   (B) 32 30   (C) 30 28   (D) 16 32   (E) 16 14

18. 25 30 35 30 25 30 35 ..... (A) 30 40   (B) 25 30   (C) 25 20   (D) 35 30   (E) 30 25

19. 19 19 19 57 57 57 171 ... (A) 171 513   (B) 513 513   (C) 171 171   (D) 171 57   (E) 57 18

20. 75 69 63 57 51 45 39 ..... (A) 36 33   (B) 39 36   (C) 39 33   (D) 33 27   (E) 33 33

21. 6 15 23 30 36 41 45 .... (A) 48 50   (B) 49 53   (C) 45 41   (D) 46 47   (E) 47 49

22. 12 58 25 51 38 44 51 ..... (A) 64 37   (B) 37 64   (C) 51 51   (D) 51 64   (E) 51 37

23. 1 2 4 8 16 32 64 .... (A) 64 32   (B) 64 64   (C) 64 128   (D) 128 256   (E) 128 128

24. 5 86 7 81 10 77 14 .... (A) 16 80   (B) 70 25   (C) 79 13   (D) 19 74   (E) 74 19

PRACTICE TEST II

Time: 20 Minutes • 24 Questions

> **Directions:** *For each question below, there is at the left a series of numbers that follows some definite order and at the right five sets of two numbers each. You are to look at the numbers in the series at the left and find out what order they follow. Then decide what the next two numbers in the series would be if the series were continued. Circle the letter of the correct answer.*

1. 5 7 30 9 11 30 13 .... (A) 15 16   (B) 15 17   (C) 14 17   (D) 15 30   (E) 30 17

2. 5 7 11 13 17 19 23 .... (A) 27 29   (B) 25 29   (C) 25 27   (D) 27 31   (E) 29 31

3. 9 15 10 17 12 19 15 21 19 . (A) 23 24   (B) 25 23   (C) 17 23   (D) 23 31   (E) 21 24

4. 34 37 30 33 26 29 22 .... (A) 17 8   (B) 18 11   (C) 25 28   (D) 25 20   (E) 25 18

5. 10 16 12 14 14 12 16 .... (A) 14 12   (B) 10 18   (C) 10 14   (D) 14 18   (E) 14 16

6. 11 12 18 11 13 19 11 14 .... (A) 18 11   (B) 16 11   (C) 20 11   (D) 11 21   (E) 17 11

7. 20 9 8 19 10 9 18 11 10 ..... (A) 19 11   (B) 17 10   (C) 19 12   (D) 17 12   (E) 19 10

8. 28 27 26 31 30 29 34 .... (A) 36 32   (B) 32 31   (C) 33 32   (D) 33 36   (E) 35 36

9. 12 24 15 30 21 42 33 .... (A) 66 57   (B) 44 56   (C) 28 43   (D) 47 69   (E) 24 48

10. 46 76 51 70 56 64 61 .... (A) 61 68   (B) 69 71   (C) 58 65   (D) 66 71   (E) 58 66

11. 37 28 28 19 19 10 10 .... (A) 9 9   (B) 1 1   (C) 10 9   (D) 10 1   (E) 9 1

12. 1 2 3 6 4 5 6 15 7 .... (A) 8 15   (B) 7 8   (C) 8 9   (D) 9 17   (E) 9 24

13. 55 51 12 56 52 12 57 .... (A) 57 12   (B) 12 53   (C) 58 12   (D) 53 12   (E) 12 57

14. 75 75 8 50 50 9 25 .... (A) 25 25   (B) 25 10   (C) 10 25   (D) 25 12   (E) 10 10

15. 1 2 3 4 5 5 4 .... (A) 3 2   (B) 5 4   (C) 4 5   (D) 5 6   (E) 4 4

16. 3 6 9 4 7 10 5 .... (A) 8 9   (B) 9 6   (C) 8 11   (D) 9 12   (E) 11 8

17. 5 7 9 18 20 22 44 .... (A) 60 66   (B) 66 80   (C) 66 68   (D) 88 90   (E) 46 48

18. 94 82 72 64 58 54 .... (A) 52 50   (B) 54 52   (C) 50 46   (D) 52 52   (E) 54 50

19. 85 85 86 85 86 87 85 .... (A) 85 86   (B) 86 87   (C) 87 89   (D) 87 86   (E) 84 83

20. 99 89 79 69 59 49 39 .... (A) 29 19   (B) 39 29   (C) 38 37   (D) 39 38   (E) 19 9

21. 33 42 41 39 48 47 45 .... (A) 42 041   (B) 44 42   (C) 54 53   (D) 54 52   (E) 54 63

22. 85 89 89 84 88 88 83 .... (A) 83 87   (B) 83 83   (C) 87 87   (D) 87 82   (E) 87 83

23. 1 2 3 3 4 5 5 6 7 .... (A) 7 7   (B) 8 8   (C) 8 9   (D) 7 6   (E) 7 8

24. 5 10 15 15 20 15 25 .... (A) 30 35   (B) 15 30   (C) 15 15   (D) 30 15   (E) 30 30

PRACTICE TEST ANSWERS

PRACTICE TEST I

		Practice Test I Answer Key			
1. B	5. C	9. E	13. D	17. B	21. A
2. A	6. D	10. B	14. A	18. E	22. B
3. E	7. A	11. D	15. E	19. C	23. D
4. B	8. C	12. E	16. D	20. D	24. E

PRACTICE TEST I EXPLANATIONS

1. **The correct answer is (B).** There are two series. The first series descends one number at a time, beginning with 19. The second series enters between each two numbers of the first series. The second series increases by +1. Thus, the series are: 19 18 17 16 15 14 and 12 13 14.

2. **The correct answer is (A).** The repeating pattern is +8, –3, –5.

3. **The correct answer is (E).** This is a difficult problem. The first series begins with 18 and decreases by 2: 18 16 14, and so forth. The second series begins with 15 and descends by 1: 15 14 13, and so forth. The number 6 separates each pair of descending numbers.

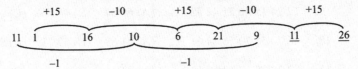

4. **The correct answer is (B).** The even numbers repeat themselves as they increase; the odd numbers simply increase by 2, alternating with the evens.

5. **The correct answer is (C).** Just add three to each number to get the next number.

6. **The correct answer is (D).** One series increases by 1: 15 16 17 18. The other series, which intervenes with two numbers to the first series' one, increases by 2: 5 7 9 11 13.

7. **The correct answer is (A).** The rule for the first series is –3. The rule for the alternating series is –1.

8. **The correct answer is (C).** There are two series here. The first reads 11 10 9. The second series starts at 1 and follows the rule +15, –10, +15, –10. The second series takes two steps to the first series' one. The solution to this problem is best seen by diagramming.

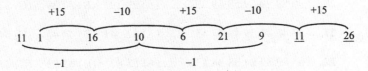

9. **The correct answer is (E).** The pattern is: +7, –3; +7, –3; and so on. Or, you might see alternating series, both increasing by +4.

10. **The correct answer is (B).** You might see two series. One series decreases at the rate of 11; the other decreases at the rate of 1. Or, you might see a series of the multiples of 11 each divided by 11.

11. **The correct answer is (D).** The pattern is +4, repeat the number, +4; +4, repeat the number, +4; +4, repeat the number, +4, and so on.

12. **The correct answer is (E).** The pattern is: −10, −10, −9, −9, −8, −8, −7, −7, −6, and so on.

13. **The correct answer is (D).** The pattern is: +2, +2, ×3; +2, +2, ×3, and so on.

14. **The correct answer is (A).** The pattern is: −5, −4, −3; −5, −4, −3; −5, and so on.

15. **The correct answer is (E).** The pattern is: repeat the number, +7, repeat the number, +6, repeat the number, +5, repeat the number, +4, and so on.

16. **The correct answer is (D).** There are two alternating series. The first series descends at the rate of 4. The alternating series ascends at the rate of 8.

17. **The correct answer is (B).** The pattern is: −2, −2, repeat the number, ×2; −2, −2, repeat the number, ×2; −2, and so on.

18. **The correct answer is (E).** The pattern is: +5, +5, −5, −5; +5, +5, −5, −5; and so on. Or you might see the repeat of the four numbers 25, 30, 35, 30.

19. **The correct answer is (C).** The pattern is: repeat the number three times, ×3; repeat the number three times, ×3; repeat the number three times, ×3.

20. **The correct answer is (D).** The pattern is simply: −6, −6, −6, and so on.

21. **The correct answer is (A).** The pattern is: +9, +8, +7, +6, +5, +4, +3, +2, +1.

22. **The correct answer is (B).** There are two alternating series. The first series increases at the rate of +13. The alternating series decreases at the rate of −7.

23. **The correct answer is (D).** The pattern is: ×2, ×2, ×2, and so on.

24. **The correct answer is (E).** There are two alternating series. The pattern of the first series is: +2, +3, +4, +5. The pattern of the alternating series is: −5, −4, −3, −2.

DETERMINE YOUR RAW SCORE

Practice Test I: Your score is based on the number of questions answered correctly:

Enter number right _____

Raw Score = _____

Practice Test II Answer Key					
1. D	5. B	9. A	13. D	17. E	21. C
2. B	6. C	10. E	14. B	18. D	22. C
3. A	7. D	11. B	15. A	19. B	23. E
4. E	8. C	12. C	16. C	20. A	24. D

PRACTICE TEST II EXPLANATIONS

1. **The correct answer is (D).** The series increases by 2. The number 30 appears after each two numbers in the series.

2. **The correct answer is (B).** The pattern is: +2, +4; +2, +4; +2, +4; and so on.

3. **The correct answer is (A).** There are two alternating series that advance according to different rules. The first series begins with 9. The rule for this series is +1, +2, +3, +4, +5. The alternating series begins with 15 and advances in steady increments of 2.

4. **The correct answer is (E).** There are two alternating series, one series beginning with 34 and the other with 37. Both series decrease by subtracting 4 each time.

5. **The correct answer is (B).** The two series are moving in opposite directions. The first series begins with 10 and increases by 2. The alternating series begins with 16 and decreases by 2.

6. **The correct answer is (C).** You might be able to figure this one by reading it rhythmically. If not, consider that there are two series, one beginning with 12, the other with 18. Both series advance by 1. The number 11 separates each progression of the two series.

7. **The correct answer is (D).** There are two series alternating at the rate of 1 to 2. The first series decreases by 1: 20 19 18 17. The other series goes one step backward and two steps forward, or − 1, +2. Read: 9^{-1} 8^{+2} 10^{-1} 9^{+2} 11^{-1} 10^{+2} 12.

8. **The correct answer is (C).** The pattern is −1, −1, +5, and repeat; −1, −1, +5, and repeat again.

9. **The correct answer is (A).** The pattern is: ×2, −9; ×2, −9; and so on.

10. **The correct answer is (E).** There are two alternating series. The first series increases by 5. The alternating series decreases at the rate of 6.

11. **The correct answer is (B).** The pattern is −9 and repeat the number; −9 and repeat the number; −9 and repeat the number.

12. **The correct answer is (C).** The series is: 1 2 3 4 5 6 7 8, and so on. After each three numbers in the series we find the sum of those three numbers. So: 1 + 2 + 3 = 6; 4 + 5 + 6 = 15; 7 + 8 + 9 = 24; 10, and so on.

13. **The correct answer is (D).** The pattern is −4, +5, and the number 12; −4, +5, and the number 12, and so on.

14. **The correct answer is (B).** There are two series. One series proceeds: repeat the number, −25; repeat the number, −25. The other series simply advances by 1.

15. **The correct answer is (A).** The series proceeds upward from 1 to 5, and then turns around and descends, one number at a time.

16. **The correct answer is (C).** There are two interpretations for this series. You may see +3, +3, –5; +3, +3, –5, and so on. Or, you might see a series of +3, +3 mini-series, each mini-series beginning at a number one higher than the beginning number of the previous mini-series.

17. **The correct answer is (E).** The pattern is: +2, +2, ×2; +2, +2, ×2, and so on.

18. **The correct answer is (D).** The pattern is: –12, –10, –8, –6, –4, –2, –0, and so on.

19. **The correct answer is (B).** Each mini-series begins with 85. With each cycle the series progresses to one more number: 85; 85 86; 85 86 87; 85 86 87 88, and so on.

20. **The correct answer is (A).** This is a simple –10 series.

21. **The correct answer is (C).** The pattern is: +9, –1, –2; +9, –1, –2, and so on.

22. **The correct answer is (C).** The pattern is +4, repeat the number, –5; +4, repeat the number, –5; +4, and so on. You might instead have seen two descending series, one beginning with 85 and descending by 1, the other beginning with 89 and repeating itself before each descent.

23. **The correct answer is (E).** This is a deceptive series. Actually, the series consists of a series of mini-series, each beginning with the last number of the previous mini-series. If you group the numbers, you can see: 1 2 3; 3 4 5; 5 6 7; 7 8, and so on.

24. **The correct answer is (D).** The series is a +5 series with the number 15 interposing after each two numbers of the series. If you substitute X for the interposing 15, you can see that the series reads: 5 10 X 15 20 X 25 30 X.

DETERMINE YOUR RAW SCORE

Practice Test II: Your score is based on the number of questions answered correctly:

Enter number right _____

Raw Score = _____

SELF-EVALUATION CHART

For each practice test, see how your raw score falls on the following scale. You should not be satisfied with less than "Excellent." Review all appropriate study material, and then retake the test(s) where you need improvement.

IF your raw score was between	THEN your work was
25–24	Excellent
18–20	Good
14–17	Average
11–13	Fair
1–10	Poor

CHAPTER 17

Following Oral Instructions Practice Tests

TAKING THE TIMED TEST

Because of the nature of this question type, you're going to need someone to help you practice with Oral Instructions questions. However, you can still simulate the actual conditions of the real test, if you follow these steps:

1. Before starting the test, give your reader (the person who is helping you practice for this question type) at least 10 to 15 minutes to practice reading the oral instructions (preferably, in a separate room), so he or she can get comfortable with the material.

2. Choose a workspace that is quiet, well lit, and uncluttered. Make sure that you also have a comfortable sitting or standing place for your reader.

3. Given that you are depending on the assistance of another person for this question type, be sure to schedule a time when the both of you are not rushed, so you can relax and concentrate on the task at hand.

4. Proceed through the entire test without repeating any instructions!

5. After finishing the test, check your answers against the correctly completed answer grid and worksheet. Circle any incorrect answers and mistakes on your worksheet.

If you really want to be fully prepared for this question type, you might also arrange to have someone read and record the instructions on tape. Depending on where you take the test, you might have a live reader, or you might have to take this section of the test by listening to a prerecorded tape.

TIMED PRACTICE TEST

The answer sheet, worksheet, and oral instructions for this practice test are on the following pages. **You will have 25 minutes to complete the test.**

ANSWER SHEET

1. Ⓐ Ⓑ Ⓒ Ⓓ Ⓔ	23. Ⓐ Ⓑ Ⓒ Ⓓ Ⓔ	45. Ⓐ Ⓑ Ⓒ Ⓓ Ⓔ	67. Ⓐ Ⓑ Ⓒ Ⓓ Ⓔ
2. Ⓐ Ⓑ Ⓒ Ⓓ Ⓔ	24. Ⓐ Ⓑ Ⓒ Ⓓ Ⓔ	46. Ⓐ Ⓑ Ⓒ Ⓓ Ⓔ	68. Ⓐ Ⓑ Ⓒ Ⓓ Ⓔ
3. Ⓐ Ⓑ Ⓒ Ⓓ Ⓔ	25. Ⓐ Ⓑ Ⓒ Ⓓ Ⓔ	47. Ⓐ Ⓑ Ⓒ Ⓓ Ⓔ	69. Ⓐ Ⓑ Ⓒ Ⓓ Ⓔ
4. Ⓐ Ⓑ Ⓒ Ⓓ Ⓔ	26. Ⓐ Ⓑ Ⓒ Ⓓ Ⓔ	48. Ⓐ Ⓑ Ⓒ Ⓓ Ⓔ	70. Ⓐ Ⓑ Ⓒ Ⓓ Ⓔ
5. Ⓐ Ⓑ Ⓒ Ⓓ Ⓔ	27. Ⓐ Ⓑ Ⓒ Ⓓ Ⓔ	49. Ⓐ Ⓑ Ⓒ Ⓓ Ⓔ	71. Ⓐ Ⓑ Ⓒ Ⓓ Ⓔ
6. Ⓐ Ⓑ Ⓒ Ⓓ Ⓔ	28. Ⓐ Ⓑ Ⓒ Ⓓ Ⓔ	50. Ⓐ Ⓑ Ⓒ Ⓓ Ⓔ	72. Ⓐ Ⓑ Ⓒ Ⓓ Ⓔ
7. Ⓐ Ⓑ Ⓒ Ⓓ Ⓔ	29. Ⓐ Ⓑ Ⓒ Ⓓ Ⓔ	51. Ⓐ Ⓑ Ⓒ Ⓓ Ⓔ	73. Ⓐ Ⓑ Ⓒ Ⓓ Ⓔ
8. Ⓐ Ⓑ Ⓒ Ⓓ Ⓔ	30. Ⓐ Ⓑ Ⓒ Ⓓ Ⓔ	52. Ⓐ Ⓑ Ⓒ Ⓓ Ⓔ	74. Ⓐ Ⓑ Ⓒ Ⓓ Ⓔ
9. Ⓐ Ⓑ Ⓒ Ⓓ Ⓔ	31. Ⓐ Ⓑ Ⓒ Ⓓ Ⓔ	53. Ⓐ Ⓑ Ⓒ Ⓓ Ⓔ	75. Ⓐ Ⓑ Ⓒ Ⓓ Ⓔ
10. Ⓐ Ⓑ Ⓒ Ⓓ Ⓔ	32. Ⓐ Ⓑ Ⓒ Ⓓ Ⓔ	54. Ⓐ Ⓑ Ⓒ Ⓓ Ⓔ	76. Ⓐ Ⓑ Ⓒ Ⓓ Ⓔ
11. Ⓐ Ⓑ Ⓒ Ⓓ Ⓔ	33. Ⓐ Ⓑ Ⓒ Ⓓ Ⓔ	55. Ⓐ Ⓑ Ⓒ Ⓓ Ⓔ	77. Ⓐ Ⓑ Ⓒ Ⓓ Ⓔ
12. Ⓐ Ⓑ Ⓒ Ⓓ Ⓔ	34. Ⓐ Ⓑ Ⓒ Ⓓ Ⓔ	56. Ⓐ Ⓑ Ⓒ Ⓓ Ⓔ	78. Ⓐ Ⓑ Ⓒ Ⓓ Ⓔ
13. Ⓐ Ⓑ Ⓒ Ⓓ Ⓔ	35. Ⓐ Ⓑ Ⓒ Ⓓ Ⓔ	57. Ⓐ Ⓑ Ⓒ Ⓓ Ⓔ	79. Ⓐ Ⓑ Ⓒ Ⓓ Ⓔ
14. Ⓐ Ⓑ Ⓒ Ⓓ Ⓔ	36. Ⓐ Ⓑ Ⓒ Ⓓ Ⓔ	58. Ⓐ Ⓑ Ⓒ Ⓓ Ⓔ	80. Ⓐ Ⓑ Ⓒ Ⓓ Ⓔ
15. Ⓐ Ⓑ Ⓒ Ⓓ Ⓔ	37. Ⓐ Ⓑ Ⓒ Ⓓ Ⓔ	59. Ⓐ Ⓑ Ⓒ Ⓓ Ⓔ	81. Ⓐ Ⓑ Ⓒ Ⓓ Ⓔ
16. Ⓐ Ⓑ Ⓒ Ⓓ Ⓔ	38. Ⓐ Ⓑ Ⓒ Ⓓ Ⓔ	60. Ⓐ Ⓑ Ⓒ Ⓓ Ⓔ	82. Ⓐ Ⓑ Ⓒ Ⓓ Ⓔ
17. Ⓐ Ⓑ Ⓒ Ⓓ Ⓔ	39. Ⓐ Ⓑ Ⓒ Ⓓ Ⓔ	61. Ⓐ Ⓑ Ⓒ Ⓓ Ⓔ	83. Ⓐ Ⓑ Ⓒ Ⓓ Ⓔ
18. Ⓐ Ⓑ Ⓒ Ⓓ Ⓔ	40. Ⓐ Ⓑ Ⓒ Ⓓ Ⓔ	62. Ⓐ Ⓑ Ⓒ Ⓓ Ⓔ	84. Ⓐ Ⓑ Ⓒ Ⓓ Ⓔ
19. Ⓐ Ⓑ Ⓒ Ⓓ Ⓔ	41. Ⓐ Ⓑ Ⓒ Ⓓ Ⓔ	63. Ⓐ Ⓑ Ⓒ Ⓓ Ⓔ	85. Ⓐ Ⓑ Ⓒ Ⓓ Ⓔ
20. Ⓐ Ⓑ Ⓒ Ⓓ Ⓔ	42. Ⓐ Ⓑ Ⓒ Ⓓ Ⓔ	64. Ⓐ Ⓑ Ⓒ Ⓓ Ⓔ	86. Ⓐ Ⓑ Ⓒ Ⓓ Ⓔ
21. Ⓐ Ⓑ Ⓒ Ⓓ Ⓔ	43. Ⓐ Ⓑ Ⓒ Ⓓ Ⓔ	65. Ⓐ Ⓑ Ⓒ Ⓓ Ⓔ	87. Ⓐ Ⓑ Ⓒ Ⓓ Ⓔ
22. Ⓐ Ⓑ Ⓒ Ⓓ Ⓔ	44. Ⓐ Ⓑ Ⓒ Ⓓ Ⓔ	66. Ⓐ Ⓑ Ⓒ Ⓓ Ⓔ	88. Ⓐ Ⓑ Ⓒ Ⓓ Ⓔ

WORKSHEET

> *Directions:* Listen carefully to the instructions read to you, and mark each item on this worksheet as directed. Then, complete each question by marking the answer sheet as directed. For each answer, you will darken the answer sheet for a number-letter combination.

1. 16   88   3   51   46   71   24

2. C   A   E   D   B

3. [__ B]   [__ D]   [__ C]   [__ A]   [__ E]

4. (56 __) (13 __) (85 __) (37 __) (44 __) (32 __) (41 __)

5. [B $9.00]   [C $42.00]   [E $19.00]

6. 87 ___   27 ___   64 ___   PLANE   TRAIN   BUS

7. 46   35   39   43   42   38

8. G   D   P   F   E   C   L   J

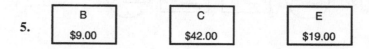

9. △2   ☆20   ○11   □5

10. 74   21   53   57   42   51

11. [18 __]   [47 __]   [56 __]   [31 __]

12. 64   82   90   75   81   76

13. [27 __]   (19 __)   (32 __)   [12 __]

14. 24B   36A   44C   20E   26D

15. 89 _____   61 _____

16. T   T   V   W   V   T   V   T   W   V   V

17.

5:36	_____
5:21	_____
5:43	_____
5:59	_____
5:38	_____

18. (__E) (__D) (__A) (__B) (__C)

19. (__C) [__A] [__B] (__E)

ORAL INSTRUCTIONS

On the job you will have to listen to directions and then do what you have been told to do. In this test, I will read instructions to you. Try to understand them as I read them; I cannot repeat them. Once we begin, you may not ask any questions until the end of the test.

On the job you won't have to deal with pictures, numbers, and letters like those in the test, but you will have to listen to instructions and follow them. We are using this test to see how well you can follow instructions.

You are to mark your test booklet according to the instructions that I'll read to you. After each set of instructions, I'll give you time to record your answers on the separate answer sheet.

The actual test begins now.

Look at line 1 on your worksheet. (Pause slightly.) Draw a line under the sixth number in line 1. (Pause 2 seconds.) Now, on your answer sheet, darken space E for the number under which you just drew a line. (Pause 5 seconds.)

Look at line 1 again. (Pause slightly.) Draw two lines under the third number on the line. (Pause 2 seconds.) Now, on your answer sheet, darken space B as in baker for the number under which you drew two lines. (Pause 5 seconds.)

Look at line 2 on your worksheet. (Pause slightly.) Find the letter that is fifth in the alphabet and circle it. (Pause 2 seconds.) Now darken that letter for number 77 on your answer sheet. (Pause 5 seconds.)

Look at line 3 on your worksheet. (Pause slightly.) Write the number 17 in the third box. (Pause 2 seconds.) Now, on your answer sheet, darken the number-letter combination that is in the box in which you just wrote. (Pause 5 seconds.)

Look at line 3 again. (Pause slightly.) In the fourth box, write the number of hours in a day. (Pause 2 seconds.) Now, on your answer sheet, darken the number-letter combination that is in the box in which you just wrote. (Pause 5 seconds.)

Look at line 4 on your worksheet. (Pause slightly.) Write D as in dog in the circle right next to the second-lowest number. (Pause 5 seconds.) Now, on your answer sheet, darken the space for the number-letter combination in the circle in which you just wrote. (Pause 5 seconds.)

Look at line 4 again. (Pause slightly.) Write the letter C on the line in the middle circle. (Pause 2 seconds.) Now, on your answer sheet, darken the space for the number-letter combination in the circle in which you just wrote. (Pause 5 seconds.)

Look at line 5 on your worksheet. Each box represents a letter carrier and the amount of money that he or she collected on the route in one day. (Pause slightly.) Find the carrier who collected the smallest amount of money that day and circle his or her letter. (Pause 2 seconds.) On your answer sheet, darken the number-letter combination in the box in which you circled a letter. (Pause 5 seconds.)

Look at line 6 on your worksheet. (Pause slightly.) Write the first letter of the third means of transportation on the second line. (Pause 8 seconds.) Write the last letter of the first means of transportation on the first line. (Pause 8 seconds.) Write the middle letter of the middle means of transportation on the last line. (Pause 8 seconds.) Now, on your answer sheet, darken the number-letter combinations on the three lines. (Pause 15 seconds.)

Look at line 7 on your worksheet. (Pause slightly.) Reading right to left, find the first number that is higher than the number 39 and draw a box around the number. (Pause 5 seconds.) Now, on your answer sheet, darken D as in dog for the number around which you just drew a box. (Pause 5 seconds.)

Look at line 8 on your worksheet. (Pause slightly.) Find, on line 8, the letter that appears first in the alphabet and underline that letter. (Pause 5 seconds.) Now, on your answer sheet, darken that letter for space number 1. (Pause 5 seconds.)

Look at line 9 on your worksheet. (Pause slightly.) In the figure with the least number of points, write the letter A. (Pause 2 seconds.) In the figure with the greatest number of points, write the letter E. (Pause 2 seconds.) Now, on your answer sheet, darken the number-letter combinations in the two figures in which you just wrote. (Pause 10 seconds.)

Look at line 10 on your worksheet. (Pause slightly.) If the third number in line 10 should, in normal counting, appear before the fourth number in line 10, write the letter B as in baker above the third number; if not, write the letter A above the fourth number. (Pause 5 seconds.) Now, on your answer sheet, darken the number-letter combination of the number you just wrote. (Pause 5 seconds.)

Look at line 11 on your worksheet. (Pause slightly.) Write the letter A in the second box. (Pause 2 seconds.) Now, on your answer sheet, darken the number-letter combination in the box in which you just wrote. (Pause 5 seconds.)

Look at line 11 again. (Pause slightly.) If the number in the smallest box is greater than the number in the first box, write the letter C in the largest box (pause 5 seconds); if not, write the letter D as in dog in the largest box. (Pause 2 seconds.) Now, on your answer sheet, darken the number-letter combination in the box in which you just wrote. (Pause 5 seconds.)

Look at line 12 on your worksheet. (Pause slightly.) Draw one line under each number that falls between 75 and 90 and is even. (Pause 8 seconds.) Now, on your answer sheet, blacken space D as in dog for each number under which you drew one line. (Pause 10 seconds.)

Look at line 12 again. (Pause slightly.) Draw two lines under each number that falls between 75 and 90 and is odd. (Pause 8 seconds.) Now, on your answer sheet, darken space E for each number under which you drew two lines. (Pause 5 seconds.)

Look at line 13 on your worksheet. (Pause slightly.) Write the letter A in the left-hand circle. (Pause 2 seconds.) Now, on your answer sheet, darken the space for the number-letter combination in the figure in which you just wrote. (Pause 5 seconds.)

Look at line 13 again. (Pause slightly.) Write the letter B as in baker in the right-hand square. (Pause 2 seconds.) Now, on your answer sheet, darken the space for the number-letter combination in the figure in which you just wrote. (Pause 5 seconds.)

Look at line 14 on your worksheet. (Pause slightly.) Write the answer to this question at the end of line 14: $22 \times 2 =$. (Pause 2 seconds.) Find the answer that you wrote among the numbers on line 14 (pause 2 seconds) and darken that number-letter combination on your answer sheet. (Pause 5 seconds.)

Look at line 15 on your worksheet. (Pause slightly.) If 3 is less than 5 and more than 7, write the letter E next to number 89 (pause 5 seconds); if not, write the letter E next to number 61. (Pause 2 seconds.) Now, on your answer sheet, darken the number-letter combination of the line on which you just wrote. (Pause 5 seconds.)

Look at line 16 on your worksheet. (Pause slightly.) Count the number of V's on line 16 and write the number at the end of the line. (Pause 2 seconds.) Now, add 11 to that number and, on your answer sheet, darken space D as in dog for the number of V's plus 11. (Pause 10 seconds.)

Look at line 17 on your worksheet. (Pause slightly.) Each time represents the scheduled arrival time of a mail truck. Write the letter A on the line beside the earliest scheduled time. (Pause 2 seconds.) Write the letter C next to the latest scheduled time. (Pause 2 seconds.) Now, on your answer sheet, darken the number-letter combinations of the last two digits of the times beside which you wrote letters. (Pause 10 seconds.)

Look at line 18 on your worksheet. (Pause slightly.) If in one day there are more hours before noon than after noon, write the number 47 in the second circle (pause 2 seconds); if not, write the number 38 in the first circle. (Pause 2 seconds.) Now, on your answer sheet, blacken the space for the number-letter combination in the circle in which you just wrote. (Pause 5 seconds.)

Look at line 18 again. (Pause slightly.) Write the number 69 in the second circle from the right. (Pause 2 seconds.) Now, on your answer sheet, darken the space for the number-letter combination in the circle in which you just wrote. (Pause 5 seconds.)

Look at line 19 on your worksheet. (Pause slightly.) Write the smallest of these numbers in the first box: 84, 35, 73. (Pause 5 seconds.) Now, on your answer sheet, darken the space for the number-letter combination in the figure in which you just wrote. (Pause 5 seconds.)

PRACTICE TEST ANSWERS

1. Ⓐ Ⓑ ● Ⓓ Ⓔ	23. Ⓐ Ⓑ Ⓒ Ⓓ Ⓔ	45. Ⓐ Ⓑ Ⓒ Ⓓ Ⓔ	67. Ⓐ Ⓑ Ⓒ Ⓓ Ⓔ
2. Ⓐ Ⓑ Ⓒ Ⓓ Ⓔ	24. ● Ⓑ Ⓒ Ⓓ Ⓔ	46. Ⓐ Ⓑ Ⓒ Ⓓ Ⓔ	68. Ⓐ Ⓑ Ⓒ Ⓓ Ⓔ
3. Ⓐ ● Ⓒ Ⓓ Ⓔ	25. Ⓐ Ⓑ Ⓒ Ⓓ Ⓔ	47. ● Ⓑ Ⓒ Ⓓ Ⓔ	69. Ⓐ ● Ⓒ Ⓓ Ⓔ
4. Ⓐ Ⓑ Ⓒ Ⓓ Ⓔ	26. Ⓐ Ⓑ Ⓒ Ⓓ Ⓔ	48. Ⓐ Ⓑ Ⓒ Ⓓ Ⓔ	70. Ⓐ Ⓑ Ⓒ Ⓓ Ⓔ
5. Ⓐ Ⓑ Ⓒ Ⓓ Ⓔ	27. Ⓐ ● Ⓒ Ⓓ Ⓔ	49. Ⓐ Ⓑ Ⓒ Ⓓ Ⓔ	71. Ⓐ Ⓑ Ⓒ Ⓓ ●
6. Ⓐ Ⓑ Ⓒ Ⓓ Ⓔ	28. Ⓐ Ⓑ Ⓒ Ⓓ Ⓔ	50. Ⓐ Ⓑ Ⓒ Ⓓ Ⓔ	72. Ⓐ Ⓑ Ⓒ Ⓓ Ⓔ
7. Ⓐ Ⓑ Ⓒ Ⓓ Ⓔ	29. Ⓐ Ⓑ Ⓒ Ⓓ Ⓔ	51. Ⓐ Ⓑ Ⓒ Ⓓ Ⓔ	73. Ⓐ Ⓑ Ⓒ Ⓓ Ⓔ
8. Ⓐ Ⓑ Ⓒ Ⓓ Ⓔ	30. Ⓐ Ⓑ Ⓒ Ⓓ Ⓔ	52. Ⓐ Ⓑ Ⓒ Ⓓ Ⓔ	74. Ⓐ Ⓑ Ⓒ Ⓓ Ⓔ
9. Ⓐ ● Ⓒ Ⓓ Ⓔ	31. Ⓐ Ⓑ Ⓒ Ⓓ Ⓔ	53. Ⓐ ● Ⓒ Ⓓ Ⓔ	75. Ⓐ Ⓑ Ⓒ Ⓓ Ⓔ
10. Ⓐ Ⓑ Ⓒ Ⓓ Ⓔ	32. Ⓐ Ⓑ Ⓒ ● Ⓔ	54. Ⓐ Ⓑ Ⓒ Ⓓ Ⓔ	76. Ⓐ Ⓑ Ⓒ ● Ⓔ
11. ● Ⓑ Ⓒ Ⓓ Ⓔ	33. Ⓐ Ⓑ Ⓒ Ⓓ Ⓔ	55. Ⓐ Ⓑ Ⓒ Ⓓ Ⓔ	77. Ⓐ Ⓑ Ⓒ Ⓓ ●
12. Ⓐ ● Ⓒ Ⓓ Ⓔ	34. Ⓐ Ⓑ Ⓒ Ⓓ Ⓔ	56. Ⓐ Ⓑ ● Ⓓ Ⓔ	78. Ⓐ Ⓑ Ⓒ Ⓓ Ⓔ
13. Ⓐ Ⓑ Ⓒ Ⓓ Ⓔ	35. ● Ⓑ Ⓒ Ⓓ Ⓔ	57. Ⓐ Ⓑ Ⓒ Ⓓ Ⓔ	79. Ⓐ Ⓑ Ⓒ Ⓓ Ⓔ
14. Ⓐ Ⓑ Ⓒ Ⓓ Ⓔ	36. Ⓐ Ⓑ Ⓒ Ⓓ Ⓔ	58. Ⓐ Ⓑ Ⓒ Ⓓ Ⓔ	80. Ⓐ Ⓑ Ⓒ Ⓓ Ⓔ
15. Ⓐ Ⓑ Ⓒ Ⓓ Ⓔ	37. Ⓐ Ⓑ ● Ⓓ Ⓔ	59. Ⓐ Ⓑ ● Ⓓ Ⓔ	81. Ⓐ Ⓑ Ⓒ Ⓓ ●
16. Ⓐ Ⓑ Ⓒ ● Ⓔ	38. Ⓐ Ⓑ Ⓒ Ⓓ ●	60. Ⓐ Ⓑ Ⓒ Ⓓ Ⓔ	82. Ⓐ Ⓑ Ⓒ ● Ⓔ
17. Ⓐ Ⓑ ● Ⓓ Ⓔ	39. Ⓐ Ⓑ Ⓒ Ⓓ Ⓔ	61. Ⓐ Ⓑ Ⓒ Ⓓ ●	83. Ⓐ Ⓑ Ⓒ Ⓓ Ⓔ
18. Ⓐ Ⓑ Ⓒ Ⓓ Ⓔ	40. Ⓐ Ⓑ Ⓒ Ⓓ Ⓔ	62. Ⓐ Ⓑ Ⓒ Ⓓ Ⓔ	84. Ⓐ Ⓑ Ⓒ Ⓓ Ⓔ
19. ● Ⓑ Ⓒ Ⓓ Ⓔ	41. Ⓐ Ⓑ Ⓒ Ⓓ Ⓔ	63. Ⓐ Ⓑ Ⓒ Ⓓ Ⓔ	85. Ⓐ Ⓑ Ⓒ Ⓓ Ⓔ
20. Ⓐ Ⓑ Ⓒ Ⓓ ●	42. Ⓐ Ⓑ Ⓒ ● Ⓔ	64. ● Ⓑ Ⓒ Ⓓ Ⓔ	86. Ⓐ Ⓑ Ⓒ Ⓓ Ⓔ
21. ● Ⓑ Ⓒ Ⓓ Ⓔ	43. Ⓐ Ⓑ Ⓒ Ⓓ Ⓔ	65. Ⓐ Ⓑ Ⓒ Ⓓ Ⓔ	87. Ⓐ Ⓑ Ⓒ Ⓓ ●
22. Ⓐ Ⓑ Ⓒ Ⓓ Ⓔ	44. Ⓐ Ⓑ ● Ⓓ Ⓔ	66. Ⓐ Ⓑ Ⓒ Ⓓ Ⓔ	88. Ⓐ Ⓑ Ⓒ Ⓓ Ⓔ

CORRECTLY FILLED WORKSHEET

1. 16   88   <u>3</u>   51   46   <u>71</u>   24

2. C   A   Ⓔ   D   B

3. | ___ B | | ___ D | | <u>17</u> C | | <u>24</u> A | | ___ E |

4. (56 ___) (13 ___) (85 ___) (37 <u>C</u>) (44 ___) (32 <u>D</u>) (41 ___)

5. | Ⓑ $9.00 | | C $42.00 | | E $19.00 |

6. 87 <u>E</u>   27 <u>B</u>   64 <u>A</u>   PLANE   TRAIN   BUS

7. 46   35   39   43 | 42 | 38

8. G   D   P   F   E   <u>C</u>   L   J

9. △2   ☆ <u>E</u>20   Ⓐ11   □5

10. 74   21   <u>B</u>53   57   42   51

11. | 18 ___ | | 47 <u>A</u> | | 56 <u>C</u> | | 31 ___ |

12. 64   <u>82</u>   90   75   <u>81</u>   76

13. | 27 ___ | (19 <u>A</u>) (32 ___) | 12 <u>B</u> |

14. 24B   36A   44C   20E   26D   **44**

15. 89 _____   61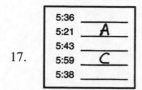

16. T T V W V T V T W V V **S**

17.

18.

19. (__ C) [35 A] [__ B] (__ E)

CHAPTER 18

Full-Length Practice Exam: Exam 470 and Exam 460

MODEL EXAMINATION

EXAM 470
Clerk
City Carrier
Distribution Clerk, Machine (Letter-Sorting Machine Operator)
Flat Sorting Machine Operator
Mail Handler
Mail Processor
Mark-up Clerk, Automated

EXAM 460
Rural Carrier

PART A—ADDRESS CHECKING ANSWER SHEET

1. Ⓐ Ⓓ	20. Ⓐ Ⓓ	39. Ⓐ Ⓓ	58. Ⓐ Ⓓ	77. Ⓐ Ⓓ
2. Ⓐ Ⓓ	21. Ⓐ Ⓓ	40. Ⓐ Ⓓ	59. Ⓐ Ⓓ	78. Ⓐ Ⓓ
3. Ⓐ Ⓓ	22. Ⓐ Ⓓ	41. Ⓐ Ⓓ	60. Ⓐ Ⓓ	79. Ⓐ Ⓓ
4. Ⓐ Ⓓ	23. Ⓐ Ⓓ	42. Ⓐ Ⓓ	61. Ⓐ Ⓓ	80. Ⓐ Ⓓ
5. Ⓐ Ⓓ	24. Ⓐ Ⓓ	43. Ⓐ Ⓓ	62. Ⓐ Ⓓ	81. Ⓐ Ⓓ
6. Ⓐ Ⓓ	25. Ⓐ Ⓓ	44. Ⓐ Ⓓ	63. Ⓐ Ⓓ	82. Ⓐ Ⓓ
7. Ⓐ Ⓓ	26. Ⓐ Ⓓ	45. Ⓐ Ⓓ	64. Ⓐ Ⓓ	83. Ⓐ Ⓓ
8. Ⓐ Ⓓ	27. Ⓐ Ⓓ	46. Ⓐ Ⓓ	65. Ⓐ Ⓓ	84. Ⓐ Ⓓ
9. Ⓐ Ⓓ	28. Ⓐ Ⓓ	47. Ⓐ Ⓓ	66. Ⓐ Ⓓ	85. Ⓐ Ⓓ
10. Ⓐ Ⓓ	29. Ⓐ Ⓓ	48. Ⓐ Ⓓ	67. Ⓐ Ⓓ	86. Ⓐ Ⓓ
11. Ⓐ Ⓓ	30. Ⓐ Ⓓ	49. Ⓐ Ⓓ	68. Ⓐ Ⓓ	87. Ⓐ Ⓓ
12. Ⓐ Ⓓ	31. Ⓐ Ⓓ	50. Ⓐ Ⓓ	69. Ⓐ Ⓓ	88. Ⓐ Ⓓ
13. Ⓐ Ⓓ	32. Ⓐ Ⓓ	51. Ⓐ Ⓓ	70. Ⓐ Ⓓ	89. Ⓐ Ⓓ
14. Ⓐ Ⓓ	33. Ⓐ Ⓓ	52. Ⓐ Ⓓ	71. Ⓐ Ⓓ	90. Ⓐ Ⓓ
15. Ⓐ Ⓓ	34. Ⓐ Ⓓ	53. Ⓐ Ⓓ	72. Ⓐ Ⓓ	91. Ⓐ Ⓓ
16. Ⓐ Ⓓ	35. Ⓐ Ⓓ	54. Ⓐ Ⓓ	73. Ⓐ Ⓓ	92. Ⓐ Ⓓ
17. Ⓐ Ⓓ	36. Ⓐ Ⓓ	55. Ⓐ Ⓓ	74. Ⓐ Ⓓ	93. Ⓐ Ⓓ
18. Ⓐ Ⓓ	37. Ⓐ Ⓓ	56. Ⓐ Ⓓ	75. Ⓐ Ⓓ	94. Ⓐ Ⓓ
19. Ⓐ Ⓓ	38. Ⓐ Ⓓ	57. Ⓐ Ⓓ	76. Ⓐ Ⓓ	95. Ⓐ Ⓓ

PART B—MEMORY FOR ADDRESSES ANSWER SHEETS

PRACTICE I ANSWER SHEET

1 Ⓐ Ⓑ Ⓒ Ⓓ Ⓔ	23 Ⓐ Ⓑ Ⓒ Ⓓ Ⓔ	45 Ⓐ Ⓑ Ⓒ Ⓓ Ⓔ	67 Ⓐ Ⓑ Ⓒ Ⓓ Ⓔ
2 Ⓐ Ⓑ Ⓒ Ⓓ Ⓔ	24 Ⓐ Ⓑ Ⓒ Ⓓ Ⓔ	46 Ⓐ Ⓑ Ⓒ Ⓓ Ⓔ	68 Ⓐ Ⓑ Ⓒ Ⓓ Ⓔ
3 Ⓐ Ⓑ Ⓒ Ⓓ Ⓔ	25 Ⓐ Ⓑ Ⓒ Ⓓ Ⓔ	47 Ⓐ Ⓑ Ⓒ Ⓓ Ⓔ	69 Ⓐ Ⓑ Ⓒ Ⓓ Ⓔ
4 Ⓐ Ⓑ Ⓒ Ⓓ Ⓔ	26 Ⓐ Ⓑ Ⓒ Ⓓ Ⓔ	48 Ⓐ Ⓑ Ⓒ Ⓓ Ⓔ	70 Ⓐ Ⓑ Ⓒ Ⓓ Ⓔ
5 Ⓐ Ⓑ Ⓒ Ⓓ Ⓔ	27 Ⓐ Ⓑ Ⓒ Ⓓ Ⓔ	49 Ⓐ Ⓑ Ⓒ Ⓓ Ⓔ	71 Ⓐ Ⓑ Ⓒ Ⓓ Ⓔ
6 Ⓐ Ⓑ Ⓒ Ⓓ Ⓔ	28 Ⓐ Ⓑ Ⓒ Ⓓ Ⓔ	50 Ⓐ Ⓑ Ⓒ Ⓓ Ⓔ	72 Ⓐ Ⓑ Ⓒ Ⓓ Ⓔ
7 Ⓐ Ⓑ Ⓒ Ⓓ Ⓔ	29 Ⓐ Ⓑ Ⓒ Ⓓ Ⓔ	51 Ⓐ Ⓑ Ⓒ Ⓓ Ⓔ	73 Ⓐ Ⓑ Ⓒ Ⓓ Ⓔ
8 Ⓐ Ⓑ Ⓒ Ⓓ Ⓔ	30 Ⓐ Ⓑ Ⓒ Ⓓ Ⓔ	52 Ⓐ Ⓑ Ⓒ Ⓓ Ⓔ	74 Ⓐ Ⓑ Ⓒ Ⓓ Ⓔ
9 Ⓐ Ⓑ Ⓒ Ⓓ Ⓔ	31 Ⓐ Ⓑ Ⓒ Ⓓ Ⓔ	53 Ⓐ Ⓑ Ⓒ Ⓓ Ⓔ	75 Ⓐ Ⓑ Ⓒ Ⓓ Ⓔ
10 Ⓐ Ⓑ Ⓒ Ⓓ Ⓔ	32 Ⓐ Ⓑ Ⓒ Ⓓ Ⓔ	54 Ⓐ Ⓑ Ⓒ Ⓓ Ⓔ	76 Ⓐ Ⓑ Ⓒ Ⓓ Ⓔ
11 Ⓐ Ⓑ Ⓒ Ⓓ Ⓔ	33 Ⓐ Ⓑ Ⓒ Ⓓ Ⓔ	55 Ⓐ Ⓑ Ⓒ Ⓓ Ⓔ	77 Ⓐ Ⓑ Ⓒ Ⓓ Ⓔ
12 Ⓐ Ⓑ Ⓒ Ⓓ Ⓔ	34 Ⓐ Ⓑ Ⓒ Ⓓ Ⓔ	56 Ⓐ Ⓑ Ⓒ Ⓓ Ⓔ	78 Ⓐ Ⓑ Ⓒ Ⓓ Ⓔ
13 Ⓐ Ⓑ Ⓒ Ⓓ Ⓔ	35 Ⓐ Ⓑ Ⓒ Ⓓ Ⓔ	57 Ⓐ Ⓑ Ⓒ Ⓓ Ⓔ	79 Ⓐ Ⓑ Ⓒ Ⓓ Ⓔ
14 Ⓐ Ⓑ Ⓒ Ⓓ Ⓔ	36 Ⓐ Ⓑ Ⓒ Ⓓ Ⓔ	58 Ⓐ Ⓑ Ⓒ Ⓓ Ⓔ	80 Ⓐ Ⓑ Ⓒ Ⓓ Ⓔ
15 Ⓐ Ⓑ Ⓒ Ⓓ Ⓔ	37 Ⓐ Ⓑ Ⓒ Ⓓ Ⓔ	59 Ⓐ Ⓑ Ⓒ Ⓓ Ⓔ	81 Ⓐ Ⓑ Ⓒ Ⓓ Ⓔ
16 Ⓐ Ⓑ Ⓒ Ⓓ Ⓔ	38 Ⓐ Ⓑ Ⓒ Ⓓ Ⓔ	60 Ⓐ Ⓑ Ⓒ Ⓓ Ⓔ	82 Ⓐ Ⓑ Ⓒ Ⓓ Ⓔ
17 Ⓐ Ⓑ Ⓒ Ⓓ Ⓔ	39 Ⓐ Ⓑ Ⓒ Ⓓ Ⓔ	61 Ⓐ Ⓑ Ⓒ Ⓓ Ⓔ	83 Ⓐ Ⓑ Ⓒ Ⓓ Ⓔ
18 Ⓐ Ⓑ Ⓒ Ⓓ Ⓔ	40 Ⓐ Ⓑ Ⓒ Ⓓ Ⓔ	62 Ⓐ Ⓑ Ⓒ Ⓓ Ⓔ	84 Ⓐ Ⓑ Ⓒ Ⓓ Ⓔ
19 Ⓐ Ⓑ Ⓒ Ⓓ Ⓔ	41 Ⓐ Ⓑ Ⓒ Ⓓ Ⓔ	63 Ⓐ Ⓑ Ⓒ Ⓓ Ⓔ	85 Ⓐ Ⓑ Ⓒ Ⓓ Ⓔ
20 Ⓐ Ⓑ Ⓒ Ⓓ Ⓔ	42 Ⓐ Ⓑ Ⓒ Ⓓ Ⓔ	64 Ⓐ Ⓑ Ⓒ Ⓓ Ⓔ	86 Ⓐ Ⓑ Ⓒ Ⓓ Ⓔ
21 Ⓐ Ⓑ Ⓒ Ⓓ Ⓔ	43 Ⓐ Ⓑ Ⓒ Ⓓ Ⓔ	65 Ⓐ Ⓑ Ⓒ Ⓓ Ⓔ	87 Ⓐ Ⓑ Ⓒ Ⓓ Ⓔ
22 Ⓐ Ⓑ Ⓒ Ⓓ Ⓔ	44 Ⓐ Ⓑ Ⓒ Ⓓ Ⓔ	66 Ⓐ Ⓑ Ⓒ Ⓓ Ⓔ	88 Ⓐ Ⓑ Ⓒ Ⓓ Ⓔ

PRACTICE II ANSWER SHEET

1 Ⓐ Ⓑ Ⓒ Ⓓ Ⓔ	23 Ⓐ Ⓑ Ⓒ Ⓓ Ⓔ	45 Ⓐ Ⓑ Ⓒ Ⓓ Ⓔ	67 Ⓐ Ⓑ Ⓒ Ⓓ Ⓔ
2 Ⓐ Ⓑ Ⓒ Ⓓ Ⓔ	24 Ⓐ Ⓑ Ⓒ Ⓓ Ⓔ	46 Ⓐ Ⓑ Ⓒ Ⓓ Ⓔ	68 Ⓐ Ⓑ Ⓒ Ⓓ Ⓔ
3 Ⓐ Ⓑ Ⓒ Ⓓ Ⓔ	25 Ⓐ Ⓑ Ⓒ Ⓓ Ⓔ	47 Ⓐ Ⓑ Ⓒ Ⓓ Ⓔ	69 Ⓐ Ⓑ Ⓒ Ⓓ Ⓔ
4 Ⓐ Ⓑ Ⓒ Ⓓ Ⓔ	26 Ⓐ Ⓑ Ⓒ Ⓓ Ⓔ	48 Ⓐ Ⓑ Ⓒ Ⓓ Ⓔ	70 Ⓐ Ⓑ Ⓒ Ⓓ Ⓔ
5 Ⓐ Ⓑ Ⓒ Ⓓ Ⓔ	27 Ⓐ Ⓑ Ⓒ Ⓓ Ⓔ	49 Ⓐ Ⓑ Ⓒ Ⓓ Ⓔ	71 Ⓐ Ⓑ Ⓒ Ⓓ Ⓔ
6 Ⓐ Ⓑ Ⓒ Ⓓ Ⓔ	28 Ⓐ Ⓑ Ⓒ Ⓓ Ⓔ	50 Ⓐ Ⓑ Ⓒ Ⓓ Ⓔ	72 Ⓐ Ⓑ Ⓒ Ⓓ Ⓔ
7 Ⓐ Ⓑ Ⓒ Ⓓ Ⓔ	29 Ⓐ Ⓑ Ⓒ Ⓓ Ⓔ	51 Ⓐ Ⓑ Ⓒ Ⓓ Ⓔ	73 Ⓐ Ⓑ Ⓒ Ⓓ Ⓔ
8 Ⓐ Ⓑ Ⓒ Ⓓ Ⓔ	30 Ⓐ Ⓑ Ⓒ Ⓓ Ⓔ	52 Ⓐ Ⓑ Ⓒ Ⓓ Ⓔ	74 Ⓐ Ⓑ Ⓒ Ⓓ Ⓔ
9 Ⓐ Ⓑ Ⓒ Ⓓ Ⓔ	31 Ⓐ Ⓑ Ⓒ Ⓓ Ⓔ	53 Ⓐ Ⓑ Ⓒ Ⓓ Ⓔ	75 Ⓐ Ⓑ Ⓒ Ⓓ Ⓔ
10 Ⓐ Ⓑ Ⓒ Ⓓ Ⓔ	32 Ⓐ Ⓑ Ⓒ Ⓓ Ⓔ	54 Ⓐ Ⓑ Ⓒ Ⓓ Ⓔ	76 Ⓐ Ⓑ Ⓒ Ⓓ Ⓔ
11 Ⓐ Ⓑ Ⓒ Ⓓ Ⓔ	33 Ⓐ Ⓑ Ⓒ Ⓓ Ⓔ	55 Ⓐ Ⓑ Ⓒ Ⓓ Ⓔ	77 Ⓐ Ⓑ Ⓒ Ⓓ Ⓔ
12 Ⓐ Ⓑ Ⓒ Ⓓ Ⓔ	34 Ⓐ Ⓑ Ⓒ Ⓓ Ⓔ	56 Ⓐ Ⓑ Ⓒ Ⓓ Ⓔ	78 Ⓐ Ⓑ Ⓒ Ⓓ Ⓔ
13 Ⓐ Ⓑ Ⓒ Ⓓ Ⓔ	35 Ⓐ Ⓑ Ⓒ Ⓓ Ⓔ	57 Ⓐ Ⓑ Ⓒ Ⓓ Ⓔ	79 Ⓐ Ⓑ Ⓒ Ⓓ Ⓔ
14 Ⓐ Ⓑ Ⓒ Ⓓ Ⓔ	36 Ⓐ Ⓑ Ⓒ Ⓓ Ⓔ	58 Ⓐ Ⓑ Ⓒ Ⓓ Ⓔ	80 Ⓐ Ⓑ Ⓒ Ⓓ Ⓔ
15 Ⓐ Ⓑ Ⓒ Ⓓ Ⓔ	37 Ⓐ Ⓑ Ⓒ Ⓓ Ⓔ	59 Ⓐ Ⓑ Ⓒ Ⓓ Ⓔ	81 Ⓐ Ⓑ Ⓒ Ⓓ Ⓔ
16 Ⓐ Ⓑ Ⓒ Ⓓ Ⓔ	38 Ⓐ Ⓑ Ⓒ Ⓓ Ⓔ	60 Ⓐ Ⓑ Ⓒ Ⓓ Ⓔ	82 Ⓐ Ⓑ Ⓒ Ⓓ Ⓔ
17 Ⓐ Ⓑ Ⓒ Ⓓ Ⓔ	39 Ⓐ Ⓑ Ⓒ Ⓓ Ⓔ	61 Ⓐ Ⓑ Ⓒ Ⓓ Ⓔ	83 Ⓐ Ⓑ Ⓒ Ⓓ Ⓔ
18 Ⓐ Ⓑ Ⓒ Ⓓ Ⓔ	40 Ⓐ Ⓑ Ⓒ Ⓓ Ⓔ	62 Ⓐ Ⓑ Ⓒ Ⓓ Ⓔ	84 Ⓐ Ⓑ Ⓒ Ⓓ Ⓔ
19 Ⓐ Ⓑ Ⓒ Ⓓ Ⓔ	41 Ⓐ Ⓑ Ⓒ Ⓓ Ⓔ	63 Ⓐ Ⓑ Ⓒ Ⓓ Ⓔ	85 Ⓐ Ⓑ Ⓒ Ⓓ Ⓔ
20 Ⓐ Ⓑ Ⓒ Ⓓ Ⓔ	42 Ⓐ Ⓑ Ⓒ Ⓓ Ⓔ	64 Ⓐ Ⓑ Ⓒ Ⓓ Ⓔ	86 Ⓐ Ⓑ Ⓒ Ⓓ Ⓔ
21 Ⓐ Ⓑ Ⓒ Ⓓ Ⓔ	43 Ⓐ Ⓑ Ⓒ Ⓓ Ⓔ	65 Ⓐ Ⓑ Ⓒ Ⓓ Ⓔ	87 Ⓐ Ⓑ Ⓒ Ⓓ Ⓔ
22 Ⓐ Ⓑ Ⓒ Ⓓ Ⓔ	44 Ⓐ Ⓑ Ⓒ Ⓓ Ⓔ	66 Ⓐ Ⓑ Ⓒ Ⓓ Ⓔ	88 Ⓐ Ⓑ Ⓒ Ⓓ Ⓔ

PRACTICE III ANSWER SHEET

1 Ⓐ Ⓑ Ⓒ Ⓓ Ⓔ	23 Ⓐ Ⓑ Ⓒ Ⓓ Ⓔ	45 Ⓐ Ⓑ Ⓒ Ⓓ Ⓔ	67 Ⓐ Ⓑ Ⓒ Ⓓ Ⓔ
2 Ⓐ Ⓑ Ⓒ Ⓓ Ⓔ	24 Ⓐ Ⓑ Ⓒ Ⓓ Ⓔ	46 Ⓐ Ⓑ Ⓒ Ⓓ Ⓔ	68 Ⓐ Ⓑ Ⓒ Ⓓ Ⓔ
3 Ⓐ Ⓑ Ⓒ Ⓓ Ⓔ	25 Ⓐ Ⓑ Ⓒ Ⓓ Ⓔ	47 Ⓐ Ⓑ Ⓒ Ⓓ Ⓔ	69 Ⓐ Ⓑ Ⓒ Ⓓ Ⓔ
4 Ⓐ Ⓑ Ⓒ Ⓓ Ⓔ	26 Ⓐ Ⓑ Ⓒ Ⓓ Ⓔ	48 Ⓐ Ⓑ Ⓒ Ⓓ Ⓔ	70 Ⓐ Ⓑ Ⓒ Ⓓ Ⓔ
5 Ⓐ Ⓑ Ⓒ Ⓓ Ⓔ	27 Ⓐ Ⓑ Ⓒ Ⓓ Ⓔ	49 Ⓐ Ⓑ Ⓒ Ⓓ Ⓔ	71 Ⓐ Ⓑ Ⓒ Ⓓ Ⓔ
6 Ⓐ Ⓑ Ⓒ Ⓓ Ⓔ	28 Ⓐ Ⓑ Ⓒ Ⓓ Ⓔ	50 Ⓐ Ⓑ Ⓒ Ⓓ Ⓔ	72 Ⓐ Ⓑ Ⓒ Ⓓ Ⓔ
7 Ⓐ Ⓑ Ⓒ Ⓓ Ⓔ	29 Ⓐ Ⓑ Ⓒ Ⓓ Ⓔ	51 Ⓐ Ⓑ Ⓒ Ⓓ Ⓔ	73 Ⓐ Ⓑ Ⓒ Ⓓ Ⓔ
8 Ⓐ Ⓑ Ⓒ Ⓓ Ⓔ	30 Ⓐ Ⓑ Ⓒ Ⓓ Ⓔ	52 Ⓐ Ⓑ Ⓒ Ⓓ Ⓔ	74 Ⓐ Ⓑ Ⓒ Ⓓ Ⓔ
9 Ⓐ Ⓑ Ⓒ Ⓓ Ⓔ	31 Ⓐ Ⓑ Ⓒ Ⓓ Ⓔ	53 Ⓐ Ⓑ Ⓒ Ⓓ Ⓔ	75 Ⓐ Ⓑ Ⓒ Ⓓ Ⓔ
10 Ⓐ Ⓑ Ⓒ Ⓓ Ⓔ	32 Ⓐ Ⓑ Ⓒ Ⓓ Ⓔ	54 Ⓐ Ⓑ Ⓒ Ⓓ Ⓔ	76 Ⓐ Ⓑ Ⓒ Ⓓ Ⓔ
11 Ⓐ Ⓑ Ⓒ Ⓓ Ⓔ	33 Ⓐ Ⓑ Ⓒ Ⓓ Ⓔ	55 Ⓐ Ⓑ Ⓒ Ⓓ Ⓔ	77 Ⓐ Ⓑ Ⓒ Ⓓ Ⓔ
12 Ⓐ Ⓑ Ⓒ Ⓓ Ⓔ	34 Ⓐ Ⓑ Ⓒ Ⓓ Ⓔ	56 Ⓐ Ⓑ Ⓒ Ⓓ Ⓔ	78 Ⓐ Ⓑ Ⓒ Ⓓ Ⓔ
13 Ⓐ Ⓑ Ⓒ Ⓓ Ⓔ	35 Ⓐ Ⓑ Ⓒ Ⓓ Ⓔ	57 Ⓐ Ⓑ Ⓒ Ⓓ Ⓔ	79 Ⓐ Ⓑ Ⓒ Ⓓ Ⓔ
14 Ⓐ Ⓑ Ⓒ Ⓓ Ⓔ	36 Ⓐ Ⓑ Ⓒ Ⓓ Ⓔ	58 Ⓐ Ⓑ Ⓒ Ⓓ Ⓔ	80 Ⓐ Ⓑ Ⓒ Ⓓ Ⓔ
15 Ⓐ Ⓑ Ⓒ Ⓓ Ⓔ	37 Ⓐ Ⓑ Ⓒ Ⓓ Ⓔ	59 Ⓐ Ⓑ Ⓒ Ⓓ Ⓔ	81 Ⓐ Ⓑ Ⓒ Ⓓ Ⓔ
16 Ⓐ Ⓑ Ⓒ Ⓓ Ⓔ	38 Ⓐ Ⓑ Ⓒ Ⓓ Ⓔ	60 Ⓐ Ⓑ Ⓒ Ⓓ Ⓔ	82 Ⓐ Ⓑ Ⓒ Ⓓ Ⓔ
17 Ⓐ Ⓑ Ⓒ Ⓓ Ⓔ	39 Ⓐ Ⓑ Ⓒ Ⓓ Ⓔ	61 Ⓐ Ⓑ Ⓒ Ⓓ Ⓔ	83 Ⓐ Ⓑ Ⓒ Ⓓ Ⓔ
18 Ⓐ Ⓑ Ⓒ Ⓓ Ⓔ	40 Ⓐ Ⓑ Ⓒ Ⓓ Ⓔ	62 Ⓐ Ⓑ Ⓒ Ⓓ Ⓔ	84 Ⓐ Ⓑ Ⓒ Ⓓ Ⓔ
19 Ⓐ Ⓑ Ⓒ Ⓓ Ⓔ	41 Ⓐ Ⓑ Ⓒ Ⓓ Ⓔ	63 Ⓐ Ⓑ Ⓒ Ⓓ Ⓔ	85 Ⓐ Ⓑ Ⓒ Ⓓ Ⓔ
20 Ⓐ Ⓑ Ⓒ Ⓓ Ⓔ	42 Ⓐ Ⓑ Ⓒ Ⓓ Ⓔ	64 Ⓐ Ⓑ Ⓒ Ⓓ Ⓔ	86 Ⓐ Ⓑ Ⓒ Ⓓ Ⓔ
21 Ⓐ Ⓑ Ⓒ Ⓓ Ⓔ	43 Ⓐ Ⓑ Ⓒ Ⓓ Ⓔ	65 Ⓐ Ⓑ Ⓒ Ⓓ Ⓔ	87 Ⓐ Ⓑ Ⓒ Ⓓ Ⓔ
22 Ⓐ Ⓑ Ⓒ Ⓓ Ⓔ	44 Ⓐ Ⓑ Ⓒ Ⓓ Ⓔ	66 Ⓐ Ⓑ Ⓒ Ⓓ Ⓔ	88 Ⓐ Ⓑ Ⓒ Ⓓ Ⓔ

MEMORY FOR ADDRESSES—SCORED EXAM ANSWER SHEET

1 Ⓐ Ⓑ Ⓒ Ⓓ Ⓔ   23 Ⓐ Ⓑ Ⓒ Ⓓ Ⓔ   45 Ⓐ Ⓑ Ⓒ Ⓓ Ⓔ   67 Ⓐ Ⓑ Ⓒ Ⓓ Ⓔ

2 Ⓐ Ⓑ Ⓒ Ⓓ Ⓔ   24 Ⓐ Ⓑ Ⓒ Ⓓ Ⓔ   46 Ⓐ Ⓑ Ⓒ Ⓓ Ⓔ   68 Ⓐ Ⓑ Ⓒ Ⓓ Ⓔ

3 Ⓐ Ⓑ Ⓒ Ⓓ Ⓔ   25 Ⓐ Ⓑ Ⓒ Ⓓ Ⓔ   47 Ⓐ Ⓑ Ⓒ Ⓓ Ⓔ   69 Ⓐ Ⓑ Ⓒ Ⓓ Ⓔ

4 Ⓐ Ⓑ Ⓒ Ⓓ Ⓔ   26 Ⓐ Ⓑ Ⓒ Ⓓ Ⓔ   48 Ⓐ Ⓑ Ⓒ Ⓓ Ⓔ   70 Ⓐ Ⓑ Ⓒ Ⓓ Ⓔ

5 Ⓐ Ⓑ Ⓒ Ⓓ Ⓔ   27 Ⓐ Ⓑ Ⓒ Ⓓ Ⓔ   49 Ⓐ Ⓑ Ⓒ Ⓓ Ⓔ   71 Ⓐ Ⓑ Ⓒ Ⓓ Ⓔ

6 Ⓐ Ⓑ Ⓒ Ⓓ Ⓔ   28 Ⓐ Ⓑ Ⓒ Ⓓ Ⓔ   50 Ⓐ Ⓑ Ⓒ Ⓓ Ⓔ   72 Ⓐ Ⓑ Ⓒ Ⓓ Ⓔ

7 Ⓐ Ⓑ Ⓒ Ⓓ Ⓔ   29 Ⓐ Ⓑ Ⓒ Ⓓ Ⓔ   51 Ⓐ Ⓑ Ⓒ Ⓓ Ⓔ   73 Ⓐ Ⓑ Ⓒ Ⓓ Ⓔ

8 Ⓐ Ⓑ Ⓒ Ⓓ Ⓔ   30 Ⓐ Ⓑ Ⓒ Ⓓ Ⓔ   52 Ⓐ Ⓑ Ⓒ Ⓓ Ⓔ   74 Ⓐ Ⓑ Ⓒ Ⓓ Ⓔ

9 Ⓐ Ⓑ Ⓒ Ⓓ Ⓔ   31 Ⓐ Ⓑ Ⓒ Ⓓ Ⓔ   53 Ⓐ Ⓑ Ⓒ Ⓓ Ⓔ   75 Ⓐ Ⓑ Ⓒ Ⓓ Ⓔ

10 Ⓐ Ⓑ Ⓒ Ⓓ Ⓔ   32 Ⓐ Ⓑ Ⓒ Ⓓ Ⓔ   54 Ⓐ Ⓑ Ⓒ Ⓓ Ⓔ   76 Ⓐ Ⓑ Ⓒ Ⓓ Ⓔ

11 Ⓐ Ⓑ Ⓒ Ⓓ Ⓔ   33 Ⓐ Ⓑ Ⓒ Ⓓ Ⓔ   55 Ⓐ Ⓑ Ⓒ Ⓓ Ⓔ   77 Ⓐ Ⓑ Ⓒ Ⓓ Ⓔ

12 Ⓐ Ⓑ Ⓒ Ⓓ Ⓔ   34 Ⓐ Ⓑ Ⓒ Ⓓ Ⓔ   56 Ⓐ Ⓑ Ⓒ Ⓓ Ⓔ   78 Ⓐ Ⓑ Ⓒ Ⓓ Ⓔ

13 Ⓐ Ⓑ Ⓒ Ⓓ Ⓔ   35 Ⓐ Ⓑ Ⓒ Ⓓ Ⓔ   57 Ⓐ Ⓑ Ⓒ Ⓓ Ⓔ   79 Ⓐ Ⓑ Ⓒ Ⓓ Ⓔ

14 Ⓐ Ⓑ Ⓒ Ⓓ Ⓔ   36 Ⓐ Ⓑ Ⓒ Ⓓ Ⓔ   58 Ⓐ Ⓑ Ⓒ Ⓓ Ⓔ   80 Ⓐ Ⓑ Ⓒ Ⓓ Ⓔ

15 Ⓐ Ⓑ Ⓒ Ⓓ Ⓔ   37 Ⓐ Ⓑ Ⓒ Ⓓ Ⓔ   59 Ⓐ Ⓑ Ⓒ Ⓓ Ⓔ   81 Ⓐ Ⓑ Ⓒ Ⓓ Ⓔ

16 Ⓐ Ⓑ Ⓒ Ⓓ Ⓔ   38 Ⓐ Ⓑ Ⓒ Ⓓ Ⓔ   60 Ⓐ Ⓑ Ⓒ Ⓓ Ⓔ   82 Ⓐ Ⓑ Ⓒ Ⓓ Ⓔ

17 Ⓐ Ⓑ Ⓒ Ⓓ Ⓔ   39 Ⓐ Ⓑ Ⓒ Ⓓ Ⓔ   61 Ⓐ Ⓑ Ⓒ Ⓓ Ⓔ   83 Ⓐ Ⓑ Ⓒ Ⓓ Ⓔ

18 Ⓐ Ⓑ Ⓒ Ⓓ Ⓔ   40 Ⓐ Ⓑ Ⓒ Ⓓ Ⓔ   62 Ⓐ Ⓑ Ⓒ Ⓓ Ⓔ   84 Ⓐ Ⓑ Ⓒ Ⓓ Ⓔ

19 Ⓐ Ⓑ Ⓒ Ⓓ Ⓔ   41 Ⓐ Ⓑ Ⓒ Ⓓ Ⓔ   63 Ⓐ Ⓑ Ⓒ Ⓓ Ⓔ   85 Ⓐ Ⓑ Ⓒ Ⓓ Ⓔ

20 Ⓐ Ⓑ Ⓒ Ⓓ Ⓔ   42 Ⓐ Ⓑ Ⓒ Ⓓ Ⓔ   64 Ⓐ Ⓑ Ⓒ Ⓓ Ⓔ   86 Ⓐ Ⓑ Ⓒ Ⓓ Ⓔ

21 Ⓐ Ⓑ Ⓒ Ⓓ Ⓔ   43 Ⓐ Ⓑ Ⓒ Ⓓ Ⓔ   65 Ⓐ Ⓑ Ⓒ Ⓓ Ⓔ   87 Ⓐ Ⓑ Ⓒ Ⓓ Ⓔ

22 Ⓐ Ⓑ Ⓒ Ⓓ Ⓔ   44 Ⓐ Ⓑ Ⓒ Ⓓ Ⓔ   66 Ⓐ Ⓑ Ⓒ Ⓓ Ⓔ   88 Ⓐ Ⓑ Ⓒ Ⓓ Ⓔ

PART C—NUMBER SERIES ANSWER SHEET

1. Ⓐ Ⓑ Ⓒ Ⓓ Ⓔ   7. Ⓐ Ⓑ Ⓒ Ⓓ Ⓔ   13. Ⓐ Ⓑ Ⓒ Ⓓ Ⓔ   19. Ⓐ Ⓑ Ⓒ Ⓓ Ⓔ
2. Ⓐ Ⓑ Ⓒ Ⓓ Ⓔ   8. Ⓐ Ⓑ Ⓒ Ⓓ Ⓔ   14. Ⓐ Ⓑ Ⓒ Ⓓ Ⓔ   20. Ⓐ Ⓑ Ⓒ Ⓓ Ⓔ
3. Ⓐ Ⓑ Ⓒ Ⓓ Ⓔ   9. Ⓐ Ⓑ Ⓒ Ⓓ Ⓔ   15. Ⓐ Ⓑ Ⓒ Ⓓ Ⓔ   21. Ⓐ Ⓑ Ⓒ Ⓓ Ⓔ
4. Ⓐ Ⓑ Ⓒ Ⓓ Ⓔ   10. Ⓐ Ⓑ Ⓒ Ⓓ Ⓔ   16. Ⓐ Ⓑ Ⓒ Ⓓ Ⓔ   22. Ⓐ Ⓑ Ⓒ Ⓓ Ⓔ
5. Ⓐ Ⓑ Ⓒ Ⓓ Ⓔ   11. Ⓐ Ⓑ Ⓒ Ⓓ Ⓔ   17. Ⓐ Ⓑ Ⓒ Ⓓ Ⓔ   23. Ⓐ Ⓑ Ⓒ Ⓓ Ⓔ
6. Ⓐ Ⓑ Ⓒ Ⓓ Ⓔ   12. Ⓐ Ⓑ Ⓒ Ⓓ Ⓔ   18. Ⓐ Ⓑ Ⓒ Ⓓ Ⓔ   24. Ⓐ Ⓑ Ⓒ Ⓓ Ⓔ

PART D—FOLLOWING ORAL INSTRUCTIONS ANSWER SHEET

1 Ⓐ Ⓑ Ⓒ Ⓓ Ⓔ   23 Ⓐ Ⓑ Ⓒ Ⓓ Ⓔ   45 Ⓐ Ⓑ Ⓒ Ⓓ Ⓔ   67 Ⓐ Ⓑ Ⓒ Ⓓ Ⓔ
2 Ⓐ Ⓑ Ⓒ Ⓓ Ⓔ   24 Ⓐ Ⓑ Ⓒ Ⓓ Ⓔ   46 Ⓐ Ⓑ Ⓒ Ⓓ Ⓔ   68 Ⓐ Ⓑ Ⓒ Ⓓ Ⓔ
3 Ⓐ Ⓑ Ⓒ Ⓓ Ⓔ   25 Ⓐ Ⓑ Ⓒ Ⓓ Ⓔ   47 Ⓐ Ⓑ Ⓒ Ⓓ Ⓔ   69 Ⓐ Ⓑ Ⓒ Ⓓ Ⓔ
4 Ⓐ Ⓑ Ⓒ Ⓓ Ⓔ   26 Ⓐ Ⓑ Ⓒ Ⓓ Ⓔ   48 Ⓐ Ⓑ Ⓒ Ⓓ Ⓔ   70 Ⓐ Ⓑ Ⓒ Ⓓ Ⓔ
5 Ⓐ Ⓑ Ⓒ Ⓓ Ⓔ   27 Ⓐ Ⓑ Ⓒ Ⓓ Ⓔ   49 Ⓐ Ⓑ Ⓒ Ⓓ Ⓔ   71 Ⓐ Ⓑ Ⓒ Ⓓ Ⓔ
6 Ⓐ Ⓑ Ⓒ Ⓓ Ⓔ   28 Ⓐ Ⓑ Ⓒ Ⓓ Ⓔ   50 Ⓐ Ⓑ Ⓒ Ⓓ Ⓔ   72 Ⓐ Ⓑ Ⓒ Ⓓ Ⓔ
7 Ⓐ Ⓑ Ⓒ Ⓓ Ⓔ   29 Ⓐ Ⓑ Ⓒ Ⓓ Ⓔ   51 Ⓐ Ⓑ Ⓒ Ⓓ Ⓔ   73 Ⓐ Ⓑ Ⓒ Ⓓ Ⓔ
8 Ⓐ Ⓑ Ⓒ Ⓓ Ⓔ   30 Ⓐ Ⓑ Ⓒ Ⓓ Ⓔ   52 Ⓐ Ⓑ Ⓒ Ⓓ Ⓔ   74 Ⓐ Ⓑ Ⓒ Ⓓ Ⓔ
9 Ⓐ Ⓑ Ⓒ Ⓓ Ⓔ   31 Ⓐ Ⓑ Ⓒ Ⓓ Ⓔ   53 Ⓐ Ⓑ Ⓒ Ⓓ Ⓔ   75 Ⓐ Ⓑ Ⓒ Ⓓ Ⓔ
10 Ⓐ Ⓑ Ⓒ Ⓓ Ⓔ   32 Ⓐ Ⓑ Ⓒ Ⓓ Ⓔ   54 Ⓐ Ⓑ Ⓒ Ⓓ Ⓔ   76 Ⓐ Ⓑ Ⓒ Ⓓ Ⓔ
11 Ⓐ Ⓑ Ⓒ Ⓓ Ⓔ   33 Ⓐ Ⓑ Ⓒ Ⓓ Ⓔ   55 Ⓐ Ⓑ Ⓒ Ⓓ Ⓔ   77 Ⓐ Ⓑ Ⓒ Ⓓ Ⓔ
12 Ⓐ Ⓑ Ⓒ Ⓓ Ⓔ   34 Ⓐ Ⓑ Ⓒ Ⓓ Ⓔ   56 Ⓐ Ⓑ Ⓒ Ⓓ Ⓔ   78 Ⓐ Ⓑ Ⓒ Ⓓ Ⓔ
13 Ⓐ Ⓑ Ⓒ Ⓓ Ⓔ   35 Ⓐ Ⓑ Ⓒ Ⓓ Ⓔ   57 Ⓐ Ⓑ Ⓒ Ⓓ Ⓔ   79 Ⓐ Ⓑ Ⓒ Ⓓ Ⓔ
14 Ⓐ Ⓑ Ⓒ Ⓓ Ⓔ   36 Ⓐ Ⓑ Ⓒ Ⓓ Ⓔ   58 Ⓐ Ⓑ Ⓒ Ⓓ Ⓔ   80 Ⓐ Ⓑ Ⓒ Ⓓ Ⓔ
15 Ⓐ Ⓑ Ⓒ Ⓓ Ⓔ   37 Ⓐ Ⓑ Ⓒ Ⓓ Ⓔ   59 Ⓐ Ⓑ Ⓒ Ⓓ Ⓔ   81 Ⓐ Ⓑ Ⓒ Ⓓ Ⓔ
16 Ⓐ Ⓑ Ⓒ Ⓓ Ⓔ   38 Ⓐ Ⓑ Ⓒ Ⓓ Ⓔ   60 Ⓐ Ⓑ Ⓒ Ⓓ Ⓔ   82 Ⓐ Ⓑ Ⓒ Ⓓ Ⓔ
17 Ⓐ Ⓑ Ⓒ Ⓓ Ⓔ   39 Ⓐ Ⓑ Ⓒ Ⓓ Ⓔ   61 Ⓐ Ⓑ Ⓒ Ⓓ Ⓔ   83 Ⓐ Ⓑ Ⓒ Ⓓ Ⓔ
18 Ⓐ Ⓑ Ⓒ Ⓓ Ⓔ   40 Ⓐ Ⓑ Ⓒ Ⓓ Ⓔ   62 Ⓐ Ⓑ Ⓒ Ⓓ Ⓔ   84 Ⓐ Ⓑ Ⓒ Ⓓ Ⓔ
19 Ⓐ Ⓑ Ⓒ Ⓓ Ⓔ   41 Ⓐ Ⓑ Ⓒ Ⓓ Ⓔ   63 Ⓐ Ⓑ Ⓒ Ⓓ Ⓔ   85 Ⓐ Ⓑ Ⓒ Ⓓ Ⓔ
20 Ⓐ Ⓑ Ⓒ Ⓓ Ⓔ   42 Ⓐ Ⓑ Ⓒ Ⓓ Ⓔ   64 Ⓐ Ⓑ Ⓒ Ⓓ Ⓔ   86 Ⓐ Ⓑ Ⓒ Ⓓ Ⓔ
21 Ⓐ Ⓑ Ⓒ Ⓓ Ⓔ   43 Ⓐ Ⓑ Ⓒ Ⓓ Ⓔ   65 Ⓐ Ⓑ Ⓒ Ⓓ Ⓔ   87 Ⓐ Ⓑ Ⓒ Ⓓ Ⓔ
22 Ⓐ Ⓑ Ⓒ Ⓓ Ⓔ   44 Ⓐ Ⓑ Ⓒ Ⓓ Ⓔ   66 Ⓐ Ⓑ Ⓒ Ⓓ Ⓔ   88 Ⓐ Ⓑ Ⓒ Ⓓ Ⓔ

PART A—ADDRESS CHECKING

SAMPLE QUESTIONS

You will be allowed 3 minutes to read the directions and answer the five sample questions that follow. On the actual test, however, you will have only 6 minutes to answer 95 questions, so see how quickly you can compare addresses and still get the correct answer.

> **Directions:** *For each question, compare the address in the left column with the address in the right column. If the two addresses are ALIKE IN EVERY WAY, mark A on your answer sheet. If the two addresses are DIFFERENT IN ANY WAY, mark D on your answer sheet.*

1	... 4836 Mineola Blvd	4386 Mineola Blvd
2	... 3062 W 197th St	3062 W 197th Rd
3	... Columbus OH 43210	Columbus OH 43210
4	... 9413 Alcan Hwy So	9413 Alcan Hwy So
5	... 4186 Carrier Ln	4186 Carreer Ln

```
    SAMPLE ANSWER SHEET
 1. Ⓐ  ⓓ       4. Ⓐ  ⓓ
 2. Ⓐ  ⓓ       5. Ⓐ  ⓓ
 3. Ⓐ  ⓓ
```

```
       CORRECT ANSWERS
 1. Ⓐ  ●        4. ●  ⓓ
 2. Ⓐ  ●        5. Ⓐ  ●
 3. ●  ⓓ
```

ADDRESS CHECKING

Time: 6 Minutes • 95 Questions

> **Directions:** *For each question, compare the address in the left column with the address in the right column. If the two addresses are ALIKE IN EVERY WAY, blacken space A on your answer sheet. If the two addresses are DIFFERENT IN ANY WAY, blacken space D on your answer sheet. Correct answers for this test are on page 204.*

1	... 462 Midland Ave	462 Midland Ave
2	... 2319 Sherry Dr	3219 Sherry Dr
3	... 1015 Kimball Ave	1015 Kimball Av
4	... Wappinger Falls NY 12590	Wappinger Falls NY 12590
5	... 1255 North Ave	1225 North Ave
6	... 1826 Tibbets Rd	1826 Tibetts Rd
7	... 603 N Division St	603 N Division St
8	... 2304 Manhattan Ave	2034 Manhattan Ave
9	... Worcester MA 01610	Worcester ME 01610

10	... 1186 Vernon Drive	1186 Vernon Drive
11	... 209 Peter Bont Rd	209 Peter Bent Rd
12	... Miami Beach FL 33139	Miami Beach FL 33193
13	... 1100 West Ave	1100 East Ave
14	... 2063 Winyah Ter	2036 Winyah Ter
15	... 3483 Suncrest Ave	3483 Suncrest Dr
16	... 234 Rochambeau Rd	234 Roshambeau Rd
17	... 306 N Terrace Blvd	306 N Terrace Blvd
18	... 1632 Paine St	1632 Pain St
19	... Palm Springs CA 92262	Palm Spring CA 92262
20	... 286 Marietta Ave	286 Marrietta Ave
21	... 2445 Pigott Rd	2445 Pigott Rd
22	... 2204 PineBrook Blvd	2204 Pinebrook Blvd
23	... Buffalo NY 42113	Buffulo NY 42113
24	... 487 Warburton Ave	487 Warburton Ave
25	... 9386 North St	9386 North Ave
26	... 2272 Glandale Rd	2772 Glandale Rd
27	... 9236 Puritan Dr	9236 Puritan Pl
28	... Watertown MA 02172	Watertown MA 02172
29	... 7803 Kimball Ave	7803 Kimbal Ave
30	... 1362 Colonial Pkwy	1362 Colonial Pkwy
31	... 115 Rolling Hills Rd	115 Rolling Hills Rd
32	... 218 Rockledge Rd	2181 Rockledge Rd
33	... 8346 N Broadway	8346 W Broadway
34	... West Chester PA 19380	West Chester PA 19830
35	... 9224 Highland Way	9244 Highland Way
36	... 8383 Mamaroneck Ave	8383 Mamaroneck Ave
37	... 276 Furnace Dock Rd	276 Furnace Dock Rd
38	... 4137 Loockerman St	4137 Lockerman St
39	... 532 Broadhollow Rd	532 Broadhollow Rd
40	... Sunrise FL 33313	Sunrise FL 33133

41	... 148 Cortlandt Rd	148 Cortland Rd
42	... 5951 W Hartsdale Rd	5951 W Hartsdale Ave
43	... 5231 Alta Vista Cir	5321 Alta Vista Cir
44	... 6459 Chippewa Rd	6459 Chippewa Rd
45	... 1171 S Highland Rd	1771 S Highland Rd
46	... Dover DE 19901	Dover DL 19901
47	... 2363 Old Farm Ln	2363 Old Farm Ln
48	... 1001 Hemingway Dr	1001 Hemmingway Dr
49	... 1555 Morningside Ave	1555 Morningslide Ave
50	... Purchase NY 10577	Purchase NY 10577
51	... 1189 E 9th St	1189 E 9th St
52	... 168 Old Lyme Rd	186 Old Lyme Rd
53	... 106 Notingham Rd	106 Nottingham Rd
54	... 1428 Midland Ave	1428 Midland Ave
55	... Elmhurst NY 11373	Elmherst NY 11373
56	... 1450 West Chester Pike	1450 West Chester Pike
57	... 3357 NW Main St	3357 NE Main St
58	... 5062 Marietta Ave	5062 Marrietta Ave
59	... 1890 NE 3rd Ct	1980 NE 3rd Ct
60	... Wilmington DE 19810	Wilmington DE 19810
61	... 1075 Central Park Av	1075 Central Park W
62	... 672 Bacon Hill Rd	672 Beacon Hill Rd
63	... 1725 W 17th St	1725 W 17th St
64	... Bronxville NY 10708	Bronxville NJ 10708
65	... 2066 Old Wilmot Rd	2066 Old Wilmont Rd
66	... 3333 S State St	3333 S State St
67	... 1483 Meritoria Dr	1438 Meritoria Dr
68	... 2327 E 23rd St	2327 E 27th St
69	... Baltimore MD 21215	Baltimore MD 21215
70	... 137 Clarence Rd	137 Claremont Rd
71	... 3516 N Ely Ave	3516 N Ely Ave

72	... 111 Beechwood St	1111 Beechwood St
73	... 143 N Highland Ave	143 N Highland Ave
74	... Miami Beach FL 33179	Miami FL 33179
75	... 6430 Spring Mill Rd	6340 Spring Mill Rd
76	... 1416 87th Ave	1416 78th Ave
77	... 4204 S Lexington Ave	4204 Lexington Ave
78	... 3601 Clarks Lane	3601 Clark Lane
79	... Indianapolis IN 46260	Indianapolis IN 46260
80	... 4256 Fairfield Ave	4256 Fairfield Ave
81	... Jamaica NY 11435	Jamiaca NY 11435
82	... 1809 83rd St	1809 83rd St
83	... 3288 Page Ct	3288 Paige Ct
84	... 2436 S Broadway	2436 S Broadway
85	... 6309 The Green	6309 The Green
86	... Kew Gardens NY 11415	Kew Garden NY 11415
87	... 4370 W 158th St	4370 W 158th St
88	... 4263 3rd Ave	4623 3rd Ave
89	... 1737 Fisher Ave	1737 Fischer Ave
90	... Bronx NY 10475	Bronx NY 10475
91	... 5148 West End Ave	5184 West End Ave
92	... 1011 Ocean Ave	1011 Ocean Ave
93	... 1593 Webster Dr	1593 Webster Dr
94	... Darien CT 06820	Darien CT 06820
95	... 1626 E 115th St	1662 E 115th St

END OF ADDRESS CHECKING

PART B—MEMORY FOR ADDRESSES

SAMPLE QUESTIONS

The sample questions for this part are based on the addresses in the five boxes below. Your task is to mark on your answer sheet the letter of the box in which each address belongs. You will have 5 minutes now to study the locations of the addresses. Then cover the boxes and try to mark the location of the sample questions. You may look back at the boxes if you cannot yet mark the address locations from memory.

The exam itself provides three practice sessions before the question set that really counts. Practice I and Practice III supply you with the boxes and permit you to refer to them if necessary. Practice II and the Memory for Addresses Test itself do not permit you to look at the boxes. The test itself is based on memory.

A	B	C	D	E
4100–4199 Plum	1000–1399 Plum	4200–4599 Plum	1400–4099 Plum	4600–5299 Plum
Bardack	Greenhouse	Flynn	Pepper	Cedar
4200–4599 Ash	4600–5299 Ash	1400–4099 Ash	1000–1399 Ash	4100–4199 Ash
Lemon	Dalby	Race	Clown	Hawk
1000–1399 Neff	4100–4199 Neff	4600–5299 Neff	4200–4599 Neff	1400–4099 Neff

1. 1400–4099 Plum
2. 1000–1399 Neff
3. Lemon
4. Flynn
5. 4200–4599 Ash

6. 4600–5299 Ash
7. Cedar
8. Pepper
9. 4100–4199 Plum
10. 4600–5299 Neff

11. 1000–1399 Plum
12. Clown
13. Greenhouse
14. 4100–4199 Ash

SAMPLE ANSWER SHEET

1. Ⓐ Ⓑ Ⓒ Ⓓ Ⓔ   8. Ⓐ Ⓑ Ⓒ Ⓓ Ⓔ
2. Ⓐ Ⓑ Ⓒ Ⓓ Ⓔ   9. Ⓐ Ⓑ Ⓒ Ⓓ Ⓔ
3. Ⓐ Ⓑ Ⓒ Ⓓ Ⓔ   10. Ⓐ Ⓑ Ⓒ Ⓓ Ⓔ
4. Ⓐ Ⓑ Ⓒ Ⓓ Ⓔ   11. Ⓐ Ⓑ Ⓒ Ⓓ Ⓔ
5. Ⓐ Ⓑ Ⓒ Ⓓ Ⓔ   12. Ⓐ Ⓑ Ⓒ Ⓓ Ⓔ
6. Ⓐ Ⓑ Ⓒ Ⓓ Ⓔ   13. Ⓐ Ⓑ Ⓒ Ⓓ Ⓔ
7. Ⓐ Ⓑ Ⓒ Ⓓ Ⓔ   14. Ⓐ Ⓑ Ⓒ Ⓓ Ⓔ

CORRECT ANSWERS

1. Ⓐ Ⓑ Ⓒ ● Ⓔ   8. Ⓐ Ⓑ Ⓒ ● Ⓔ
2. ● Ⓑ Ⓒ Ⓓ Ⓔ   9. ● Ⓑ Ⓒ Ⓓ Ⓔ
3. ● Ⓑ Ⓒ Ⓓ Ⓔ   10. Ⓐ Ⓑ ● Ⓓ Ⓔ
4. Ⓐ Ⓑ ● Ⓓ Ⓔ   11. Ⓐ ● Ⓒ Ⓓ Ⓔ
5. ● Ⓑ Ⓒ Ⓓ Ⓔ   12. Ⓐ Ⓑ Ⓒ ● Ⓔ
6. Ⓐ ● Ⓒ Ⓓ Ⓔ   13. Ⓐ ● Ⓒ Ⓓ Ⓔ
7. Ⓐ Ⓑ Ⓒ Ⓓ ●   14. Ⓐ Ⓑ Ⓒ Ⓓ ●

MEMORY FOR ADDRESSES PRACTICE TESTS

Directions: The five boxes below are labeled A, B, C, D, and E. In each box are three sets of number spans with names and two names that are not associated with numbers. In the next 3 MINUTES, you must try to memorize the box location of each name and number span. The position of a name or number span within its box is not important. You need only remember the letter of the box in which the item is to be found. You will use these names and numbers to answer three sets of practice questions that are NOT scored and one actual test that is scored. Correct answers begin on page 205.

A	B	C	D	E
4100–4199 Plum	1000–1399 Plum	4200–4599 Plum	1400–4099 Plum	4600–5299 Plum
Bardack	Greenhouse	Flynn	Pepper	Cedar
4200–4599 Ash	4600–5299 Ash	1400–4099 Ash	1000–1399 Ash	4100–4199 Ash
Lemon	Dalby	Race	Clown	Hawk
1000–1399 Neff	4100–4199 Neff	4600–5299 Neff	4200–4599 Neff	1400–4099 Neff

PRACTICE I

Directions: *Use the next 3 MINUTES to mark on your answer shee[t] which each item that follows is to be found. Try to mark each item wit[h] boxes. If, however, you get stuck, you may refer to the boxes during you find that you must look at the boxes, try to memorize as you do so. This tes[t] only. It will not be scored.*

1.	4600–5299 Ash	31.	1400–4099 Neff	61.	4100–4199 Ash
2.	4600–5299 Neff	32.	4600–5299 Neff	62.	Bardack
3.	1400–4099 Plum	33.	1400–4099 Ash	63.	Dalby
4.	Cedar	34.	Flynn	64.	Clown
5.	Bardack	35.	Lemon	65.	4200–4599 Ash
6.	1400–4099 Neff	36.	Clown	66.	1400–4099 Ash
7.	1400–4099 Ash	37.	4100–4199 Plum	67.	4200–4599 Plum
8.	1000–1399 Plum	38.	1000–1399 Ash	68.	Hawk
9.	Greenhouse	39.	4100–4199 Neff	69.	4100–4199 Neff
10.	Lemon	40.	Greenhouse	70.	1400–4099 Neff
11.	4600–5299 Plum	41.	Hawk	71.	1000–1399 Plum
12.	4200–4599 Ash	42.	4600–5299 Plum	72.	Pepper
13.	4600–5299 Neff	43.	1000–1399 Neff	73.	1000–1399 Neff
14.	Dalby	44.	1400–4099 Ash	74.	4100–4199 Ash
15.	Hawk	45.	4600–5299 Ash	75.	Dalby
16.	4100–4199 Plum	46.	Cedar	76.	Cedar
17.	4200–4599 Plum	47.	Greenhouse	77.	4100–4199 Plum
18.	4600–5299 Ash	48.	1400–4099 Plum	78.	1400–4099 Ash
19.	4200–4599 Neff	49.	4200–4599 Neff	79.	1400–4099 Plum
20.	Race	50.	1000–1399 Ash	80.	1400–4099 Neff
21.	Pepper	51.	Race	81.	Pepper
22.	4100–4199 Ash	52.	Flynn	82.	Hawk
23.	1000–1399 Neff	53.	4600–5299 Ash	83.	4600–5299 Ash
24.	1000–1399 Plum	54.	4600–5299 Plum	84.	4600–5299 Plum
25.	Cedar	55.	4600–5299 Neff	85.	1000–1399 Ash
26.	Dalby	56.	Pepper	86.	1000–1399 Neff
27.	4600–5299 Plum	57.	Lemon	87.	Cedar
28.	1400–4099 Plum	58.	1000–1399 Plum	88.	Greenhouse
29.	Bardack	59.	4100–4199 Plum		
30.	4200–4599 Ash	60.	1000–1399 Neff		

PRACTICE II

> **Directions:** *The next 88 questions constitute another practice exercise. You should mark your answers on your answer sheet. Again, the time limit is 3 MINUTES. This time, however, you must NOT look at the boxes while answering the questions. You must rely on your memory in marking the box location of each item. This practice test will not be scored.*

1.	4100–4199 Plum	31.	4100–4199 Neff	61.	4200–4599 Ash
2.	1400–4099 Neff	32.	1400–4099 Plum	62.	Pepper
3.	1400–4099 Ash	33.	4200–4599 Neff	63.	Clown
4.	Clown	34.	Dalby	64.	4600–5299 Ash
5.	Greenhouse	35.	Flynn	65.	1000–1399 Neff
6.	4100–4199 Neff	36.	4200–4599 Ash	66.	1000–1399 Plum
7.	1000–1399 Ash	37.	4600–5299 Plum	67.	Race
8.	4100–4199 Ash	38.	4100–4199 Plum	68.	Dalby
9.	Race	39.	Bardack	69.	1400–4099 Ash
10.	Flynn	40.	Hawk	70.	4100–4199 Ash
11.	4600–5299 Plum	41.	1000–1399 Plum	71.	4600–5299 Plum
12.	1000–1399 Neff	42.	1000–1399 Neff	72.	4600–5299 Neff
13.	4200–4599 Ash	43.	1000–1399 Ash	73.	Cedar
14.	1000–1399 Plum	44.	Greenhouse	74.	1400–4099 Neff
15.	Cedar	45.	Clown	75.	Greenhouse
16.	Dalby	46.	4600–5299 Ash	76.	4100–4199 Plum
17.	Pepper	47.	4100–4199 Ash	77.	4200–4599 Neff
18.	4600–5299 Neff	48.	1400–4099 Neff	78.	4200–4599 Ash
19.	4200–4599 Neff	49.	Race	79.	Clown
20.	1400–4099 Plum	50.	Cedar	80.	Dalby
21.	Bardack	51.	Flynn	81.	4200–4599 Plum
22.	Lemon	52.	Hawk	82.	1400–4099 Ash
23.	Hawk	53.	4100–4199 Neff	83.	1000–1399 Neff
24.	4200–4599 Plum	54.	1000–1399 Ash	84.	Pepper
25.	4600–5299 Ash	55.	4100–4199 Plum	85.	Bardack
26.	4200–4599 Plum	56.	1400–4099 Plum	86.	4100–4199 Plum
27.	4600–5299 Neff	57.	4200–4599 Plum	87.	1400–4099 Neff
28.	1400–4099 Ash	58.	Bardack	88.	4100–4199 Ash
29.	Lemon	59.	4600–5299 Neff		
30.	Pepper	60.	4200–4599 Neff		

PRACTICE III

Directions: *The names and address are repeated for you in the boxes below. Each name and each number span is in the same box in which you found it in the original set. You will now be allowed 5 MINUTES to study the locations again. Do your best to memorize the letter of the box in which each item is located. This is your last chance to see the boxes.*

A	B	C	D	E
4100–4199 Plum Bardack 4200–4599 Ash Lemon 1000–1399 Neff	1000–1399 Plum Greenhouse 4600–5299 Ash Dalby 4100–4199 Neff	4200–4599 Plum Flynn 1400–4099 Ash Race 4600–5299 Neff	1400–4099 Plum Pepper 1000–1399 Ash Clown 4200–4599 Neff	4600–5299 Plum Cedar 4100–4199 Ash Hawk 1400–4099 Neff

Directions: *This is your last practice test. Mark the location of each of the 88 items on your answer sheet. You will have 5 MINUTES to answer these questions. Do NOT look back at the boxes. This practice test will not be scored.*

1.	1400–4099 Ash	22.	1000–1399 Plum	43.	Greenhouse
2.	4600–5299 Plum	23.	4200–4599 Ash	44.	Pepper
3.	1000–1399 Neff	24.	Lemon	45.	4100–4199 Plum
4.	Pepper	25.	Race	46.	1400–4099 Neff
5.	Greenhouse	26.	4600–5299 Neff	47.	4600–5299 Ash
6.	4100–4199 Plum	27.	4600–5299 Plum	48.	1000–1399 Ash
7.	1400–4099 Neff	28.	Dalby	49.	Clown
8.	4600–5299 Ash	29.	Cedar	50.	Bardack
9.	1000–1399 Ash	30.	4200–4599 Neff	51.	Lemon
10.	Bardack	31.	1000–1399 Plum	52.	4200–4599 Plum
11.	Lemon	32.	1400–4099 Ash	53.	4600–5299 Neff
12.	Hawk	33.	4200–4599 Neff	54.	Hawk
13.	1000–1399 Plum	34.	1400–4099 Plum	55.	Flynn
14.	4200–4599 Neff	35.	4100–4199 Neff	56.	Race
15.	4200–4599 Ash	36.	Ceda	57.	1400–4099 Plum
16.	4100–4199 Neff	37.	Clown	58.	1000–1399 Neff
17.	1400–4099 Plum	38.	Dalby	59.	4100–4199 Ash
18.	4100–4199 Ash	39.	4200–4599 Ash	60.	1400–4099 Ash
19.	Clown	40.	4100–4199 Ash	61.	1400–4099 Plum
20.	Flynn	41.	4600–5299 Plum	62.	4100–4199 Neff
21.	4600–5299 Ash	42.	1000–1399 Neff	63.	1400–4099 Neff

64.	Hawk	73.	4100–4199 Ash	82.	4100–4199 Plum
65.	Lemon	74.	Greenhouse	83.	4600–5299 Neff
66.	1000–1399 Plum	75.	Race	84.	Flynn
67.	4100–4199 Neff	76.	4200–4599 Neff	85.	Clown
68.	4600–5299 Ash	77.	1000–1399 Ash	86.	1400–4099 Ash
69.	Pepper	78.	4200–4599 Plum	87.	4600–5299 Plum
70.	Dalby	79.	Bardack	88.	4100–4199 Plum
71.	1000–1399 Neff	80.	Cedar		
72.	4600–5299 Plum	81.	4200–4599 Ash		

MEMORY FOR ADDRESSES—SCORED EXAM

Time: 5 Minutes • 88 Questions

> **Directions:** *Mark your answers on the answer sheet provided at the beginning of the chapter. This test will be scored. You are NOT permitted to look at the boxes. Work from memory, as quickly and as accurately as you can. Correct answers are on page 206.*

1.	1400–4099 Neff	24.	Greenhouse	47.	4100–4199 Ash
2.	4100–4199 Plum	25.	4200–4599 Neff	48.	4100–4199 Plum
3.	1400–4099 Ash	26.	1000–1399 Plum	49.	1000–1399 Neff
4.	Pepper	27.	1400–4099 Neff	50.	4100–4199 Neff
5.	Dalby	28.	4200–4599 Ash	51.	Hawk
6.	4200–4599 Plum	29.	Hawk	52	Greenhouse
7.	4600–5299 Neff	30.	Flynn	53.	Dalby
8.	4100–4199 Ash	31.	4100–4199 Plum	54.	1400–4099 Ash
9.	4200–4599 Ash	32.	4200–4599 Neff	55.	4600–5299 Ash
10.	Bardack	33.	1400–4099 Ash	56.	4200–4599 Plum
11.	Hawk	34.	Clown	57.	Clown
12.	4600–5299 Plum	35.	Dalby	58.	Race
13.	1000–1399 Neff	36.	4100–4199 Ash	59.	1000–1399 Ash
14.	1000–1399 Ash	37.	4100–4199 Neff	60.	4600–5299 Plum
15.	Clown	38.	1400–4099 Plum	61.	Bardack
16.	Flynn	39.	Cedar	62.	4200–4599 Neff
17.	4600–5299 Ash	40.	Bardack	63.	Flynn
18.	1400–4099 Plum	41.	1000–1399 Plum	64.	Pepper
19.	1000–1399 Plum	42.	4600–5299 Neff	65.	1400–4099 Neff
20.	Cedar	43.	1400–4099 Plum	66.	4100–4199 Ash
21.	Race	44.	Lemon	67.	4600–5299 Neff
22.	Lemon	45.	Cedar	68.	1000–1399 Plum
23.	4100–4199 Neff	46.	4200–4599 Ash	69.	4100–4199 Plum

70. 4600–5299 Ash	**77.** 4100–4199 Ash	**84.** 4200–4599 Plum
71. 4600–5299 Neff	**78.** 4600–5299 Plum	**85.** Flynn
72. Lemon	**79.** Greenhouse	**86.** Clown
73. Pepper	**80.** Dalby	**87.** 4200–4599 Ash
74. Cedar	**81.** 1000–1399 Plum	**88.** 4100–4199 Ash
75. 1400–4099 Ash	**82.** 1000–1399 Ash	
76. 1400–4099 Neff	**83.** 4100–4199 Neff	

END OF MEMORY FOR ADDRESSES

PART C—NUMBER SERIES

SAMPLE QUESTIONS

The following sample questions show you the type of question that will be used in Part C. You will have 3 minutes to answer the sample questions below and to study the explanations.

> **Directions:** *Each number series question consists of a series of numbers that follows some definite order. The numbers progress from left to right according to some rule. One pair of numbers to the right of the series comprises the next two numbers in the series. Study each series to try to find a pattern to the series and to figure out the rule that governs the progression. Choose the answer pair that continues the series according to the pattern established and mark its letter on your answer sheet.*

1. 23 25 27 29 31 33 35 .... (A) 35 36 (B) 35 37   (C) 36 37   (D) 37 38   (E) 37 39

The correct answer is (E). This series progresses by adding 2. 35 + 2 = 37 + 2 = 39.

2. 3 3 6 6 12 12 24 .... (A) 24 36 (B) 36 36   (C) 24 24   (D) 24 48   (E) 48 48

The correct answer is (D). The series requires you to repeat a number, then multiply it by 2.

3. 11 13 16 20 25 31 38 .... (A) 46 55 (B) 45 55   (C) 40 42   (D) 47 58   (E) 42 46

The easiest way to solve this problem is to write the degree and direction of change between the numbers. By doing this, you see that the pattern is +2, +3, +4, +5, +6, +7. Continue the series by continuing the pattern: 38 + 8 = 46 + 9 = 55. The correct answer is (A).

4. 76 72 72 68 64 64 60 .... (A) 60 56 (B) 60 60   (C) 56 56   (D) 56 52   (E) 56 54

Here, the pattern is: –4, repeat the number,–4; –4, repeat the number, –4. To find that choice (C) is the answer you must realize that you are at the beginning of the pattern. 60 – 4 = 56, then repeat the number 56.

5. 92 94 96 92 94 96 92 .... (A) 92 94 (B) 94 96   (C) 96 92   (D) 96 94   (E) 96 98

The series consists of the sequence 92 94 96 repeated over and over again. Choice (B) is the answer because 94 96 continues the sequence after 92.

SAMPLE ANSWER SHEET
1. Ⓐ Ⓑ Ⓒ Ⓓ Ⓔ
2. Ⓐ Ⓑ Ⓒ Ⓓ Ⓔ
3. Ⓐ Ⓑ Ⓒ Ⓓ Ⓔ
4. Ⓐ Ⓑ Ⓒ Ⓓ Ⓔ
5. Ⓐ Ⓑ Ⓒ Ⓓ Ⓔ

CORRECT ANSWERS
1. Ⓐ Ⓑ Ⓒ Ⓓ ●
2. Ⓐ Ⓑ Ⓒ ● Ⓔ
3. ● Ⓑ Ⓒ Ⓓ Ⓔ
4. Ⓐ Ⓑ ● Ⓓ Ⓔ
5. Ⓐ ● Ⓒ Ⓓ Ⓔ

NUMBER SERIES
Time: 20 Minutes • 24 Questions

Directions: Each number series question consists of a series of numbers that follows some definite order. The numbers progress from left to right according to some rule. One lettered pair of numbers comprises the next two numbers in the series. Study each series to try to find a pattern to the series and to figure out the rule that governs the progression. Choose the answer pair that continues the series according to the pattern established and mark its letter on your answer sheet. Correct answers are on page 207.

1. 8 9 9 8 10 10 8 .... (A) 11 8   (B) 8 13   (C) 8 11   (D) 11 11   (E) 8 8

2. 10 10 11 11 12 12 13 .... (A) 15 15   (B) 13 13   (C) 14 14   (D) 13 14   (E) 14 15

3. 6 6 10 6 6 12 6 .... (A) 6 14   (B) 13 6   (C) 14 6   (D) 6 13   (E) 6 6

4. 17 11 5 16 10 4 15 .... (A) 13 9   (B) 13 11   (C) 8 5   (D) 9 5   (E) 9 3

5. 1 3 2 4 3 5 4 .... (A) 6 8   (B) 5 6   (C) 6 5   (D) 3 4   (E) 3 5

6. 11 11 10 12 12 11 13 .... (A) 12 14   (B) 14 12   (C) 14 14   (D) 13 14   (E) 13 12

7. 18 5 6 18 7 8 18 .... (A) 9 9   (B) 9 10   (C) 18 9   (D) 8 9   (E) 18 7

8. 8 1 9 3 10 5 11 .... (A) 7 12   (B) 6 12   (C) 12 6   (D) 7 8   (E) 6 7

9. 14 12 10 20 18 16 32 30 ... (A) 60 18   (B) 32 64   (C) 30 28   (D) 28 56   (E) 28 28

10. 67 59 52 44 37 29 22 .... (A) 15 7   (B) 14 8   (C) 14 7   (D) 15 8   (E) 16 11

11. 17 79 20 74 23 69 26 .... (A) 64 29   (B) 65 30   (C) 29 64   (D) 23 75   (E) 26 64

12. 3 5 10 8 4 6 12 10 5 .... (A) 8 16   (B) 7 14   (C) 10 20   (D) 10 5   (E) 7 9

13. 58 52 52 46 46 40 40 .... (A) 34 28   (B) 28 28   (C) 40 34   (D) 35 35   (E) 34 34

14. 32 37 33 33 38 34 34 .... (A) 38 43   (B) 34 39   (C) 39 35   (D) 39 39   (E) 34 40

15. 15 17 19 16 18 20 17 .... (A) 14 16   (B) 19 21   (C) 17 19   (D) 16 18   (E) 19 16

16. 5 15 7 21 13 39 31 .... (A) 93 85   (B) 62 69   (C) 39 117   (D) 93 87   (E) 31 93

17. 84 76 70 62 56 48 42 .... (A) 42 36   (B) 34 26   (C) 36 28   (D) 36 24   (E) 34 28

18. 47 23 43 27 39 31 35 .... (A) 31 27   (B) 39 43   (C) 39 35   (D) 35 31   (E) 31 35

19. 14 23 31 38 44 49 53 .... (A) 55 57   (B) 57 61   (C) 56 58   (D) 57 59   (E) 58 62

20. 5 6 8 8 9 11 11 12 .... (A) 12 13   (B) 14 14   (C) 14 15   (D) 14 16   (E) 12 14

21. 9 18 41 41 36 72 41 .... (A) 108 108   (B) 41 108   (C) 41 144   (D) 144 144   (E) 72 41

22. 13 15 17 13 15 17 13 .... (A) 17 15   (B) 13 15   (C) 17 13   (D) 15 13   (E) 15 17

23. 13 92 17 89 21 86 25 .... (A) 83 29   (B) 24 89   (C) 29 83   (D) 25 83   (E) 89 21

24. 10 20 23 13 26 29 19 .... (A) 9 12   (B) 38 41   (C) 22 44   (D) 44 33   (E) 36 39

END OF NUMBER SERIES

PART D—FOLLOWING ORAL INSTRUCTIONS

DIRECTIONS AND SAMPLE QUESTIONS

LISTENING TO INSTRUCTIONS

When you are ready to try these sample questions, give the following instructions to a friend and have the friend read them aloud to you at the rate of 80 words per minute. Do not read them to yourself. Your friend will need a watch with a second hand. Listen carefully and do exactly what your friend tells you to do with the worksheet and answer sheet. Your friend will tell you some things to do with each item on the worksheet. After each set of instructions, your friend will give you time to mark your answer by darkening a circle on the sample answer sheet. Because B and D sound very much alike, your friend will say "B as in baker" when he or she means B and "D as in dog" when he or she means D.

TO THE PERSON WHO IS TO READ THE INSTRUCTIONS: The instructions are to be read at the rate of 80 words per minute. Do not read aloud the material that is in parentheses. Do not repeat any instructions.

READ ALOUD TO THE CANDIDATE

Look at line 1 on your worksheet. (Pause slightly.) Draw two lines under the middle number on line 1. (Pause 2 seconds.) Now, on your answer sheet, find the number under which you just drew two lines and darken space D as in dog for that number. (Pause 5 seconds.)

Look at line 2 on your worksheet. (Pause slightly.) Write the letter A in the left-hand circle. (Pause 2 seconds.) Now, on your answer sheet, darken the space for the number-letter combination in the circle in which you just wrote. (Pause 5 seconds.)

Look at line 3 on your worksheet. (Pause slightly.) Count the number of times the letter E appears on line 3 and write the number at the end of the line. (Pause 2 seconds.) Now, on your answer sheet, darken space C for the number you just wrote. (Pause 5 seconds.)

Look at line 4 on your worksheet. (Pause slightly.) If an hour is longer than a day, write the letter B as in baker on the line next to the first number on line 4; if not, write the letter E on the line next to the third number. (Pause 5 seconds.) Now, on your answer sheet, darken the space for the number-letter combination you just wrote. (Pause 5 seconds.)

Look at line 4 again. (Pause slightly.) Write the second letter of the alphabet on the line next to the middle number. (Pause 2 seconds.) Now, on your answer sheet, darken the space for the number-letter combination you just wrote. (Pause 5 seconds.)

SAMPLE WORKSHEET

> **Directions:** *Listening carefully to each set of instructions, mark each item on this worksheet as directed. Then complete each question by marking the sample answer sheet below as directed. For each answer, you will darken the answer for a number-letter combination. Should you fall behind and miss an instruction, don't become excited. Let that one go and listen for the next one. If you start to darken a space for a number and you find that you have already darkened another space for that number, either erase the first mark and darken the space for the new combination, or let the first mark stay and do not darken a space for the new combination. Write with a pencil that has a clean eraser. When you finish, you should have no more than one space darkened for each number.*

1. 9 7 12 14 1

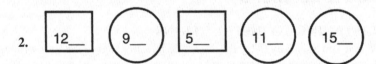

2.

3. WARNING. BEWARE OF DOG. __

4. 4____   13____   6____

SAMPLE ANSWER SHEET

1. Ⓐ Ⓑ Ⓒ Ⓓ Ⓔ	6. Ⓐ Ⓑ Ⓒ Ⓓ Ⓔ	11. Ⓐ Ⓑ Ⓒ Ⓓ Ⓔ
2. Ⓐ Ⓑ Ⓒ Ⓓ Ⓔ	7. Ⓐ Ⓑ Ⓒ Ⓓ Ⓔ	12. Ⓐ Ⓑ Ⓒ Ⓓ Ⓔ
3. Ⓐ Ⓑ Ⓒ Ⓓ Ⓔ	8. Ⓐ Ⓑ Ⓒ Ⓓ Ⓔ	13. Ⓐ Ⓑ Ⓒ Ⓓ Ⓔ
4. Ⓐ Ⓑ Ⓒ Ⓓ Ⓔ	9. Ⓐ Ⓑ Ⓒ Ⓓ Ⓔ	14. Ⓐ Ⓑ Ⓒ Ⓓ Ⓔ
5. Ⓐ Ⓑ Ⓒ Ⓓ Ⓔ	10. Ⓐ Ⓑ Ⓒ Ⓓ Ⓔ	15. Ⓐ Ⓑ Ⓒ Ⓓ Ⓔ

CORRECT ANSWERS TO SAMPLE QUESTIONS

1. Ⓐ Ⓑ Ⓒ Ⓓ Ⓔ	6. Ⓐ Ⓑ Ⓒ Ⓓ ●	11. Ⓐ Ⓑ Ⓒ Ⓓ Ⓔ
2. Ⓐ Ⓑ ● Ⓓ Ⓔ	7. Ⓐ Ⓑ Ⓒ Ⓓ Ⓔ	12. Ⓐ Ⓑ Ⓒ ● Ⓔ
3. Ⓐ Ⓑ Ⓒ Ⓓ Ⓔ	8. Ⓐ Ⓑ Ⓒ Ⓓ Ⓔ	13. Ⓐ ● Ⓒ Ⓓ Ⓔ
4. Ⓐ Ⓑ Ⓒ Ⓓ Ⓔ	9. ● Ⓑ Ⓒ Ⓓ Ⓔ	14. Ⓐ Ⓑ Ⓒ Ⓓ Ⓔ
5. Ⓐ Ⓑ Ⓒ Ⓓ Ⓔ	10. Ⓐ Ⓑ Ⓒ Ⓓ Ⓔ	15. Ⓐ Ⓑ Ⓒ Ⓓ Ⓔ

CORRECTLY FILLED WORKSHEET

1. 9   7   <u>12</u>   14   1

2. [12__]   (9**A**)   [5__]   (11__)   (15__)

3. WARNING. BEWARE OF DOG. <u>**2**</u>

4. 4__   13_**B**_   6_**E**_

FOLLOWING ORAL INSTRUCTIONS
Time: 25 Minutes

LISTENING TO INSTRUCTIONS

> *Directions:* *When you are ready to try this test of the Model Exam, give the following instructions to a friend and have the friend read them aloud to you at the rate of 80 words per minute. Do NOT read them to yourself. Your friend will need a watch with a second hand. Listen carefully and do exactly what your friend tells you to do with the worksheet and with the answer sheet. Your friend will tell you some things to do with each item on the worksheet. After each set of instructions, your friend will give you time to mark your answer by darkening a circle on the answer sheet. Because B and D sound very much alike, your friend will say "B as in baker" when he or she means B, and "D as in dog" when he or she means D.*

Before proceeding further, tear out the worksheet on page 203. Then, hand this book to your friend.

TO THE PERSON WHO IS TO READ THE INSTRUCTIONS: The instructions are to be read at the rate of 80 words per minute. Do not read aloud the material that is in parentheses. Once you have begun the test itself, do not repeat any instructions. The next three paragraphs consist of approximately 120 words. Read these three paragraphs aloud to the candidate in about 1½ minutes. You may reread these paragraphs as often as necessary to establish an 80 words-per-minute reading speed.

READ ALOUD TO THE CANDIDATE

On the job you will have to listen to directions and then do what you have been told to do. In this test, I will read instructions to you. Try to understand them as I read them; I cannot repeat them. After we begin, you may not ask any questions until the end of the test.

On the job you won't have to deal with pictures, numbers, and letters like those in the test, but you will have to listen to instructions and follow them. We are using this test to see how well you can follow instructions.

You are to mark your test booklet according to the instructions that I'll read to you. After each set of instructions, I'll give you time to record your answers on the separate answer sheet.

The actual test begins now.

Look at line 1 on your worksheet. (Pause slightly.) Draw one line under the first number on line 1. (Pause 2 seconds.) Now, on your answer sheet, darken space E for the number under which you just drew one line. (Pause 5 seconds.)

Look at line 1 again. (Pause slightly.) Draw two lines under the lowest number on line 1. (Pause 2 seconds.) Now, on your answer sheet, darken space B as in baker for the number under which you just drew two lines. (Pause 5 seconds.)

Look at line 2 on your worksheet. (Pause slightly.) Write the number 38 in front of the letter that comes second in the alphabet. (Pause 2 seconds.) Now, on your answer sheet, darken the space for the number-letter combination you just wrote. (Pause 5 seconds.)

Look at line 3 on your worksheet. The numbers represent afternoon pickup times at corner mailboxes. (Pause slightly.) Draw a line under the latest pickup time. (Pause 2 seconds.) Now, on your answer sheet, darken the letter A for the last two digits, the minutes, of the time under which you just drew a line. (Pause 5 seconds.)

Look at line 3 again. (Pause slightly.) Find the earliest pickup time and add together all the digits of that time. Write the sum of the digits on the line at the end of line 3. (Pause 2 seconds.) Now, on your answer sheet, darken letter D as in dog for the number you just wrote. (Pause 5 seconds.)

Look at line 4 on your worksheet. (Pause slightly.) In the first circle, write the answer to this question: How many hours are there in a day? (Pause 2 seconds.) In the third circle, write the answer to this question: How many working hours are there in a five-day, 8-hours-per-day work-week? (Pause 5 seconds.) Now, on your answer sheet, darken the number-letter combinations that appear in both circles that you wrote in. (Pause 10 seconds.)

Look at line 5 on your worksheet. (Pause slightly.) If a yard is longer than 10 inches, write the letter C in the triangle. If not, write E. (Pause 2 seconds.) Now, on your answer sheet, darken the space for the number-letter combination in the triangle. (Pause 5 seconds.)

Look at line 5 again. (Pause slightly.) If you are older than 36 months, write the letter A in the rectangle. If not, write the letter B as in baker in the square. (Pause 5 seconds.) Now, on your answer sheet, darken the space for the number-letter combination in the figure you just wrote in. (Pause 5 seconds.)

Look at line 6 on your worksheet. (Pause slightly.) Write the letter E beside the number that is second from the last on line 6. (Pause 2 seconds.) Now, on your answer sheet, darken the space for the number-letter combination you just wrote. (Pause 5 seconds.)

Look at line 7 on your worksheet. The numbers on line 7 represent a bar code. (Pause slightly.) Draw a line under each 0 in the bar code. (Pause 5 seconds.) Count the number of lines you have drawn, add 50, and write that number at the end of line 7. (Pause 5 seconds.) Now, on your answer sheet, darken space E for the number you just wrote. (Pause 5 seconds.)

Look at line 8 on your worksheet. The numbers in the mailsacks represent the weight of the mailsacks in pounds. (Pause slightly.) Write the letter D as in dog in the heaviest mailsack. (Pause 2 seconds.) Now, on your answer sheet, darken the space for the number-letter combination in the mailsack in which you just wrote. (Pause 5 seconds.)

Look at line 9 on your worksheet. (Pause slightly.) Mark an X through the second number on line 9 and an X through every other number thereafter on line 9. (Pause 5 seconds.) Now, on your answer sheet, darken space A for the first number you drew an X through. (Pause 5 seconds.)

Look at line 9 again. (Pause slightly.) For all other numbers through which you drew an X, mark C on your answer sheet. (Pause 15 seconds.)

Look at line 10 on your worksheet. (Pause slightly.) Write the number 1 in the second figure in line 10. (Pause 2 seconds.) Now, on your answer sheet, darken the space for the number-letter combination in the figure in which you just wrote. (Pause 5 seconds.)

Look at line 10 again. (Pause slightly.) Write the number 12 in the first circle on line 10. (Pause 2 seconds.) Now, on your answer sheet, darken the space for the number-letter combination in the figure in which you just wrote. (Pause 5 seconds.)

Look at line 11 on your worksheet. (Pause slightly.) Write the letter A in the figure with fewer sides. (Pause 2 seconds.) Now, on your answer sheet, darken the space for the number-letter combination in the figure in which you just wrote. (Pause 5 seconds.)

Look at line 12 on your worksheet. (Pause slightly.) If 3 is less than 5 and 10 is more than 2, write the number 79 in the first box. (Pause 5 seconds.) If not, write the number 76 in the second box. (Pause 5 seconds.) Now, on your answer sheet, darken the space for the number-letter combination in the box in which you just wrote. (Pause 5 seconds.)

Look at line 13 on your worksheet. (Pause slightly.) Write the first letter of the third word in the second box. (Pause 5 seconds.) Write the third letter of the second word in the first box. (Pause 5 seconds.) Write the second letter of the first word in the third box. (Pause 5 seconds.) Now, on your answer sheet, darken the spaces for the number-letter combinations in the three boxes. (Pause 15 seconds.)

Look at line 14 on your worksheet. (Pause slightly.) If it is possible to purchase two 29-cent stamps for 55 cents, write the number 72 on the second line. (Pause 5 seconds.) If not, write the number 19 on the first line. (Pause 5 seconds.) Now, on your answer sheet, darken the space for the number-letter combination you just wrote. (Pause 5 seconds.)

Look at line 15 on your worksheet. (Pause slightly.) Write the larger of these two numbers, 65 and 46, in the smaller box. (Pause 2 seconds.) Now, on your answer sheet, darken the space for the number-letter combination in the figure in which you just wrote. (Pause 5 seconds.)

Look at line 15 again. (Pause slightly.) Write the sum of 10 plus 20 in the first box. (Pause 2 seconds.) Now, on your answer sheet, darken the space for the number-letter combination in the figure in which you just wrote. (Pause 5 seconds.)

Look at line 16 on your worksheet. (Pause slightly.) Circle the fourth number on line 16. (Pause 2 seconds.) Now, on your answer sheet, darken the space for letter C for the number you just circled. (Pause 5 seconds.)

Look at line 17 on your worksheet. (Pause slightly.) If the number in the oval is greater than the number in the square, write the letter A in the circle. (Pause 5 seconds.) If not, write the letter B as in baker in the square. (Pause 5 seconds.) Now, on your answer sheet, darken the space for the number-letter combination in the figure in which you just wrote. (Pause 5 seconds.)

Look at line 17 again. (Pause slightly.) If the number in the triangle is less than 25, write the letter D as in dog in the triangle. (Pause 2 seconds.) If not, write the letter C in the oval. (Pause 2 seconds.) Now, on your answer sheet, darken the space for the number-letter combination in the figure you just wrote in. (Pause 5 seconds.)

Look at line 18 on your worksheet. (Pause slightly.) Find the letter on line 18 that does not appear in the word GRADE and circle that letter. (Pause 2 seconds.) Now, on your answer sheet, find the number 44 and darken the space for the letter you just circled. (Pause 5 seconds.)

Look at line 19 on your worksheet. (Pause slightly.) Listen to the following numbers and write the smallest number beside the second letter: 59, 62, 49, 54, 87. (Pause 5 seconds.) Now, on your answer sheet, darken the number-letter combination you just wrote. (Pause 5 seconds.)

FOLLOWING ORAL INSTRUCTIONS

WORKSHEET

> **Directions:** *Listening carefully to each set of instructions, mark each item on this worksheet as directed. Then complete each question by marking the answer sheet as directed. For each answer you will darken the answer for a number-letter combination. Should you fall behind and miss an instruction, don't become excited. Let that one go and listen for the next one. If you start to darken a space for a number and you find that you have already darkened another space for that number, either erase the first mark and darken the space for the new combination or let the first mark stay and do not darken a space for the new combination. Write with a pencil that has a clean eraser. When you finish, you should have no more than one space darkened for each number. Correct answers are on page 210.*

1. 75   14   9   27   54   12

2. ___B   ___D   ___C   ___A   ___E

3. 5:43   4:32   3:58   6:27

4. (__C) (__D) (__A) (__E)

5. | 33___ | /81___\   (17___) | 3___ |

6. 35___   16___   10___   52___   6___   80___

7. 7   1   0   5   0   3   3   0   6   8   0   4   0

8. (61__) (39__) (45__) (58__) (47__)

9. 17   51   37   46   76   87   12   5

10. | __A | | __B | (__D) (__E) (__C)

11. ⬡86___   ⬡68___

12. [___ B]   [___ D]

13. [33___]   [85___]   [57___]   SACK   CODE   EXAM

14. ___B   ___E

15. [___ E]   (___ A)   [___ D]   (___ C)

16. 45   19   81   22   10   76

17. [29___]   (73___)   △ 10__   ⬭ 72___

18. D   G   E   B   R   A

19. ___A   ___E   ___C   ___B

END OF EXAMINATION

CORRECT ANSWERS FOR MODEL EXAMINATION

PART A—ADDRESS CHECKING

Part A Answer Key						
1. A	15. D	29. D	43. D	57. D	71. A	85. A
2. D	16. D	30. A	44. A	58. D	72. D	86. D
3. D	17. A	31. A	45. D	59. D	73. A	87. A
4. A	18. D	32. D	46. D	60. A	74. D	88. D
5. D	19. D	33. D	47. A	61. D	75. D	89. D
6. D	20. D	34. D	48. D	62. D	76. D	90. A
7. A	21. A	35. D	49. D	63. A	77. D	91. D
8. D	22. D	36. A	50. A	64. D	78. D	92. A
9. D	23. D	37. A	51. A	65. D	79. A	93. A
10. A	24. A	38. D	52. D	66. A	80. A	94. A
11. D	25. D	39. A	53. D	67. D	81. D	95. D
12. D	26. D	40. D	54. A	68. D	82. A	
13. D	27. D	41. D	55. D	69. A	83. D	
14. D	28. A	42. D	56. A	70. D	84. A	

ANALYZING YOUR ERRORS

This Address Checking Test contains 35 addresses that are exactly alike and 60 addresses that are different. The chart below shows the types of differences that occur in each of the addresses that do not match. Check your answers against this chart to see which kind of difference you missed most often. Note also the questions in which you thought you saw a difference but in which there really was none. Becoming aware of your errors helps you to eliminate those errors on the actual exam.

Type of Difference	Question Numbers	Number of Questions You Missed
Difference in NUMBERS	2, 3, 8, 12, 14, 26, 32, 34, 35, 40, 43, 45, 52, 59, 67, 68, 72, 75, 76, 88, 91, 95	
Difference in ABBREVIATIONS	3, 9, 15, 25, 27, 33, 42, 46, 57, 61, 64, 77	
Difference in NAMES	6, 11, 13, 16, 18, 19, 20, 22, 23, 29, 38, 41, 48, 49, 53, 55, 58, 62, 65, 70, 74, 78, 81, 83, 86, 89	
No Difference	1, 4, 7, 10, 17, 21, 24, 28, 30, 31, 36, 37, 39, 44, 47, 50, 51, 54, 56, 60, 63, 66, 69, 71, 73, 79, 80, 82, 84, 85, 87, 90, 92, 93, 94	

PART B—MEMORY FOR ADDRESSES

Part B Answer Key

PRACTICE I

1. B	14. B	27. E	40. B	53. B	66. C	79. D
2. C	15. E	28. D	41. E	54. E	67. C	80. E
3. D	16. A	29. A	42. E	55. C	68. E	81. D
4. E	17. C	30. A	43. A	56. D	69. B	82. E
5. A	18. B	31. E	44. C	57. A	70. E	83. B
6. E	19. D	32. C	45. B	58. B	71. B	84. E
7. C	20. C	33. C	46. E	59. A	72. D	85. D
8. B	21. D	34. C	47. B	60. A	73. A	86. A
9. B	22. E	35. A	48. D	61. E	74. E	87. E
10. A	23. A	36. D	49. D	62. A	75. B	88. B
11. E	24. B	37. A	50. D	63. B	76. E	
12. A	25. E	38. D	51. C	64. D	77. A	
13. C	26. B	39. B	52. C	65. A	78. C	

PRACTICE II

1. A	14. B	27. C	40. E	53. B	66. B	79. D
2. E	15. E	28. C	41. B	54. D	67. C	80. B
3. C	16. B	29. A	42. A	55. A	68. B	81. C
4. D	17. D	30. D	43. D	56. D	69. C	82. C
5. B	18. C	31. B	44. B	57. C	70. E	83. A
6. B	19. D	32. D	45. D	58. A	71. E	84. D
7. D	20. D	33. D	46. B	59. C	72. C	85. A
8. E	21. A	34. B	47. E	60. D	73. E	86. A
9. C	22. A	35. C	48. E	61. A	74. E	87. E
10. C	23. E	36. A	49. C	62. D	75. B	88. E
11. E	24. C	37. E	50. E	63. D	76. A	
12. A	25. B	38. A	51. C	64. B	77. D	
13. A	26. C	39. A	52. E	65. A	78. A	

Part B—Answer Key (Cont.)

PRACTICE III

1. C	14. D	27. E	40. E	53. C	66. B	79. A
2. E	15. A	28. B	41. E	54. E	67. B	80. E
3. A	16. B	29. E	42. A	55. C	68. B	81. A
4. D	17. D	30. D	43. B	56. C	69. D	82. A
5. B	18. E	31. B	44. D	57. D	70. B	83. C
6. A	19. D	32. C	45. A	58. A	71. A	84. C
7. E	20. C	33. D	46. E	59. E	72. E	85. D
8. B	21. B	34. D	47. B	60. C	73. E	86. C
9. D	22. B	35. B	48. D	61. D	74. B	87. E
10. A	23. A	36. E	49. D	62. B	75. C	88. A
11. A	24. A	37. D	50. A	63. E	76. D	
12. E	25. C	38. B	51. A	64. E	77. D	
13. B	26. C	39. A	52. C	65. A	78. C	

MEMORY FOR ADDRESSES—SCORED EXAM

1. E	14. D	27. E	40. A	53. B	66. E	79. B
2. A	15. D	28. A	41. B	54. C	67. C	80. B
3. C	16. C	29. E	42. C	55. B	68. B	81. B
4. D	17. B	30. C	43. D	56. C	69. A	82. D
5. B	18. D	31. A	44. A	57. D	70. B	83. B
6. C	19. B	32. D	45. E	58. C	71. C	84. C
7. C	20. E	33. C	46. A	59. D	72. A	85. C
8. E	21. C	34. D	47. E	60. E	73. D	86. D
9. A	22. A	35. B	48. A	61. A	74. E	87. A
10. A	23. B	36. E	49. A	62. D	75. C	88. E
11. E	24. B	37. B	50. B	63. C	76. E	
12. E	25. D	38. D	51. E	64. D	77. E	
13. A	26. B	39. E	52. B	65. E	78. E	

PART C—NUMBER SERIES

Part C Answer Key						
1. D	5. C	9. D	13. E	16. A	19. C	22. E
2. D	6. E	10. C	14. C	17. E	20. B	23. A
3. A	7. B	11. A	15. B	18. D	21. C	24. B
4. E	8. A	12. B				

EXPLANATIONS

1.   **The correct answer is (D).** The series really begins with 9 and consists of repeated numbers moving upward in order. The number 8 is inserted between each pair of repeated numbers in the series.

2.   **The correct answer is (D).** The numbers repeat themselves and move up in order.

3.   **The correct answer is (A).** 6 6 is a repetitive theme. Between each set of 6s, the numbers move up by +2.

4.   **The correct answer is (E).** The full sequence is a number of sets of miniseries. Each miniseries consists of three numbers decreasing by –6. Each succeeding miniseries begins with a number one lower than the previous miniseries.

5.   **The correct answer is (C).** Two alternating series each increase by +1. The first series starts at 1 and the second series starts at 3.

6.   **The correct answer is (E).** Two series alternate. The first series consists of repeating numbers that move up by +1. The alternating series consists of numbers that move up by +1 without repeating.

7.   **The correct answer is (B).** The series proceeds 5 6 7 8 9 10, with the number 18 appearing between each two numbers.

8.   **The correct answer is (A).** The first series ascends one number at a time starting from 8. The alternating series ascends by +2 starting from 1.

9.   **The correct answer is (D).** The pattern is: –2, –2, ×2; –2, –2, ×2....

10.   **The correct answer is (C).** The pattern is: –8, –7; –8, –7; –8, –7....

11.   **The correct answer is (A).** Two series alternate. The first series ascends by +3; the alternating series descends by –5.

12.   **The correct answer is (B).** This is a tough one. The pattern is +2, ×2, –2, ÷2; +2, ×2, –2, ÷2....

13.   **The correct answer is (E).** The pattern is: –6, repeat the number; –6, repeat the number....

14. **The correct answer is (C).** The pattern is: +5, –4, repeat the number; +5, –4, repeat the number....

15. **The correct answer is (B).** The pattern is: +2, +2, –3; +2, +2, –3....

16. **The correct answer is (A).** The pattern is: ×3, –8; ×3, –8; ×3, –8....

17. **The correct answer is (E).** The pattern is: –8, –6; –8, –6; –8, –6....

18. **The correct answer is (D).** There are two alternating series. The first series descends by –4 starting from 47; the alternating series ascends by +4, starting from 23.

19. **The correct answer is (C).** The pattern is: +9, +8, +7, +6, +5, +4, +3, +2, +1.

20. **The correct answer is (B).** The pattern is: +1, +2, repeat the number; + 1, +2, repeat the number....

21. **The correct answer is (C).** This is really a times 2 series with the number 41 appearing twice after each two numbers in the series. Thus: 9×2=18; 18×2=36; 36×2=72; 72×2=144.

22. **The correct answer is (E).** The sequence 13 15 17 repeats itself over and over.

23. **The correct answer is (A).** Two series alternate. The first series ascends by +4; the alternating series descends by –3.

24. **The correct answer is (B).** The pattern is: ×2, +3, –10; ×2, +3, –10; ×2, +3, –10....

PART D—FOLLOWING ORAL INSTRUCTIONS

CORRECTLY FILLED ANSWER GRID

1 Ⓐ ● Ⓒ Ⓓ Ⓔ	23 Ⓐ Ⓑ Ⓒ Ⓓ Ⓔ	45 Ⓐ Ⓑ Ⓒ Ⓓ Ⓔ	67 Ⓐ Ⓑ Ⓒ Ⓓ Ⓔ
2 Ⓐ Ⓑ Ⓒ Ⓓ Ⓔ	24 Ⓐ Ⓑ ● Ⓓ Ⓔ	46 Ⓐ Ⓑ ● Ⓓ Ⓔ	68 ● Ⓑ Ⓒ Ⓓ Ⓔ
3 ● Ⓑ Ⓒ Ⓓ Ⓔ	25 Ⓐ Ⓑ Ⓒ Ⓓ Ⓔ	47 Ⓐ Ⓑ Ⓒ Ⓓ Ⓔ	69 Ⓐ Ⓑ Ⓒ Ⓓ Ⓔ
4 Ⓐ Ⓑ Ⓒ Ⓓ Ⓔ	26 Ⓐ Ⓑ Ⓒ Ⓓ Ⓔ	48 Ⓐ Ⓑ Ⓒ Ⓓ Ⓔ	70 Ⓐ Ⓑ Ⓒ Ⓓ Ⓔ
5 Ⓐ Ⓑ ● Ⓓ Ⓔ	27 ● Ⓑ Ⓒ Ⓓ Ⓔ	49 Ⓐ Ⓑ Ⓒ Ⓓ ●	71 Ⓐ Ⓑ Ⓒ Ⓓ Ⓔ
6 Ⓐ Ⓑ Ⓒ Ⓓ ●	28 Ⓐ Ⓑ Ⓒ Ⓓ Ⓔ	50 Ⓐ Ⓑ Ⓒ Ⓓ Ⓔ	72 Ⓐ Ⓑ Ⓒ Ⓓ Ⓔ
7 Ⓐ Ⓑ Ⓒ Ⓓ Ⓔ	29 Ⓐ Ⓑ Ⓒ Ⓓ Ⓔ	51 ● Ⓑ Ⓒ Ⓓ Ⓔ	73 ● Ⓑ Ⓒ Ⓓ Ⓔ
8 Ⓐ Ⓑ Ⓒ Ⓓ Ⓔ	30 Ⓐ Ⓑ Ⓒ Ⓓ ●	52 Ⓐ Ⓑ Ⓒ Ⓓ Ⓔ	74 Ⓐ Ⓑ Ⓒ Ⓓ Ⓔ
9 Ⓐ ● Ⓒ Ⓓ Ⓔ	31 Ⓐ Ⓑ Ⓒ Ⓓ Ⓔ	53 Ⓐ Ⓑ Ⓒ Ⓓ Ⓔ	75 Ⓐ Ⓑ Ⓒ Ⓓ ●
10 Ⓐ Ⓑ Ⓒ ● Ⓔ	32 Ⓐ Ⓑ Ⓒ Ⓓ Ⓔ	54 Ⓐ Ⓑ Ⓒ Ⓓ Ⓔ	76 Ⓐ Ⓑ Ⓒ Ⓓ Ⓔ
11 Ⓐ Ⓑ Ⓒ Ⓓ Ⓔ	33 Ⓐ Ⓑ Ⓒ ● Ⓔ	55 Ⓐ Ⓑ Ⓒ Ⓓ ●	77 Ⓐ Ⓑ Ⓒ Ⓓ Ⓔ
12 Ⓐ Ⓑ Ⓒ ● Ⓔ	34 Ⓐ Ⓑ Ⓒ Ⓓ Ⓔ	56 Ⓐ Ⓑ Ⓒ Ⓓ Ⓔ	78 Ⓐ Ⓑ Ⓒ Ⓓ Ⓔ
13 Ⓐ Ⓑ Ⓒ Ⓓ Ⓔ	35 Ⓐ Ⓑ Ⓒ Ⓓ Ⓔ	57 ● Ⓑ Ⓒ Ⓓ Ⓔ	79 Ⓐ ● Ⓒ Ⓓ Ⓔ
14 Ⓐ Ⓑ Ⓒ Ⓓ Ⓔ	36 Ⓐ Ⓑ Ⓒ Ⓓ Ⓔ	58 Ⓐ Ⓑ Ⓒ Ⓓ Ⓔ	80 Ⓐ Ⓑ Ⓒ Ⓓ Ⓔ
15 Ⓐ Ⓑ Ⓒ Ⓓ Ⓔ	37 Ⓐ Ⓑ Ⓒ Ⓓ Ⓔ	59 Ⓐ Ⓑ Ⓒ Ⓓ Ⓔ	81 Ⓐ Ⓑ ● Ⓓ Ⓔ
16 Ⓐ Ⓑ Ⓒ ● Ⓔ	38 Ⓐ ● Ⓒ Ⓓ Ⓔ	60 Ⓐ Ⓑ Ⓒ Ⓓ Ⓔ	82 Ⓐ Ⓑ Ⓒ Ⓓ Ⓔ
17 Ⓐ Ⓑ Ⓒ Ⓓ Ⓔ	39 Ⓐ Ⓑ Ⓒ Ⓓ Ⓔ	61 Ⓐ Ⓑ Ⓒ ● Ⓔ	83 Ⓐ Ⓑ Ⓒ Ⓓ Ⓔ
18 Ⓐ Ⓑ Ⓒ Ⓓ Ⓔ	40 ● Ⓑ Ⓒ Ⓓ Ⓔ	62 Ⓐ Ⓑ Ⓒ Ⓓ Ⓔ	84 Ⓐ Ⓑ Ⓒ Ⓓ Ⓔ
19 Ⓐ ● Ⓒ Ⓓ Ⓔ	41 Ⓐ Ⓑ Ⓒ Ⓓ Ⓔ	63 Ⓐ Ⓑ Ⓒ Ⓓ Ⓔ	85 Ⓐ Ⓑ Ⓒ Ⓓ ●
20 Ⓐ Ⓑ Ⓒ Ⓓ Ⓔ	42 Ⓐ Ⓑ Ⓒ Ⓓ Ⓔ	64 Ⓐ Ⓑ Ⓒ Ⓓ Ⓔ	86 Ⓐ Ⓑ Ⓒ Ⓓ Ⓔ
21 Ⓐ Ⓑ Ⓒ Ⓓ Ⓔ	43 Ⓐ Ⓑ Ⓒ Ⓓ Ⓔ	65 Ⓐ Ⓑ Ⓒ ● Ⓔ	87 Ⓐ Ⓑ ● Ⓓ Ⓔ
22 Ⓐ Ⓑ ● Ⓓ Ⓔ	44 Ⓐ ● Ⓒ Ⓓ Ⓔ	66 Ⓐ Ⓑ Ⓒ Ⓓ Ⓔ	88 Ⓐ Ⓑ Ⓒ Ⓓ Ⓔ

CORRECTLY FILLED WORKSHEET

1. <u>75</u>   14 <u>9</u>   27   54   12

2. <u>38</u> B   ___D   ___C   ___A   ___E

3. 5:43   4:32   3:58   <u>6:27</u>   <u>16</u>

4. (<u>24</u>C) (___D) (<u>10</u>A) (___E)

5. [33___] △ 81 <u>C</u> ◯ 17___ [3 <u>A</u>]

6. 35___   16___   10___   52___   6 <u>E</u>   80___

7. 7 1 <u>0</u> 5 <u>0</u> 3 3 <u>0</u> 6 8 <u>0</u> 4 <u>0</u> <u>55</u>

8. (61 <u>D</u>) (39___) (45___) (58___) (47___)

9. 17   ✗   37   ✗   76   ✗   12   ✗

10. [___A] [_|_B] (<u>12</u>D) (___E) (___C)

11. [86___] ⬡ 68 <u>A</u>

12. [<u>19</u> B] [___D]

13. [33 <u>D</u>] [85 <u>E</u>] [57 <u>A</u>]   SACK   CODE   EXAM

14. <u>19</u> B   ___E

15. [<u>30</u>E] (___A) [<u>65</u>D] (___C)

16. 45   19   81   (22)   10   76

17. [29___]   (73 **A**)   /10 **D**\   (72___)

18. D   G   E   (B)   R   A

19. ___A   **49** E   ___C   ___B

SCORE SHEET

ADDRESS CHECKING: Your score on the Address Checking part is based upon the number of questions you answered correctly minus the number of questions you answered incorrectly. To determine your score, subtract the number of wrong answers from the number of correct answers.

Number Right   –   Number Wrong   =   Raw Score

_____ - _____ = _____

MEMORY FOR ADDRESSES: Your score on the Memory for Addresses part is based upon the number of questions you answered correctly minus one-fourth of the questions you answered incorrectly (number wrong divided by 4). Calculate this now:

Number Wrong   ÷ 4   =   _____

Number Right   –   Number Wrong   ÷   4   =   Raw Score

_____ - _____ = _____

NUMBER SERIES: Your score on the Number Series part is based only on the number of questions you answered correctly. Wrong answers do not count against you.

Number Right   =   Raw Score

_____ = _____

FOLLOWING ORAL INSTRUCTIONS: Your score on the Following Oral Instructions part is based only upon the number of questions you marked correctly on the answer sheet. The worksheet is not scored, and wrong answers on the answer sheet do not count against you.

Number Right   =   Raw Score

_____ = _____

TOTAL SCORE: To find your total raw score, add together the raw scores for each section of the exam.

Address Checking Score _____

\+

Memory for Addresses Score _____

\+

Number Series Score _____

\+

Following Oral Instructions Score _____

\=

Total Raw Score _____

Self-Evaluation Chart

Calculate your raw score for each test, as shown above. Then check to see where your score falls on the scale from "Poor" to "Excellent." Lightly shade in the boxes in which your scores fall.

Part	Excellent	Good	Average	Fair	Poor
Address Checking	80–95	65–79	50–64	35–49	1–34
Memory for Addresses	75–88	60–74	45–59	30–44	1–29
Number Series	21–24	18–20	14–17	11–13	1–10
Following Oral Instructions	27–31	23–26	19–22	14–18	1–13

PART V

Civil Service Career Information Resources

CHAPTER 19

How to Find a Government Job

FINDING INFORMATION ON USPS POSITIONS

Job Listings for the United States Postal Service can be found on their Web Site at www.usps.com. You can apply to take Post Office exams as well. Job vacancies are also posted on the bulletin boards of local post offices, in local newspapers, and are also available from District Offices. You can find the District Office closest to you by looking at the government pages in your local phone book.

FINDING INFORMATION ON FEDERAL JOBS

All openings for jobs within the federal government are listed on USAJOBS, the federal government's Employment Information System. USAJOBS is available on line at www.usajobs.opm.gov or by telephone at (478) 757-3000 (or TDD (478) 744-2299).

You can often apply for jobs on line and sometimes even submit your resume electronically. If you must submit your application on paper, you have some choices. You can use a standardized Federal application called the OF-612 or a resume. A Federal resume is different than what you would use to apply for a job in the private sector. You need to include much more detail. You also need to make sure to include information that is asked for on the job announcement. Job announcements for Federal jobs are generally quite long and include a tremendous amount of information about the job and it's requirements. It's important to read it carefully.

FINDING INFORMATION ON STATE AND LOCAL JOBS

Hiring procedures vary significantly from state to state and from locality to locality. For information about working for your state, you can start by looking for information on your state's Web site. Search for that site by typing the name of the state into a search engine such as Google, www.google.com/, i.e. "State of New Jersey." You can do the same to find the Web site for your village, city, town, or county.

If you can't find the information on the Web, or if you don't have Internet access, you can call or visit your municipality's office. Check the government pages in your phone book for the address or phone number. Some public libraries may also have the information you need. You can also try your State Department of Labor Office. The U.S. Department of Labor Web site lists the Web sites of these offices at www.dol.gov/dol/location.htm.

STATE INTERNET SITES

Alabama	www.state.al.us	Montana	www.mt.gov
Alaska	www.state.ak.us	Nebraska	www.state.ne.us
Arizona	www.az.gov	Nevada	silver.state.nv.us
Arkansas	www.state.ar.us	New Hampshire	www.state.nh.us
California	www.state.ca.us	New Jersey	www.state.nj.us
Colorado	www.colorado.gov	New Mexico	www.state.nm.us
Connecticut	www.state.ct.us	New York	www.state.ny.us
Delaware	www.delaware.gov	North Carolina	www.ncgov.com
District of Columbia	www.dchomepage.net	North Dakota	discovernd.com
Florida	www.myflorida.com	Ohio	www.state.oh.us
Georgia	www.georgia.gov	Oklahoma	www.state.ok.us
Hawaii	www.state.hi.us	Oregon	www.oregon.gov
Idaho	www.state.id.us	Pennsylvania	www.state.pa.us
Illinois	www.state.il.us	Rhode Island	www.state.ri.us
Indiana	www.state.in.us	South Carolina	www.myscgov.com
Iowa	www.state.ia.us	South Dakota	www.state.sd.us
Kansas	www.accesskansas.org	Tennessee	www.state.tn.us
Kentucky	www.kydirect.net	Texas	www.state.tx.us
Louisiana	www.state.la.us	Utah	www.utah.gov
Maine	www.state.me.us	Vermont	www.state.vt.us
Maryland	www.state.md.us	Virginia	www.vipnet.org
Massachusetts	www.mass.gov	Washington	access.wa.gov
Michigan	www.michigan.gov	West Virginia	www.state.wv.us
Minnesota	www.state.mn.us	Wisconsin	www.wisconsin.gov
Mississippi	www.state.ms.us	Wyoming	www.state.wy.us
Missouri	www.state.mo.us		

INTERNET SITES

There are also several Internet sites you can visit for more information. Although it is by no means exhaustive, the following list should get you started in the right direction as you learn more about what working for the USPS has to offer.

GENERAL INFORMATION

1. **Postal Facts** (www.usps.gov/history/pfact00.htm)
   Facts and figures to help you learn more about the USPS.

2. **USPS Financials**
   (www.usps.gov/financials)

3. **Postal Clerks and Mail Carriers (Occupational Outlook Handbook)**
   (stats.bls.gov/oco/ocos141.htm)

JOB LISTINGS

1. **U.S. Postal Service: Employment:** www.usps.gov/employment
   The official job listings from the USPS includes information on how to apply.

ONLINE PUBLICATIONS

1. **The Mail Handler:** www.npmhu.org/Pubs/MailHandler.htm
   Quarterly publication from the National Mail Handlers' Association.

2. **The Mail Handler Update:** www.npmhu.org/Pubs/Update.htm
   Monthly publications from the National Mail Handlers' Association.

3. **Federal Employees News Digest:** www.fendonline.com
   Federal news for government employees.

4. **Postal News from FederalTimes.com:** www.federaltimes.com/
   index.php?C=570476.php
   News of interest to those in the United States Postal Service.

UNIONS AND ASSOCIATIONS AND CONTRACT INFORMATION

1. **American Postal Workers Union (APWU) Locals:** www.apwu.org/locals/
   localframe.htm

2. **American Postal Workers Union:** www.apwu.org

3. **National Association of Letter Carriers:** www.nalc.org

4. **National Postal Mail Handlers Union:** www.npmhu.org/

5. **National Rural Letter Carriers Association:** www.nrlca.org/

COLLECTIVE BARGAINING AGREEMENTS

1. **National Association of Letter Carriers 1994–1998 Agreement:** www.nalc.org/
   depart/cau/agreemnt.html

2. **American Postal Workers Union 2000–03 Agreement:**
   www.apwu.org/departments/ir/cba/2000-2003CBA.pdf

MISCELLANEOUS

1. **Mailman "Stuff":** www.rollanet.org/~gary/index.html
   This site exists to promote the sharing of information among letter carriers.

2. **Post Office Locatior:** www.mapsonus.com/db/usps
   Find your local post office.

3. **Postal Workers' Web Ring:** l.webring.com/hub?ring=postalring
   Links to postal employees' Web sites.

STEPS TOWARD GETTING HIRED

All applicants for a Postal Service job must meet minimum age requirements and must be either citizens of the United States or must have permanent resident alien status (a Green Card). Listed below are other phases of the hiring process

THE INTERVIEW

If there is no exam and you are called directly to an interview, what you wear is very important. Take special care to look businesslike and professional. Try not to appear too casual, and certainly not sloppy. Overdressing is also inappropriate. A neat dress or suit is fine for women; men should wear a shirt and tie with suit or slacks and a jacket. Be sure to pay attention to your grooming.

If you are called for an interview, you are under serious consideration. There may still be competition for the job; someone else may be more suited than you, but you are qualified and your skills and background have appealed to someone in the hiring offices. The interview may be aimed at getting information about:

- **Your knowledge.** The interviewer wants to know what you know about the area in which you will work. For instance, if you will be doing data entry in a budget office, what do you know about the budget process? Are you at all interested in this area of financial planning? You may also be asked questions probing your knowledge of the postal service. Show that you care enough to have educated yourself about the functions of the postal service, whether it's mail handler, distribution clerk, machine operator, or another area.

- **Your judgment.** You may be faced with hypothetical situations, job-related or in interpersonal relations, and be asked, "What would you do if...?" questions. Think carefully before answering. You must be decisive but diplomatic. There are no "right or wrong" answers. The interviewer is aware that you are being put on the spot. How well you can handle this type of question is an indication of your flexibility, maturity and ability to "think on your feet," all qualities that are critical to any job.

- **Your personality.** You will have to be trained and supervised. You will have to work with others. What is your attitude? How will you fit in? The interviewer will be trying to make judgments in these areas on the basis of general conversation with you and from your responses to specific lines of questioning. Be pleasant, polite, and open with your answers, but do not volunteer a great deal of extra information. Stick to the subjects introduced by the interviewer. Answer fully, but resist the temptation to ramble on.

- **Your attitude toward work conditions.** These are practical concerns: If the job will require frequent travel for extended periods, how do you feel about it? What is your family's attitude? If you will be very unhappy about traveling, you may eventually leave the job, and your training will have been a waste of money and time. The interviewer may want to know how you will react to overtime or irregular shifts. Remember, in today's busy world, with multiple work and family commitments, you need to be very honest with yourself—and your interviewer—in regard to working outside the traditional "8 to 5" hours.

Other steps along the hiring route may be a medical examination, physical performance testing, and psychological interview, as well as written tests.

MEDICAL EXAMINATION

USPS candidates are specifically tested for alcohol and drug abuse as well as an examination for overall good health. Five extra points are added to the score of an honorably discharged veteran, and 10 extra points are added to the score of a veteran who was wounded in combat or disabled. Disabled veterans who have a compensable, service-connected disability of 10 percent or more are placed at the top of the eligibility list.

PHYSICAL EXAMINATION

Physical performance testing is limited to applicants for physically demanding jobs. Applicants for jobs that require strength and stamina are sometimes given a special test. For example, mail handlers must be able to lift mail sacks weighing up to 70 pounds. The names of applicants who pass the examinations are placed on a list in the order of their scores.

Remember that working for the government is working for the people, since government revenues come from taxes. The hiring officers have a responsibility to put the right people into the right jobs in order to spend the taxpayers' money most effectively. And, as a government employee, you have a responsibility to give the people (including yourself) their money's worth.

CHAPTER 20

Career Development with the USPS

USPS CAREER PROGRAMS

The USPS offers four specific programs to help employees develop and broaden their career opportunities. Some of these programs are open to all employees, while others are geared primarily at administrators and/or supervisors. You can find more information on all these programs at www.usps.com/employment/develop.htm. The four programs are summarized below:

- **National Center for Employee Development (NCED)**: The NCED can be thought of as the "clearinghouse" of USPS training, as it provides employees hands-on, technical instruction for work on advanced postal systems, vehicles, and mail processing equipment. With a focus on national job skills training, the NCED also offers distance-learning opportunities, and utilizes live satellite broadcasts, audio teletraining, and various Web-based technologies to bring to USPS employees an extensive and accessible mechanism for career growth and training.

- **Associate Supervisor Program (ASP)**: A sixteen-week training program, the ASP seeks, selects, and trains the best individuals for first-line supervisory positions within the USPS. An intensely individualized program, each ASP participant is teamed with a "coach" who helps to answer questions, provide leadership, and serve as a professional mentor as the candidate works through the stages of the program. The ASP combines hands-on, classroom, and onsite training to help deliver the most comprehensive and inclusive environment for grooming the future supervisors of the USPS.

- **Career Management Program (CMP)**: The best supervisors, regardless of their employer, must possess the skills (including analytical, communication, and employer-specific) to help guide those individuals they manage in their own respective career paths and interests. The CMP allows USPS supervisors the chance—and provides them with the tools—to guide those they supervise in the most complete, knowledgeable fashion possible. Initial skill assessment is a key feature of this program, so that supervisors, managers, and postmasters can best guide their employees to training that best fits their current skill level and interest.

- **Advanced Leadership Program (ALP)**: The ALP seeks to empower the best of existing USPS managers with the skills they need to become future leaders in advanced management and leadership positions within the USPS. Designed around a specific skill set, the ALP has as a central goal the development of a strong, future management base by training highly qualified existing supervisors and managers with the skills they will need for tomorrow.

With the information provided in this book, you can score high on your postal exam, learn about the benefits of working for the Postal Service, and you can search for information by using the resources listed. Best of luck on your search for a career in with the U.S. Postal Service!

APPENDIX

POSTAL TERMS GLOSSARY

Base Salary—*Basic Salary* with *COLA*

Basic Salary—annual, daily, or hourly rate of pay as indicated by the salary schedule for the employee's assigned position; excludes *COLA*

Career Appointment—an appointment to the postal career service without time limitation

Casual Appointment—a non-career limited term appointment to positions used as a supplemental work force

COLA—see *Cost of Living Adjustment*

Cost of Living Adjustment—increase in pay based on increases in the Consumer Price Index (CPI) over a base month; this increase is specified in bargaining unit agreements

Entrance Examinations—tests given to establish eligibility for employment

Grade—each pay category

Inservice Examinations—tests administered to substitute rural carriers and career postal employees to determine eligibility for advancement and reassignment; also used to establish qualification for enrollment in certain postal training courses

Merit Promotion Program—provides the means for making selections for promotions according to the relative qualifications of the employees under consideration

Performance Test—a procedure in which the applicant is directed to carry out a certain work activity related to the position under consideration

Promotion—the permanent assignment, with or without relocation, of an employee to an established position with a higher grade than the position to which the employee was previously assigned in the same schedule or in another schedule

Quality Step Increase—an increase in addition to a periodic *step increase* granted on or before expiration of required waiting periods in recognition of extra competence

Rated Application—applications and other required documents that provide a basis for evaluation against an established rating standard; based on this application, a final rating is established for each competitor

Reassignment—the permanent assignment, with or without relocation, to another established position with the same grade in the same schedule or in a different schedule

Register—a file of eligibles' names arranged in order of relative standing for appointment consideration

Step Increase—an advancement from one step to the next within a specific grade of a position; it is dependent on satisfying certain performance and waiting period criteria; see also *Quality Step Increase*

Temporary Appointment—a non-career limited term appointment up to, but not exceeding, one year in a position that includes the performance of duties assigned to nonbargaining units

Temporary Assignment—the placement of an employee in another established position, for a limited period of time, to perform duties other than those in the position description

Veteran Preference—granted to eligible applicants to be added to the ratings on examinations

NOTES

NOTES

Your everything education destination... the *all-new* Petersons.com

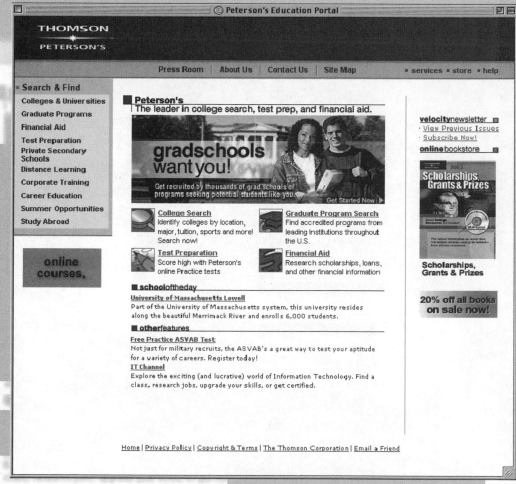